The Great Strikes of 1877

THE WORKING CLASS
IN AMERICAN HISTORY

Editorial Advisors
James R. Barrett
Alice Kessler-Harris
Nelson Lichtenstein
David Montgomery

A list of books in the series
appears at the end of this book.

The
Great Strikes
of 1877

Edited by
DAVID O. STOWELL

University of Illinois Press
URBANA AND CHICAGO

Manufactured in the United States of America
1 2 3 4 5 C P 5 4 3 2 1
∞ This book is printed on acid-free paper.

Library of Congress Cataloging-in-Publication Data
The great strikes of 1877 / edited by David O. Stowell.
p.   cm. — (The working class in American history)
Includes bibliographical references and index.
ISBN-13: 978-0-252-03241-7 (cloth : alk. paper)
ISBN-10: 0-252-03241-1 (cloth : alk. paper)
ISBN-13: 978-0-252-07477-6 (pbk. : alk. paper)
ISBN-10: 0-252-07477-7 (pbk. : alk. paper)
1. Railroad Strike, U.S., 1877. 2. Working class—United
States—Political activity—History—19th century. 3. United
States—Social conditions—1865–1918. 4. Social structure—
United States—History—19th century. 5. United States—
Ethnic relations—History—19th century.
I. Stowell, David O. (David Omar)
HD5325.R21877   G74 2008
331.892'81385097309034—dc22   2007021090

Dedicated to my two brothers,
Douglas B. Stowell and Donald M. Stowell,
&
my wife, Deborah Hodgson Stowell,
&
my niece and nephew,
Meghan E. Stowell and Andrew D. Stowell

Contents

Acknowledgments

I would like to thank each of the people whose articles appear in this volume: Joshua Brown, Steve Hoffman, Michael Kazin, David Miller, Rich Schneirov, and Shel Stromquist. Needless to say, without their time and effort, this volume would never have come to fruition. I also thank the two reviewers, especially David Montgomery (the other remains anonymous); his comments in particular improved a number of the articles, and especially my introduction. But as the saying goes, any remaining shortcomings are the sole property of the editor and the contributors. Thanks are due also to Laurie Matheson, acquisitions editor at the University of Illinois Press; she consistently and enthusiastically supported this project from start to finish—a period covering roughly three years.

My colleagues in the Department of History at Keene State College—Matt Crocker, Carl Granquist, Greg Knouff, Gerry Hayden, John Lund, Elizabeth McCahill, Margaret Orelup, Graham Warder, Tom Whitcomb, and Andy Wilson—made working on this and other scholarly endeavors easier because of their friendship and great sense of humor. It has been a pleasure to work and laugh with them for the past eleven years. Thanks also to Judy Powers, our administrative assistant: only someone with an equally great sense of humor could possibly have put up with me and still get her work accomplished. Judy also assisted with some of the formatting that initially befuddled this editor. I thank *Chicago History* and the University of California Press for permission to reprint previously published material that appears in two of the chapters.

The Great Strikes of 1877

Introduction

DAVID O. STOWELL

During and after the Civil War, worker militancy and various labor organizations experienced a revival from the hard times following the depression of 1857. The Civil War itself, writes David Montgomery, was for most
wage-workers, "a nightmare. . . . The burden of taxation fell heavily on them,
greenbacks were associated with severe inflation, and conscription not only
gave the state a claim upon their very lives but discriminatorily provided the
wealthy citizen with an escape through commutation for cash. . . . Emancipation . . . appeared to most as a threat to unleash hordes of Negro laborers
who would depress industrial wages."[1] From the socioeconomic furnace of
the war, labor emerged with a renewed sense of urgency and commitment
to improving its social, political, and economic status. Consequently, a host
of labor organizations, from trade unions and sections of the International
Workingmen's Association, to reform associations and labor parties, were
formed or reformulated to confront the plight of working people. Despite the
continued, though weakening, hegemony of the free-labor ideology, roughly
67 percent of Americans in 1870 were wage-earners or employees (38.4 percent in industry, manufacturing, and service occupations; 28.7 percent in
agriculture).[2] The central thrust of organizing efforts remained along craft
lines. Craft unionization flourished after the war, owing in part to the impact
of accelerating industrialization on group, if not class, consciousness among
growing numbers of workers, skilled and unskilled. By the Depression of
1873, there were roughly thirty national and international trade unions in the
country. The 1873 depression, though, crushed national trade union organizations, as had previous depressions in the antebellum era. By the time of the
Great Strike of 1877, only nine existed.[3] Despite the depression's devastating

impact on national labor organizations, the determination of laborers to fight for their rights and their ability to make a living wage remained. The Molly Maguires were perhaps best known to contemporaries in the 1870s as the most militant of laborers. A secret organization of Irish-immigrant miners that freely used violence in the course of a long strike in the eastern Pennsylvania coal fields in 1875–76, the Molly Maguires were crushed by the greater violence of the mine owners and the state; after a trial of dubious legitimacy, ten were hanged for murder, while fourteen others were sent to prison. The sensational nature of the strikes and violence in eastern Pennsylvania aside, more traditional "strikes" hardly disappeared during the years 1873–76. Among other labor disputes, a series of railroad strikes erupted in 1873–74, and in New York City's Tompkins Square, unemployed workers "struck" for public works projects and public relief by holding a massive rally and then fighting police sent to break up the peaceful demonstration.[4]

In the spring of 1877, the United States was still in the grip of the depression. Hunger and unemployment stalked town and countryside. The states of the former Confederacy were economically prostrate from the devastation wrought by the Civil War. Despite the depression, Reconstruction politics remained front-page news in most major newspapers throughout the nation. Indeed, the bitterly contested presidential election of 1876 between Republican Rutherford B. Hayes and Democrat Samuel J. Tilden had only recently been resolved—at least to the satisfaction of most white men, North and South. With the "Compromise of 1877," the long retreat of northern interest in the plight of former slaves was essentially complete, and the remaining handful of U.S. troops were ordered back to their barracks in Louisiana, South Carolina, and Florida following Hayes's inauguration. As a consequence of their withdrawal, the three remaining state Reconstruction governments collapsed entirely. With the "Negro question" now in the hands of southern whites, white supremacists had finished their task of regaining political power throughout the former Confederacy, though virtual absolute control would await the complete disfranchisement of black men and the completion of the all-embracing web of Jim Crow in the 1890s.[5]

The Great Strike of 1877, one of the most spectacular and frightening episodes of collective violence in American history, notwithstanding the New York City draft riots of 1863, began innocuously enough, at least on the surface.[6] On July 16, at the railroad yard in Martinsburg, West Virginia, Baltimore & Ohio Railroad trainmen reacted to a 10 percent wage cut, enacted July 1 by most railroad corporations, by dismantling a cattle train upon its entrance to the yard. Upon uncoupling the cars, the men stated that no more freight trains would be allowed to travel until their wages were restored. This job action by railroadmen quickly elicited support from segments of the Martinsburg community, both working class and middle class; that evening, a crowd gathered at the town depot and prevented the arrest of the strikers by the police. The following day, freight traffic was disrupted or stopped by striking railroad workers, and more ominously for railroad companies and ruling elites in general, by people with no wage relationship to the B & O. The strike of railroad workers spread rapidly from Martinsburg, engulfing towns and cities throughout the Northeast and the Midwest, and extending as far west as the Pacific Coast.

The strike of railroad workers, impressive in scope and intensity, triggered a series of equally widespread, popular uprisings against the railroads—the nation's preeminent industrial enterprise after the Civil War and the symbol of the capitalist nature of the American industrial revolution. Though largely viewed as the carriers of progress and prosperity, the railroads—"the great money-maker of the age"—also engendered considerable hostility. Their tracks and trains wreaked havoc in urban communities, sowing disorder in city streets, obstructing the commercial and noncommercial uses of streets, and killing and injuring thousands of people every year in various types of "accidents" involving pedestrians and horse-drawn vehicles. Consequently, crowds composed mostly of workers with no wage relationship to the railroad companies, sprinkled with substantial numbers of middle-class folk, joined striking railroad workers in stopping trains; they also engaged in violent attacks against railroad property, behavior that dismayed many if not all striking railroad employees.[7]

Given Baltimore's proximity to Martinsburg and its status as the major rail nexus for the B & O Railroad, it was the place of the first major outbreak of violence. On Friday July 20, the Great Strike (having hit various communities along the lines, such as Wheeling and Cumberland, West Virginia) hit Baltimore with a vengeance. Railroad and civil authorities had already filled Baltimore with hundreds of soldiers in expectation of "trouble," and trouble they got. On Front Street, at the armory housing a regiment of troops called out to protect railroad property, thousands of people collected. Women, children, unemployed men, and people from nearly all walks of city life gathered to voice their rage at the troops. As Robert V. Bruce put it: "The emotion that filled the crowd on Front Street was fury, engendered by the life sentence of toil and misery which the age had pronounced upon them, turned against the great-bodied and soulless corporations," and focused now on the troops defending the interests of one of those corporations: the Baltimore & Ohio Railroad Company. Catcalls, threats, and brickbats were hurled at the armory. After a short period, a portion of the regiment was ordered to leave the armory and march to the major railroad depot at Camden station. Their exit and the crowd's reaction were a deadly mixture: in response to a fusillade of stones, brickbats, and perhaps a gunshot or two, the soldiers opened fire upon the crowd. As different companies of the regiment departed the armory and marched through the streets to Camden station, battles broke out all along the route. By the time the regiment reached Camden station, half of its members had decided that the wisest course of action on this particular Friday night was to slip off and get back into civilian clothes. But the damage had been done— nearly a dozen Baltimoreans lay dead and a score injured (only one militia- man had suffered serious wounds). Among the dead were Willie Hourand, a newsboy, age fifteen; Patrick Gill, a forty-year-old immigrant tinner from Ireland; and Thomas Byrne, a salesman for a clothing store. Not a single one of the dead or wounded were railroad strikers, a testimony to the scope of the hostility big business—railroad corporations in particular—had elicited in the years since the Civil War. Though there were other disturbances that evening, especially at the Camden station, the city was generally free of the fleeting deadly violence. Indeed, by Sunday night, hundreds of federal troops patrolled the city, and an uneasy peace prevailed. Passenger train service had been restored, but the strike against freight trains held.[8]

As people in Baltimore and other cities experienced the Great Strike or its beginnings that July weekend, the seminal event of the strike was unfolding in Pittsburgh, Pennsylvania. Pittsburgh was home to another railroad giant, the Pennsylvania Railroad Company, and the company held the nearly universal antipathy of the city's working class—and a not-to-be-ignored segment of its middle class as well. Its monopoly on rail and freight traffic into and out of the city had created a deep reservoir of ill feeling. "Antimonopoly" senti- ment, a set of values with roots stretching back to the eighteenth century, ran deep throughout the country, especially as industrialization created be- hemoth corporations that crushed small businesses as easily as hapless cows "caught on the tracks" were smashed by speeding locomotives. Nowhere was antimonopoly sentiment deeper and more widespread than in Pittsburgh. In 1876, a Pittsburgh newspaper ran an editorial entitled "Railroad Vultures" in which it labeled railroad corporations and their owners "money jugglers" versed in "all known ways and byways of fraud, scheming, and speculating to accomplish the amassing of princely fortunes."[9] Pittsburgh was an industrial city; coal mines, iron and steel mills, and oil refineries dominated the city's economy. The oil industry in particular had suffered during the depression, and the oil refineries' problems were attributed to the freight rates charged by the Pennsylvania Railroad Company. Any strike of railroad workers in the city was sure to reverberate among other industrial workers, as well as among the unemployed and middle-class folk who resented the railroads for a variety of reasons. The Pennsylvania Railroad's rolling stock, roundhouses, freight houses, switchyards, and ancillary workshops covered a vast area by the Union Depot, running alongside a ridge.[10]

Pittsburgh's railroadmen knew of the strikes in other cities, and they too had suffered a pay cut. Their strike started on Thursday July 19 when a group of trainmen refused to take out any freight trains. At approximately the same time, another pivotal event was beginning in the city, an event emblematic of the hostility railroad corporations had fostered in countless cities and small towns across the nation. A crowd composed largely of non-railroadmen began to form at the Twenty-Eighth Street crossing, about one mile from the Union Depot. This crowd would play a signal role in what was to follow; indeed, they began to interfere with the movement of trains almost immediately. As trainmen refused to run freight trains and also refused to allow the use of strikebreakers—scabs—the crowd at the crossing grew in size. Indeed, striking railroadmen had to intercede to allow passenger trains to continue to run—a conscious strategy on the part of the strikers to avoid alienating the public. As the day ended, hundreds of incoming freight cars lay idle in the Pennsylvania yard. On Friday July 20 no freight trains were moving into or out of the city. The situation remained the same on the following day. Yet as elsewhere, railroad corporations were successfully soliciting the armed intervention of local, state, and federal authority. Local police forces, in Pittsburgh and other cities, were simply overwhelmed by the size of the strike and the crowds. State militias faced a problem, which was particularly pronounced in Pittsburgh: militiamen were drawn from the city, and they did not want to fire on people who might be their neighbors or coworkers. Efforts to get the Pittsburgh militia to control the strikers—and the ever-growing Twenty-Eighth Street crowd—generally failed. Militiamen either failed to show up when called or they conspicuously fraternized with the strikers and those in the crowd. Consequently, railroad officials asked for and received permission to have state militiamen from Philadelphia rushed to the city via special trains provided by the railroad company.[11] Of the many features of society revealed in stark relief by the Great Strike of 1877, none was as apparent as the state's willingness to use armed force against ordinary people on behalf of the interests of private capital.

It was no secret to the strikers and other people of Pittsburgh that militiamen from Philadelphia were headed to their city. Arriving on Saturday the 21st, these out-of-town militiamen would prove to be the trigger for the signal, terrifying event in the history of the Great Strike of 1877, one of the most wholesale acts of urban destruction ever visited on an American city

by its own residents. Unlike their Pittsburgh counterparts, the state militiamen from Philadelphia had few qualms about firing into crowds of people
anonymous to them. By late Saturday afternoon, there were six hundred
Philadelphia troops at the Union Depot. News of the troops' arrival had
brought even more people to the yards of the Pennsylvania Railroad. The
troops had only one goal: to clear the tracks so that the freight trains of the
Pennsylvania Railroad could begin running again. With fixed bayonets, they
moved on the crowds of striking railroad workers; Pittsburgh militiamen who
were openly fraternizing with their fellow residents; unemployed workers;
iron and steelworkers; and women and children, all of whom blocked the
tracks leading out of the freight yards. The crowd was hostile and refused to
be moved. A number of the militiamen charged the crowd, stabbing several
people. As a barrage of stones and rocks followed, people in the crowd grew
even angrier by the sight of unarmed people being bayoneted by out-of-
town soldiers. But the railroad company meant business, as did its soldiers,
on loan from the state, and the command to fire quickly followed the hail of
stones. When the firing was over, twenty people lay dead and nearly thirty
were wounded. Bedlam reigned. So too did growing resistance. As Philip S.
Foner wrote: "As word of the massacre spread through the city, thousands of
workers from the rolling mills, coal mines, and factories hurried to the scene
of the killings."[12] Also witnessing the massacre were a number of middle-
class people, as well as women, unemployed men, and teenagers, the latter
a common characteristic of many 1877 crowds.

The crowd, numbering in the thousands, sent the six hundred troops fleeing into the relative safety of a roundhouse. So hostile was the crowd, so
intense the barrage of missiles of all types hurled at the roundhouse, that
the Philadelphia militia considered using a Gatling gun. But the aroused
working class of Pittsburgh had better things to do: people began to empty
the standing freight cars and then set fire to not only the freight cars, but
railroad property in general. As Saturday evening passed into early Sunday
morning, a three-mile stretch of railroad property—cars, workshops, lumberyards, roundhouses—went up in a spectacular blaze that lit up the night sky
for many miles. City firemen sent to the scene were prevented by the crowd
from putting any water on the flames. When it was over, the scene evoked
images of burned-out southern cities in 1865, such as Richmond and Columbia. More than two thousand cars of every sort had been destroyed, nearly
forty buildings of various kinds lay in ashes, and more than one hundred
locomotives were ready for little more than the scrap heap. It was a scene of
unparalleled destruction that stretched for miles. The shock of the carnage,
both material and human (another twenty people had been killed by the

Philadelphia militiamen), was such that the city itself largely restored order to its streets by Monday morning. Indeed, Pittsburgh's militiamen, largely working class in composition, reassembled and marched through the streets unopposed.[13]

News of what transpired in Pittsburgh shocked and terrified the nation. Newspaper headlines screamed that "the mob" had nearly burned the city to the ground in its fury to get at railroad property, and that insurrection threatened the nation, and property everywhere was at risk. Yet the railroad workers' strike continued, as railroadmen in scores of other cities went on strike during or after the events in Baltimore and Pittsburgh. On the same weekend that the western terminus of the Pennsylvania Railroad burned to the ground, the Great Strike began in upstate New York, as railroad workers in Buffalo, Albany, and elsewhere struck. As was the case nearly everywhere, their action quickly led to worker strikes from other economic sectors, as well as people from the middle class.

Chicago and St. Louis experienced serious urban disorder consequent upon the Great Strike in the eastern cities. In St. Louis, a *general strike* followed the strike of railroad workers. For several days, the city was ruled by the Workingmen's Party of the United States, as workers in virtually every industry struck and shut the city down.[14] Chicago, the nation's slaughterhouse and a major nexus for all railroads headed west or east, had its own share of Great Strike violence, with at least one pitched battle between troops and working-class crowds claiming the lives of nearly twenty people. As Richard Schneirov's essay details, the crowds were multiethnic in character, as well as containing a significant number of women who actively partook in the violence. In Chicago, as in the nation generally, the Great Strike of 1877 was put down by the armed forces of the state, whether they were local or state militia or federal troops called out by Pres. Rutherford B. Hayes.

The violent urban disorders of the strike accelerated the repressive capacities and therefore the development of the national state. As the strikes demonstrated, there was an intimate, if unstable, connection between state and national force. Local and state militias were the option of first choice (as well as local police), but if they proved unreliable, as they sometimes did, national troops were called out to crush the violent crowds of strikers and nonstrikers. In the years and decades after the strikes, state militias—especially in states that had witnessed dramatic and widespread violence—expanded in size, and National Guard armories were built or strengthened. Militias were increasingly trained to become more efficient in quelling civil disorder. John K. Mahon's study of the development of state militias and the National Guard asserts that the Great Strike, "and the industrial warfare it induced, was the stimulant that set off the development of the modern National Guard." Although the development of the guard varied significantly from state to state, the impact of the Great Strike on expanding the essential force component of the modern national state taking shape in the late-nineteenth century is clear.[15]

The Great Strike of 1877 had profound repercussions for American culture and society and consequently continues to be the subject of scholarly examination and debate in the twentieth and twenty-first centuries. In Eric Foner's masterful study of the Reconstruction era, *Reconstruction: America's Unfinished Revolution,* the Great Strike of 1877 represents a watershed event—an event that helped push the attention of white northerners away from the "Negro problem" in the South, leaving the embers of the North's Reconstruction efforts to the heels of southern whites. In its place, northerners focused their attention on the problems of rapid economic growth and the increasingly large and turbulent working class spawned by the process of industrialization and its twins, urbanization and immigration. The strikes also heralded the violent clashes between labor and capital in Gilded Age and Progressive Era America. Other historians also view the Great Strike as a watershed event, turning the nation away from Reconstruction, toward the violent and even insurrectionary possibilities attendant upon America's capitalist socioeconomic transformation. In short, this historiographical current views the Great Strike as a turning point in U.S. history, particularly with regard to the demise of Reconstruction and the growth of an increasingly militant working class.[16]

There is a strong measure of truth to the "watershed" view of the Great Strike, but it has come at the expense of the continuity inherent in the Great Strike itself and in the nation at large during the Gilded Age. Furthermore, the explicit or implicit assertion that the strikes changed the nation's focus from one of race (in the South) to one of class (in the North) neglects the newer scholarship of historians such as Scott Reynolds Nelson and Heather Cox Richardson, which argues persuasively that there were organic, causal ties between race and class in the decision of white northerners to turn their backs on southern blacks and the demise of Reconstruction in the South.[17] Richardson, for example, argues that the demands of former slaves for land and government intervention on their behalf was interpreted by many northern politicians as a rejection of the free-labor ideology and an acceptance by the former slaves of the notion that there was an irrepressible conflict between capital and labor. Consequently, Richardson writes, white northerners dropped the "Negro question" because southern blacks were viewed as a threat to the very "core of American society."[18]

This first-ever volume of essays on the Great Strike of 1877 significantly expands our knowledge of nationwide events during the summer of 1877. The existing historiography on 1877 has been almost entirely of an eastern and midwestern focus. Three of the essays in this volume push the historiography in a much needed southerly and westward direction, examining 1877 in the Mid-South and California. The essays also begin to fill a hole in our knowledge of the strikes by examining the ethnic and racial terrain within which 1877 was interpreted and played out. The essays in this volume examine and analyze the social and political continuities, as well as changes, intrinsic to the Great Strike in specific locales and regions. These essays also shed light on the nature of the Gilded Age and subsequent decades.

Joshua Brown's essay, "The Great Uprising and Pictorial Order in Gilded Age America," analyzes pictorial, journalistic representations of the poor, laborers, and other denizens of urban America in mid-nineteenth-century America and how the Great Strike compelled a dramatic change in the standard social typing found in illustrated depictions. Basing his analysis on the unique and widely read *Frank Leslie's Illustrated Newspaper,* and on other illustrated newspapers, Brown argues that the Great Strike marked "the breaking point in Leslie's pictorial practice and the end of one phase of a pictorial order that had governed illustrated journalism up to that time." Up until the 1877 strike, pictorial journalism revealed "the poverty underlying city life while also assuring its viewers that the problem was largely the result of individual moral failure." That comforting characterization of the poor was shattered by the Great Strike. The very nature of the strike—triggered by railroad workers, but with broad middle-class support, and to a lesser extent actual "middling" participation in crowd violence—forced a new pictorial representation of those responsible for urban violence and disorder. Given that readers may very well have been in the 1877 crowds, *Leslie's Illustrated* showed the strike and its participants "without the predictable marks of moral character, social role, and motive." The Great Strike of 1877 consequently created an "unpredictability of depiction, unmooring of types, and lessening of physiognomy in the representation of the poor and workers" and precipitated a "move toward realism."

Shelton Stromquist's "'Our Rights as Workingmen': Class Traditions and Collective Action in a Nineteenth-Century Railroad Town, Hornellsville, N.Y., 1869–82" examines the Great Strike in Hornellsville, a railroad town where the "troubles" garnered secondary headlines in papers throughout the country in July 1877. Stromquist's article takes a close look at the social structure of Hornellsville and its railroad workforce. Unlike so many previous studies of the 1877 strikes, this essay places the Great Strike in the "social context of railroad workers' lives." In addition to the Great Strike, major railroad strikes occurred in Hornellsville in 1869, 1870, 1871, 1873, 1874, and 1881. The dramatic increase in railroad and industrial conflict in the decade of the 1870s produced an upsurge in union organization. Among railroad workers particularly, the strikes prior to 1877 produced a tradition of collection action, which was played out in July 1877. Railroad brakemen were in the forefront of these strikes, including the Great Strike. The formation in 1873, the year the depression began, of the Brakemen's Brotherhood served to provide an organizational vehicle for various labor actions. But as Stromquist illustrates, the Brakemen's Brotherhood was from its inception "a nascent industrial union of railroad workers." As Stromquist's article details, at root, workers—railroad workers and other laborers—fought for their self-defined "rights." The Great Strike of 1877 accelerated greatly the move toward industrial unionism, though solidarity across the lines of skill and trade had developed prior to the creation of formal organizations. Stromquist's article points toward the changes taking place in the consciousness of workers that underlay the formation of the Knights of Labor and its ascendancy in the 1880s.

Richard Schneirov's essay on the 1877 strike in Chicago, the nation's railroad transportation hub as well as the country's slaughterhouse, merges Gilded Age labor history with political history. In Chicago, the Great Strike of 1877 "brought to a crisis the increasing polarization of two emerging industrial classes: large-scale employers and allied property owners and a new immigrant, industrial working class." The crisis between these two groups, precipitated by the violence of the strike, jolted democratic politics in the city and posed a vital question for the city and, by implication, the nation at large: could the city's democratic politics, guided by professional politicians responsive to those who had no income-producing property, be "reconciled" with the new order being created by industrial capitalism? As readers will learn, Schneirov's "Chicago's Great Upheaval of 1877: Class Polarization and Democratic Politics" challenges the standard interpretation of Gilded Age politics.

Steven Hoffman's "Looking North: A Mid-South Perspective on the Great Strike" examines the 1877 strikes in three Mid-South cities: Memphis and Nashville, Tennessee, and Louisville, Kentucky. As such, it is the first article of its kind to detail the Great Strike of 1877 in a southern setting. As Hoffman illustrates, elites in these three cities viewed the Great Strike via the prism of southern sectionalism, and juxtaposed the strikes and their accompanying violence with the allegedly contented status of white and black workers in the South. However, the strikes soon prompted southern workers in these cities to strike themselves—or threaten to strike—as a way of obtaining concessions from their employers. These threatened or actual strikes were not limited to the railroad industry; workers in other economic sectors also used these two tactics to force employers to given them meaningful concessions in the area of wages and working conditions. The initial glee of southern newspaper editors at what had been almost exclusively a northern event was severely tempered by Louisville's citywide strikes, which amounted to a virtual general strike. In particular, the willingness of black sewer workers to strike and form large black crowds in the city dramatically alarmed white elites (and no doubt, non-elites). Indeed, in Louisville, a crowd overwhelmingly composed of seven hundred black strikers cast the Great Strike, at least temporarily, in something other than a mould with which to favorably compare the actions of northern and southern workers.

Michael Kazin's article on the Great Strike in San Francisco, "The July Days in San Francisco, 1877: Prelude to Kearneyism," is the only in-depth study of the 1877 strike in San Francisco, and it is a vital contribution to our understanding of collective violence and the contours of the Great Strike in the Far West, an area of the country given short shrift in the historiography of 1877. In San Francisco, workers vented their violence not at railroad property, as they did in scores of other cities and towns across the nation, but at what they defined as their chief enemy: Chinese immigrants. In short, white workers in San Francisco targeted their wrath at the terms of industrial capitalism through the scope of ethnic animosity. And as Kazin demonstrates, there was a distinctly political dimension to the San Francisco strikes, for they served as the "prelude to Kearneyism," a working-class political movement for white men only.

David Miller's essay breaks entirely new ground by examining the impact of the Great Strike on Californios (Hispanics and Mexican Americans) and southern California. In "California's Changing Society and Mexican American Conceptions of the Great Strike," Miller posits that the strikes were "a particularly salient moment in the ongoing struggle in United States history between the tensions of capitalist development and racial equality in a democratic society." For Mexican Americans, the 1877 strikes occurred as they "were near the culmination of a three-decade-long struggle to resist white hegemony." Indeed, as readers will find, the strikes served a defensive role in Californios' struggle to resist the impositions and demands of a white, capitalist "modernity."

During the Great Strike of 1877, the nation did indeed focus its attention on the nature of the working classes and the new industrial order rapidly taking shape. And after the strikes, Reconstruction was dead as a national issue. Yet, Reconstruction would have died in 1877 without the Great Strike, and the strikes themselves and their consequences in towns from Hornellsville and Chicago to Louisville and San Francisco revealed that society and politics during the Gilded Age were marked as much by continuity, perhaps more so, than by fundamental change in the existing social order. For workers, organized and unorganized, the depression would continue for nearly another two years. Organized labor rebounded in the 1880s, primarily with the rise to prominence and power of the Knights of Labor. As the Knights reached their zenith in 1886, the American Federation of Labor formed—an organization of skilled white workers organized along craft lines. The future of organized labor was to lie with the trade-union model upon which the AFL was built. Industrial unionism and the building of an alternative society—the "cooperative commonwealth" envisioned by the Knights—faded as quickly as the Knights had exploded onto the national scene in the decade following the Great Strike. Gilded Age politics were intensely partisan, particularly on the local level, despite the equilibrium of power between Republicans and Democrats on the national level—a stasis shattered by the election of 1896.

Notes

1. David Montgomery, *Beyond Equality: Labor and the Radical Republicans, 1862–1872* (New York: Alfred A. Knopf, 1967), 91.

2. Ibid., 30, 135.

3. Melvyn Dubofsky and Foster Rhea Dulles, *Labor in America: A History,* 6th ed. (Wheeling, Ill.: Harlan Davidson, 1999), 102.

4. Herbert G. Gutman, "Trouble on the Railroads in 1873–1874: Prelude to the 1877 Crisis?" in Gutman, *Work, Culture, and Society in Industrializing America: Essays in Working Class and Social History* (New York: Vintage Books, 1976); Gutman, "The Tompkins Square 'Riot' in New York City on January 13, 1874: A Re-examination of Its Causes and Its Aftermath," *Labor History* 6, no. 1 (1965): 44–70; Dubofsky and Dulles, *Labor in America,* 107–8.

5. Eric Foner, *Reconstruction: America's Unfinished Revolution, 1863–1877* (New York: Harper & Row, 1988).

6. I define the term *collective violence* following Charles Tilly's definition in *The Politics of Collective Violence* (Cambridge: Cambridge University Press, 2003), 3: the violent behavior involves at least two people, results in immediate physical/personal damage, and involves at least some prior planning or coordination among the participants. Bruce Laurie, *Artisans into Workers: Labor in Nineteenth-Century America* (Urbana: University of Illinois Press, 1997), 143–44.

7. Eric Hobsbawm, *The Age of Capital: 1848–1875* (New York: Vintage Books, 1996), 145; David O. Stowell, *Streets, Railroads, and the Great Strike of 1877* (Chicago: University of Chicago Press, 1999). For an excellent analysis of the Gilded Age, see Rebecca Edwards, *New Spirits: Americans in the Gilded Age, 1865–1905* (Oxford: Oxford University Press, 2006). On the Great Strike of 1877, see Robert V. Bruce, *1877: Year of Violence* (Chicago: Ivan R. Dee, 1989); Philip S. Foner, *The Great Labor Uprising of 1877* (New York: Pathfinder, 1977); Gutman, "Trouble on the Railroads" in Gutman, *Work, Culture, and Society;*

Nick Salvatore, "Railroad Workers and the Great Strike of 1877: The View from a Small Midwest City," *Labor History* 21, no. 4 (Fall 1980): 522–45; David Montgomery, "Strikes in Nineteenth-Century America," *Social Science History* 4, no. 1 (February 1980): 81–103; David R. Roediger, "'Not Only the Ruling Classes to Overcome, but Also the So-Called Mob': Class, Skill and Community in the St. Louis General Strike of 1877," *Journal of Social History* (Winter 1985): 213–39; Shelton Stromquist, *A Generation of Boomers: The Pattern of Railroad Labor Conflict in Nineteenth-Century America* (Urbana: University of Illinois Press, 1987); David O. Stowell, "'Small Property-Holders' and the Great Strike of 1877: Railroads, City Streets, and the Middle Classes," *Journal of Urban History* 21, no. 6 (September 1995): 741–63; William Deverell, *Railroad Crossing: Californians and the Railroad, 1850–1910* (Berkeley: University of California Press, 1994); Richard Schneirov, "Chicago's Great Upheaval of 1877," *Chicago History* (1980); Brian P. Luskey, "Riot and Respectability: The Shifting Terrain of Class Language and Status in Baltimore during the Great Strike of 1877," *American Nineteenth Century History* 4 (Fall 2003).

8. Bruce, *1877: Year of Violence,* 104, 100–114.

9. Cited in Bruce, *1877: Year of Violence,* 121.

10. Bruce, *1877: Year of Violence,* Chapter 7.

11. Ibid., Chapter 8.

12. Foner, *The Great Labor Uprising,* 73–75.

13. Foner, *The Great Labor Uprising,* 76–77; Bruce, *1877: Year of Violence,* 180.

14. Foner, *The Great Labor Uprising,* Chapter 9. See Roediger's "'Not Only the Ruling Classes to Overcome'" for a detailed analysis of the social composition of the strike's participants—and opponents.

15. John K. Mahon, *History of the Militia and National Guard* (New York: Macmillan, 1983), 113. For a different perspective on the impact of the Great Strikes on the development of the guard, see Jerry M. Cooper, *The Rise of the National Guard: The Evolution of the American Militia, 1865–1920* (Lincoln: University of Nebraska Press, 1997). On the evolution of the national state during the mid-nineteenth century, see Richard Franklin Bensel, *Yankee Leviathan: The Origins of Central State Authority in America, 1859–1877* (Cambridge: Cambridge University Press, 1990).

16. Foner, *Reconstruction.* To be sure, the watershed view of 1877 is not Foner's creation—Robert V. Bruce wrote, "Everywhere the shock of the Great Strike broke old patterns of thought and crystallized new ones. The nation put away childish things, the lead soldiers and toy drums of Reconstruction politics, and, for a season at least, faced a living issue." The majority of historians, including Foner, have followed Bruce's watershed construction. Bruce, *1877: Year of Violence,* 312. For some other watershed positions, see Nell Irvin Painter, *Standing at Armageddon: The United States, 1877–1919* (New York: W. W. Norton, 1997); Walter Licht, *Industrializing America: The Nineteenth Century* (Baltimore: Johns Hopkins University Press, 1995). For an excellent critique of a watershed view of the Great Strike, see Salvatore, "Railroad Workers and the Great Strike of 1877."

17. Scott Reynolds Nelson, *Iron Confederacies: Southern Railways, Klan Violence, and Reconstruction* (Chapel Hill: University of North Carolina Press, 1999); Heather Cox Richardson, *The Death of Reconstruction: Race, Labor, and Politics in the Post–Civil War North, 1865–1901* (Cambridge, Mass.: Harvard University Press, 2001).

18. Richardson, *The Death of Reconstruction,* xiii–xiv, 244–45.

1. The Great Uprising and Pictorial Order in Gilded Age America

JOSHUA BROWN

I became manager of the art department of FRANK LESLIE'S in 1875. . . . Notwithstanding I was the chief of the department, I often had to respond to "emergency calls" myself, and at last it came to pass that when any important event requiring illustration took place, Becker had to go. I always in those days kept a satchel, already packed, in the office, and was prepared to leave at a moment's notice. Partly because I had become the regular pictorial reporter, and partly because I was born in and was familiar with the region, I went, in 1877, to northeastern Pennsylvania to depict scenes in the sensational "Mollie Maguire" troubles.

In 1905, when Joseph Becker wrote a brief reminiscence of his forty-one-year career with *Frank Leslie's Illustrated Newspaper,* he severely condensed his role in the pictorial coverage of life, labor, and especially conflict in the anthracite coal region of eastern Pennsylvania.[1] In fact, Becker was first dispatched to the area four years before he began supervising *Leslie's* art department. From March through May 1871, four engravings attributed to him appeared in the weekly depicting strikers harassing and attacking "blackleg" replacements, along with three cuts illustrating "mining operations."[2] Then Becker seems to have moved on to other reportorial duties and, after its comparatively intensive pictorial consideration of coal miners' struggles, labor, and peril, *Leslie's* interest abruptly subsided; a three-year hiatus in coverage followed, broken only by one peaceful Fourth of July scene (not recorded by Becker) during the summer of 1873.[3]

The bitter "Long Strike" during the winter of 1874–75 brought Joseph Becker and *Frank Leslie's* back to eastern Pennsylvania. Franklin Gowen, president of the Reading Railroad, instigated the strike to destroy the miners' union, the Workingmen's Benevolent Association, and thereby gain total control of eastern Pennsylvania coal mining. For *Leslie's,* Becker's longtime familiarity with the area must have seemed particularly advantageous, as the region was steeped in suspicion, destitution, and violence engendered by Gowen's efforts.[4]

Becker's pictorial reportage of the strike began in December 1874 with a small engraving of miners' huts near Scranton. The secret society of the Molly Maguires was mentioned for the first time in the accompanying text, and both the description and the distant perspective of the cut offered an impartial view of the strikers.[5] A few months later, however, Becker's engravings and written reports (the additional textual information suggests that the artist himself was their author) took a decidedly partisan turn toward Gowen's position. Depicting himself "among the 'Mollie Maguires'" of Pottsville, Becker constructed a portrait of "anarchy in the coal regions of Pennsylvania" promoted by the Irish miners' "criminal organization," and he blamed the destitution of mining families on a "spirit of lawlessness" produced by ignorance, alcoholism, and sloth.[6] "The last loaf," the engraving ("from real life") published in the March 13, 1875, issue, presented the "sad story of the suffering that frequently befalls the families of the mistaken workmen who follow the lead of the blatant demagogues—the orators who prate of the utility of strikes."

In lines and words that recall representations of urban poverty, Becker depicted a familiar travesty of domesticity:

> The father of the family, a strong, athletic man whose labor could bring means to support his family in comfort, sits idly by his cabin-door carousing with his boon companions, while his hard-worked wife and almost starving children gather around the oven, as they place in it the last loaf, doubtful as to where the next supply of food may come from. . . . In the distance are collieries lying idle for want of workmen such as he who thus allows his family to want. What a happy home this man might make for himself and family! A neat cot, with smiling wife and happy children to greet his return from an honest day's labor, might take the place of this dismal hovel and dejected family, would he but work contentedly for a fair remuneration.[7]

Though Becker's reminiscences thirty years later revealed that his interpretation matched that of the Reading Railroad, his services extended far beyond reporting conditions of the Long Strike to *Leslie's* readers. Soon after arriving in Pennsylvania, he wrote in 1905, "I fell in with a detective, and together, unsuspected, but taking great risks, we traveled about, coming in contact with many 'Mollies,' and even getting on familiar terms with their leaders. In this way we acquired inside information which was of avail to the prosecuting officers."[8]

Figure 1.1. "Pennsylvania.—The last loaf—A scene in the coal region during the recent strike." Wood engraving based on a sketch by Joseph Becker, *Frank Leslie's Illustrated Newspaper*, March 13, 1875, 9. American Social History Project.

Becker's pictures of self-inflicted degradation and his conflation of trade unionists with ringleaders of a secret criminal organization did not go uncontested. In April 1875, in a rare public acknowledgement of reader response, *Frank Leslie's Illustrated Newspaper* addressed objections to its coverage of the Long Strike. In the wake of Becker's "pen and pencil pictures," *Frank Leslie's* received a flurry of "ill-spelled" and "violently abusive" letters from the mining districts; these, in the weekly's view, only confirmed the special artist's depictions. *Leslie's* felt obliged, however, to address the more measured protest of Hugh McGarvy, president of the State Council of the Workingmen's Benevolent Association. "[B]oth the illustration and the pen-picture of the Miners of Pennsylvania are unfair," McGarvy had complained; "the miners are not all drunkards." McGarvy went on to defend his members' morals and sobriety, stating that if they were given "fair remuneration" from their employers, "there would be no trouble. They would willingly work, and make happy families and comfortable firesides." McGarvy concluded, "I was not surprised when first I saw such things in *Harper's Weekly,* but from FRANK LESLIE'S ILLUSTRATED NEWSPAPER better things were expected. We respectfully solicit at your hands simple truth and justice for the miners as a whole."[9]

In response to this criticism, *Leslie's* conceded that strikes "are sometimes the only, and in that case, the legitimate, resort of labor in a conflict with capital." But, the weekly added, "experience proves how ruinous strikes usually are to both, and particularly to the former."[10] Two more Becker contributions on the miners' strike subsequently appeared during 1875, one in the issue following McGarvy's letter and the other not until early September; neither relinquished much rhetorical ground. The accompanying descriptions forthrightly defended the engravings' accuracy and called on "all honest laborers to aid in discountenancing deeds that tend to degrade the dignity of labor[.]"[11]

The next time *Leslie's* depicted labor conflict in the anthracite coal region was for the execution of the convicted Molly Maguire conspirators in June 1877.[12] Once again Joseph Becker journeyed to eastern Pennsylvania, although in this instance (perhaps as a cautionary measure) his sketchwork remained uncredited. As censorious as his Long Strike pictures had been, Becker's images of the Pottsville prison, the families and friends of the condemned men, the last rites, and the final march to the gallows were somber and respectful.[13] The solemn occasion, and no doubt *Leslie's* Catholic readers, prescribed this different approach. Becker's own attitude seems to have been fleetingly remorseful. "I could not bear to see these men swing," he later confessed, "and so I absented myself from their execution. Afterward I received from the executioner (the detective aforesaid) a two and a half inch section of each rope used in the hanging. I have these grim souvenirs still."[14]

Whatever the nature of *Leslie's* coverage of the Long Strike, it sharply contrasted with the cursory reporting of the two competing pictorial papers of the period. *Harper's Weekly* published only one image, "The strike in the coal mines—Meeting of 'Molly M'Guire' men," credited to Paul Frenzeny and Jules Tavernier, an atypically romantic image of the secret society that belied the weekly's contempt for Irish Catholics (as exemplified in Thomas Nast's ubiquitous political caricatures).[15] The *New York Daily Graphic* covered the strike in the anthracite region in its issue of May 22, 1875, peppering its report with anti-Irish commentary.[16]

But the significance of *Leslie's* Long Strike engravings lies less in Joseph Becker's collusion with the Pinkerton National Detective Agency than in the many letters *Leslie's* received denouncing his "pen and pencil pictures." Those letters indicate that in the decade following the Civil War, the weekly's readership extended even into isolated areas like the coalfields of Schuylkill County. Moreover, they showed specific readers firmly refusing to be reduced to a criminal, degraded social type in the pages of *Frank Leslie's*. To be sure, their protest had little immediate impact beyond tortured defenses of the engravings' depictions of violence and degradation. But Hugh McGarvy's closing remark—that "better things were expected" from *Frank Leslie's*—suggests something more. Although the paper was hardly the voice of beleaguered trade unionism, its reliance on a broad spectrum of readers compelled it to cover labor struggles, a hazardous tactic as it also attempted to bridge the increasing political, social, and cultural differences among its varied reading public. The exigencies of industrial capitalism and the resultant social conflict during the Gilded Age multiplied difference and threatened to fracture the broad readership on which the weekly relied. "The Great Uprising" of July 1877 would mark the breaking point in *Leslie's* pictorial practice and the end of one phase of a pictorial order that had governed illustrated journalism up to that time.

The Illustrated Press

Born out of the conjuncture of the transportation revolution, innovations in printing technology, an expanded literary and pictorial market, and national crisis, *Frank Leslie's Illustrated Newspaper* exemplified mid-nineteenth-century pictorial publication.[17] After running the engraving department of the *Illustrated London News* for six years, Frank Leslie (the name adopted by Suffolk-born Henry Carter when he took up wood engraving in defiance of his glove-manufacturer father) arrived in New York City in 1848 to discover no comparable news publication requiring his services.[18] Opening an

engraving establishment on Broadway, within a year Leslie found work with
an individual who would steer him down a path that dramatically departed
from the genteel approach to the news espoused by his previous employer. In
1849, P. T. Barnum hired Leslie to illustrate a lavish program to promote Jenny
Lind's whirlwind concert tour of the United States. The successful promotion
of the Swedish Nightingale's 1850–51 tour soon led to another collaboration
in 1853. Although Barnum's *Illustrated News* did not survive the first year
of its publication, Leslie (who served as its chief engraver) had amassed
enough capital by then to finally go out on his own.[19] *Frank Leslie's Ladies'
Gazette of Fashion* and *Frank Leslie's Journal of Romance*, a story magazine,
both published in 1854, turned out to be lucrative ventures, and they were
soon joined by *Frank Leslie's Illustrated Newspaper* in 1855. After weathering
the 1857 depression, Leslie's operation was put on firm financial footing by
its Civil War reportage. With its pictorial coverage of the national crisis, the
American weekly illustrated press—epitomized by *Frank Leslie's Illustrated
Newspaper* and *Harper's Weekly* (founded in 1857)—became an established
source of news, providing a picture-hungry public with thousands of images
during the four years of the war. In 1873, the *New York Daily Graphic* was
introduced, the first daily newspaper to consistently carry pictures; four of
its eight pages were devoted to news images and cartoons (albeit, compared
to *Leslie's* and *Harper's*, with less elaborate rendering or expansive coverage).
By the time the *Daily Graphic* appeared, Leslie's firm at 537 Pearl Street employed between three and four hundred people, including seventy engravers,
and published seven publications bearing his name that sometimes reached
editions numbering into the hundreds of thousands.

Frank Leslie created a pictorial publishing empire predicated on innovations in cheap printing, the subdivision of labor in the production of illustrations, and the appeal to a broad and diverse audience. Unlike his archrival,
the genteel House of Harper, Leslie teetered on the cusp of respectability,
prepared to attract the circulation necessary to support the expense of an
illustrated press by addressing the varied constituencies comprising the vastly
expanded market. Leslie viewed his publishing house as a marketplace in
itself, with specific periodicals targeted at specific audiences, his publications ranging from didactic children's magazines to the notorious *The Days'
Doings* (in which "Illustrating Current Events of Romance, Police Reports,
Important Trials, and Sporting News" was directed to a male readership,
inspired by the equally sensational *National Police Gazette*). The capstone
of his endeavors, *Frank Leslie's Illustrated Newspaper*—"giving to the public
original, accurate and faithful representations of the most prominent events
of the day"—was Leslie's most inclusive publication, addressing the broad

"middle," an elastic range of readers that, in the mid-nineteenth century, stretched from mechanics to merchants.[20]

With impressive rapidity, the sixteen-page newspaper (often accompanied by supplements and special editions) regularly depicted the events and personages of the previous week. Adopting the methods of mass production that were transforming the labor process in mid-nineteenth-century America, *Leslie's* was able to rapidly deliver illustrations of the news to the public, often within days of its occurrence. The artist's sketch was but the first step in a process of pictorial reproduction that would progressively reconfigure and transform its initial interpretation. After the art superintendent chose a sketch to be worked up into an engraving, a staff artist drew a new version on paper, rendered in outlines. The drawing was then rubbed down in reverse upon the whitewashed surface of a block of Turkish boxwood, itself composed of smaller sections of wood secured together by a system of nuts and bolts. Draftsmen applied further detail in washes and pencil (sometimes dividing up the block among artists with particular skills for rendering figures, architecture, landscapes, machinery, etc.), and then the composite block went to the engraving department, where it was unbolted and distributed to a team of engravers. The engravers laboriously carved out the design (leaving the lines in relief to print black) on their individual pieces, after which the constituent blocks were rebolted together and a supervising engraver ensured that the incised lines met across the sections. The engraved block was then sent to the composing room, where it was locked into place with handset type to create a *Frank Leslie's* page to be made into an electrotyped copper plate.[21]

Supplementing daily press coverage, the pictures in *Frank Leslie's* added the dimension of palpability to the news, displaying the faces of noted individuals, the contexts and content of events. This information was rendered with particular attention to the detail of streets, scenery, and interiors. Deriving their authenticity in the eyewitness (or earwitness) presence of the "special artist," aided by an "ambulatory" photographic staff and a vast photographic file providing architectural and topographical references, the engravings constructed news events into visual performances. The illustrations, often framed in prosceniumlike compositions, imparted a brief narrative, extending the sense of time and conveying cause and effect. On occasion, *Leslie's* published news engravings based solely on photographs, usually duly noted in their captions; in contrast to the extended narrative of the standard news cuts, the engravings that faithfully reproduced photographs often appear detached and static, marking the importance of an event rather than delineating its meaning or atmosphere. "We do not depend upon the accidental transmission of photographs, with their corpse-like literalness," *Frank Leslie's* intoned in 1859, "but upon our own special artists." Disingenuous as this remark was in the light of *Leslie's* use of photographs as source material, it nevertheless accurately described the differing representational effect of the two media.[22]

The Pictorial Order

In *Frank Leslie's* archive of places, events, and people, portraits were ubiquitous. Mathew Brady and his contemporaries may have captured the features of "illustrious Americans" on the photographic plate, but it was the illustrated press that made the faces of politicians and pundits, actors and artists, clergymen and charitable reformers, diplomats and royalty, familiar to the public. However, Brady did more than merely record; he codified the conventions of the formal public portrait into a facial map of success.[23] The idealized face of the "emulatory" photographic portrait became the standard by which the notable were represented in the pages of *Frank Leslie's* and its competitors. Individual engraved portraits based on photographs supplied by specific studios (including Brady) graced every issue. But depictions of events involving notable figures also remained in the vise of conventional photographic portraiture. The even, modulatory gaze of the posed shot tyrannized every cut, unchanging even in the most dramatic circumstances. Such engravings succeeded in supplying readers with the details of news events, delineating the assembled personages, the layout of rooms, and the composition of surrounding scenery. But the mission to preserve the official faces of notable Americans culminated in ideal heads planted onto ill-matched bodies, perpetuating (according to *New York World* illustrator Valerian Gribayedoff) photography's creation of a new genus called "homo 'uprights.'"[24]

Expressions appropriate to trying circumstances—unmasking and revealing the private, unholy countenances of the famous—were isolated on pages reserved for political caricatures and cartoons.[25] The discrete separation of idealized and caricatured portrayals of notable figures, however, did not apply to the greater balance of humanity portrayed in *Frank Leslie's Illustrated Newspaper.* When it came to the representation of events in the newly discovered terrain of the defeated South, the burgeoning settlements of the West, or the prosperous and poor neighborhoods of New York City, "anonymous" Americans took on explicit and exaggerated features, expressions, gestures, and poses. Distinguished by traits linked to specific regions of the nation (each in turn with its own variations and subgroups), the citizens differentiated into representational social types were instantly recognizable to readers. The device of typing dated back to the first years of the republic, but it had blossomed in the Jacksonian era's culture industry. The self-confident and calculating Yankee "Brother Jonathan" of New England, the independent and irrepressible western frontiersman, the rude backwoods southern "cracker," and the pugnacious and preening urban plebeian "Mose" were among the most popular of the regional characters performed on the popular stage, described in popular literature, and illustrated in the crude woodcuts of comic almanacs and the "low" aesthetics of genre painting. The distinctive features, styles of dress, and poses of these social types signified predictable and predetermined characteristics that served as components for a normative description of American society.[26]

In the antebellum period, types as visual images were subordinate to theatrical performance and literature, appearing mainly in woodcut illustrations of comic almanacs or in lithographs portraying actors as celebrated characters. The advent of the illustrated press in the 1850s rejuvenated the practice of typing, with its broader distribution, greater accessibility, and better reproduction techniques. Types appeared in visual codes that, to those versed in the science of physiognomy, revealed their innate character and motive to a vast American public. Rooted in Aristotelian precepts of the ideal, physiognomy's long history had reached a milestone in the late eighteenth century with the publication of Johann Caspar Lavater's multivolume *Physiognomische Fragmente*. The Swiss theologian's work, translated into many languages, set forth precise rules for deducing essential moral and social qualities from facial structure and expression. Establishing the ideal in the classical Greek profile, in which the nose and forehead form a vertical line denoting intelligence and spirituality, Lavater's many diagrams delineated how deviations from classical balance and symmetry compared with traits found in animals to confirm characterological flaws, from idiocy to immorality. More to the point, Lavater's diagrams served as models for artists, both in the studio and in the newspaper office, as they depicted the populace. Rendering figures whose features and physiques were imbued with the rules of physiognomy, the illustrations in the pictorial press constructed an orderly, detectable, moral map for what seemed so hidden and chaotic in mid-nineteenth-century America.[27] Through the palpability of appearance, *Frank Leslie's* and other weekly illustrated papers offered a way to comprehend and represent the increasingly complex and perplexing nineteenth-century social reality.

The imperative for reading character and social role was particularly acute in the new, heterogeneous "world of strangers" of the mid-nineteenth-century American city. The geographic growth and discomfiting mix of classes in cities like New York prompted the production of literary and visual categorizations that assured an emerging, inchoate middle class that there still was coherence in the universe: the threatening urban landscape could be read and, with this knowledge, safely traversed. The pictorial press played a crucial role in making the city seem decipherable, serving as the perfect complement to genteel rules of public behavior that required the controlled gaze of "civil inattention" in the street; in private, looking over a pictorial newspaper, the respectable reader could let his or her eyes rove promiscuously over the urban scene.[28]

Information guiding the citizen through the treacherous streets was readily available in the pictorial press, and it was New York City in particular, the home of *Frank Leslie's Illustrated Newspaper* and its competitors, that became the nation's paradigm for urban life. Society balls and political campaigns, building construction and conflagrations, theater openings and funerals, parks and processions—significant or not, events in New York predominated in *Frank Leslie's* coverage. The customs and manners of the city were portrayed through a range of social types (and their subcategories) stretching across the classes: Wall Street types tussled in the financial district; middle-class types thronged the ferries on weekend excursions; polite society types attended banquets and fancy balls; and a panoply of ethnic types engaged in their customary pastimes.

In their day-to-day lives, real New Yorkers endured the promiscuous bustle of humanity, but for readers of the illustrated press the spectacle of the mixed urban crowd faded from view. Like the expanding metropolis fragmented into enclaves defined by class and ethnicity, the panorama of the streets was viewed by the paper's readers in small bits. *Leslie's*, like the city guides of the period, mapped the city by gathering separate representations of distinct and contrasting social types, each populating its own characteristic haunts and environs. New York was perceptible only through its parts, a metropolis composed of several cities on a spectrum from sunshine to shadow: "the commercial metropolis," "the metropolis of vice," "the boarding house belt," and "the fashionable metropolis."[29] A unified pictorial sense of the city existed but, like contemporary lithographic and photographic representations, it was largely confined to idealized aerial views, promotional pictures of new Grand-Style buildings, laudatory cuts displaying urban improvements, or fantastic renditions of how the streets *should* look. There were exceptions to the pictorial segmentation of the city, but such engravings portrayed the mixed crowd to convey a sentimental or cautionary note, preserving the exclusiveness of types within the representation of the city.

Unlike the British illustrated press, which avoided the more unpleasant aspects of urban life, American pictorial papers offered a steady supply of pictures showing the dangerous city. *Frank Leslie's Illustrated Newspaper* regularly depicted accidents, fires, hazards, crime, and—especially—poverty.[30] The era's preoccupation with sanitary reform, and the heavy sales that attended *Frank Leslie's* exposés of health scandals, attested to the growing belief that hidden horrors could at any moment transcend the geographical boundaries of class to wreak havoc on the entire city. Readers needed to know the hazards lurking in the metropolis, and the value of the illustrated press lay in its ability to represent the threatening disorder of poverty, obviating the need to learn of danger through direct personal experience.[31]

From the late 1860s to the mid-1870s, readers of *Frank Leslie's* and its pictorial competitors were subjected to an archive of images that revealed the poverty underlying city life, while the periodicals also assured viewers that the problem was largely the result of individual moral failure. Invariably accompanied by descriptions of artist-reporters' journeys into darkness guided by jaded officers of the law, these engravings portrayed enduring social types, their faces and bodies diagrams of characterological failure, their lives passed in dark, crowded conditions that were the antithesis of the domestic ideal. The causes of their plight were readily apparent. Mrs. McMahan's wretched one-room "apartment" on Roosevelt Street, depicted in an 1867 cut, exhibited the destitution wrought by liquor; the sole male occupant was collapsed in an alcoholic stupor on the unswept floor.

While the averted face of the mother suckling her baby added a dollop of sentiment to the hovel's female occupants, the center of the composition was devoted to the slouching Mrs. McMahan. In her harsh, angular features, bereft of feminine virtues, the viewer ascertained the eventual fate of the younger women in the scene, its cause located in the liquor tankard weighing down Mrs. McMahan's right hand.[32] Although relieved occasionally by illustrations that showed the ministrations of charitable reformers and the operations of asylums and mission houses, the overall picture abandoned the "unregulated" adult poor who had irretrievably succumbed to vice. Only one hope for reform emerged out of the visual record of physical and spiritual collapse: the children of the poor. Whether abused by masters or neglected by deficient parents, whether prematurely driven or released from the moral confines of the family to roam unsupervised in the streets, the children of the poor were largely depicted as the blameless victims of corrupted adults. They alone still offered readers the possibility of reform.[33]

The Limits of Order

The conventions and codes in *Frank Leslie's* pictorial coverage of urban poverty indicated, to use Raymond Williams's phrase, an asymmetry in the rela-

Figure 1.2. "The Mysteries and Miseries of New York City. Interior of Mrs. M'Mahan's apartment at No. 22 Roosevelt Street." Wood engraving based on a sketch by Albert Berghaus, *Frank Leslie's Illustrated Newspaper*, February 2, 1867, cover. American Social History Project.

tions between dominant and subordinate cultures in Gilded Age America.[34] At first glance, social typing and the construction of moralistic pictorial narratives in *Leslie's* and its competitors appear as the pictorial equivalent of other social and cultural practices that served to define the new urban middle class. Pictorial publication was far too expensive for working-class institutions and periodicals into the late 1880s; trade union and radical publications could at best afford to reproduce occasional cartoons. No alternative visual news medium challenged the version of reality articulated in the commercial illustrated press. However, the nature of the asymmetry, at least for *Leslie's,* was more complicated than a split between high and low cultures would suggest. The pictorial "vocabulary" used to describe the city was based on forms that had been created in the circumscribed antebellum visual culture, which had been directed to more exclusive audiences. After the Civil War, the readership that sustained *Frank Leslie's* was increasingly defined by diversity, particularly in the face of the fluctuating fortunes and conflicting social relations of industrial capitalism. As an institution predicated on encompassing the differences embodied by its broad middle readership, *Leslie's* faced persistent volatility and perpetual conflicts. The paper's rigid pictorial conventions, especially its promulgation of recognizable and enduring social types, cracked under the weight of postbellum social and political change. At crucial moments, the device of social typing destabilized, and *Leslie's* pictorial narratives became ambiguous or contradictory. In unexpected places we find the creation of new types and the sundering of categories that should have been preserved if a middle-class ideal were holding sway.

The Panic of 1873 and the ensuing depression, the greatest crisis industrial capitalism had yet seen—lasting some five and a half years—led to an unprecedented shift in the representation of the poor. Because such a large proportion of the workforce relied on industrialized employment, this national disaster reconfigured the manner in which poverty was rendered.[35]

While *Leslie's* responded to the early years of the depression with stock figures of poverty, the persistence of economic catastrophe generated a new type of poor American for its representation. Born of the depression, the tramp presented a new brand of ambulatory corruption that threatened to become a permanent, aberrant "profession," as much deplored by the respectable mechanic as by the merchant. In many ways, the figure of the tramp was more an ominous variation on the theme of the undeserving poor than an object lesson in the exigencies of industrial capitalism. "The *genus* tramp," announced an 1876 *Frank Leslie's* editorial, "is a dangerous element in society, and ought to be dealt with accordingly." As depicted in a July 1877 engraving, the transient poor exhibited an aggressive form of degradation, no longer

Figure 1.3. "New York City.—A tramp's ablutions—An early morning scene in Madison Square." Wood engraving, *Frank Leslie's Illustrated Newspaper,* July 21, 1877, cover. American Social History Project.

content to defile only the streets and hovels of the lowly districts of the city and countryside.[36]

But in the face of continued depression, neither dependence on old adages about morality and fate nor reliance on new repressive recommendations seemed adequate. In a city like New York, where by the winter of 1873–74 some one hundred thousand people were unemployed, the reassuring predictability of "traditional" social types (or their slightly revised versions) could not be maintained. Images of the undeserving poor continued to appear in *Leslie's* pages, but they were now supplemented by engravings peopled with the "wrong" types.[37] Among the homeless poor pictured leaving the shelter of a New York City precinct-house on a frigid February 1877 morning were faces and dress that readers uneasily noted did not belong in an engraving of "vagrants."

"It has been noticed this winter," *Frank Leslie's* warily commented, "that among the applicants for lodgings at the stations an unusually large number represents a class of men and women unaccustomed to such dormitories."[38] Unlike the poor as familiarly depicted, the subjects of these and other engravings now potentially included some of *Frank Leslie's* readership. As the forces of industrial capitalism wantonly plucked victims from the population, the reliability of physiognomy to signify the "deserving" and "undeserving," the "respectable" and "degraded," faltered.

In an atmosphere increasingly characterized by division, crisis, and instability, *Frank Leslie's* could no longer count on the shared perceptions of its reading public. Engravings of poverty and want grew more ambivalent or appeared in contradictory juxtapositions, their typed subjects gaining and losing coherence as use of the physiognomic enhancement of features came under attack. As with images of disasters, the engravings of destitution and want brought a shock of recognition to many readers: depression selected its victims with the arbitrariness of a railway accident or calamity of nature. *Leslie's* readers, no longer able to sequester everyday tragedy in the realm of private failure, found pictorial social typing unreliable and inauthentic. Requiring a broad and varied readership to sustain its expensive project, an audience now suffering different fates with different perceptions of causes and effects, *Leslie's* altered its methods of representing social types. The trajectory of *Leslie's* depiction of labor in the decade of the 1870s would decisively reveal the change in the pictorial order.

Pictures of Labor

Since its first publication of a trade-union image (a double-page engraving in 1860 depicting the workers' procession in Lynn, Massachusetts, during a shoemakers' strike), *Frank Leslie's* had sporadically covered the labor movement—in contrast to the patrician *Harper's Weekly's* pictorial disregard of "the labor question." After the Civil War, the publication's generally dismissive and hostile stance toward the effort to win the eight-hour workday was expressed in numerous editorials but few engravings. Yet through the late 1860s, when *Leslie's* covered a strike or some organized trade union activity

Figure 1.4. "New York City.—Early morning at a police station—Turning out the vagrant night lodgers." Wood engraving based on a sketch by Fernando Miranda, *Frank Leslie's Illustrated Newspaper*, February 10, 1877, 377. American Social History Project.

(usually an event in New York), its portrayal was generally sympathetic.[39] The momentous year 1871 brought Joseph Becker's pictures of eastern Pennsylvania mine violence, which seemed to augur a new era of class relations uncomfortably suggestive of the wholesale strife erupting in many European capitals. But *Leslie's* engravings of the New York labor movement remained calm and uncontentious. The cover cut of the September 13, 1871, "great eight-hour labor demonstration," with its decorous procession—marchers and spectators alike dressed in respectable finery—confirmed "an orderly and impressive occasion" attended by the city's "hardy sons of toil."[40]

Nine months later, the characteristically temperate tone of pictures and words disappeared. New York City's trade unions had escalated their eight-hour demand and launched a strike wave that, by June 1872, involved more than one hundred thousand workers, the largest combined labor action to hit an American city up to that time.[41] Thousands of "laboring men," *Leslie's* commented in its June 8 issue, "are battling for what they consider their rights—the eight-hour system, with full day's pay, and in some cases, increase of wages." Some trade unionists, however, were not "content to confine themselves to the 'passive policy' of not working in order to gain their ends, but . . . have resorted to force, in order to compel others, more patient or more satisfied with the existing order of things, to do the same."[42] *Leslie's* did not indulge in direct (or, as in the case of the *New York Times* and other antiunion papers, overheated) references to the Paris Commune; nor did it link "internecine" worker strife in New York to previously published scenes in Pennsylvania. Instead, the engraving that accompanied the passage quoted above encouraged readers to draw such connections.

Artist Matt Morgan's illustration showing a confrontation among quarrymen excavating new streets in upper Manhattan did not convey chaos, as Becker's Pennsylvania cuts had done; yet, though the engraving's violence was incipient, its likely source was plainly visible. His sleeves rolled and fists clenched, the thickset strike leader bore the physiognomy, albeit in a mild form, of the "lowly" Irish; in their appearance, stance, and dress, his equally aggressive companions—especially the suspiciously sashed figure on the extreme right—resurrected visions of the Paris Communards. This engraving, the first to depict division among workers in New York City, proposed that the discord attending the eight-hour effort derived less from genuine domestic disputes than from imported conflicts.[43]

Three weeks later, *Leslie's* extended its vision of "foreignness." The engraving of the June 10, 1872, parade, which capped the ultimately unsuccessful citywide trade union effort, worked up the Continental signs of the participants.

"[T]he promised procession of 40,000 dwindled down to 4,000 men,"

Figure 1.5. "New York City.— The Eight-hour Movement—A group of workingmen on a strike in one of the up-town wards." Wood engraving, based on a sketch by Matthew Somerville Morgan, *Frank Leslie's Illustrated Newspaper*, June 8, 1872, 197. American Social History Project.

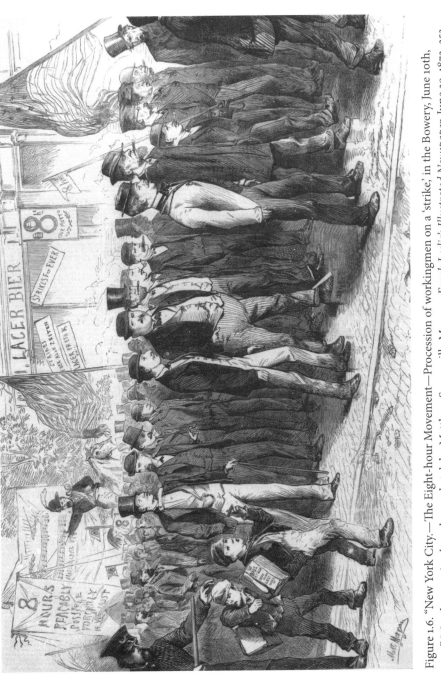

Figure 1.6. "New York City.—The Eight-hour Movement—Procession of workingmen on a 'strike,' in the Bowery, June 10th, 1872." Wood engraving based on a sketch by Matthew Somerville Morgan, *Frank Leslie's Illustrated Newspaper*, June 29, 1872, 253. American Social History Project.

Leslie's observed in the accompanying text. "As a popular movement of the workingmen, the parade was a failure. Very many, with commendable good sense, refused to take part in it, fearing that greater complications would thereby be engendered." While this perception, echoed in the *Times* and the *Tribune,* was disputed in the pro-labor *Sun,* disagreement over the numbers of participants was less important than the meaning of the scene, which downplayed the threat of violence in favor of buffoonery. Showing a grotesquely snarling figure on horseback in the background, the engraving nonetheless featured a collection of "foreign" physiognomies whose aggressiveness lay only in the absurd angle of their cigars. "It would be difficult," *Leslie's* concluded, "to convince ourselves that those who appeared were fair representatives of the workingmen of the city. They certainly did not exhibit the manly bone and sinew of the land."[44] Exhibiting a travesty of the American worker, *Leslie's* reduced the threat of disorder to the antics of two newsboys mimicking the marchers. For the exclusive male readership of Frank Leslie's sensational illustrated weekly, *The Days' Doings,* the theme of foreign infection teetered into violence, not to mention titillation, featuring a cut of the exotic and dangerous Judith Marx (emissary of the International and niece of Karl Marx) delivering "her inflammatory harangue" to a group of strikers armed "with implements of warfare as well as the tools of labor" in an Orchard Street cellar.[45]

The trade unionists depicted in the June 1872 engravings may have failed to represent the "manly bone and sinew" of the genuine American worker, but *Leslie's* could not easily oblige its readers with a pictorial alternative. For the next five years, as the nation suffered through depression and saw its labor movement decimated through unemployment and repression, *Leslie's* only once attempted to present an emblematic American worker.

Pictured in the wake of the 1873 panic and solemnly posed in front of a closed iron mill, this postbellum industrial worker seemed lost among social types, borrowing most heavily the qualities traditionally exhibited by the perennial "noble yeoman."[46] The representational gap was consistent with the disappearance of a native-born artisan social type after the Civil War; a range of "ethnic" types served as imperfect surrogates, filling the place of the worker while being rejected as "inauthentic" representations. For most of the 1870s, images of trade union organization and activity were limited to deluded or debased "Molly Maguire" Irish miners. Their urban equivalents appeared on breadlines, or in police lodging-houses, or as members of a troublesome minority merely posing as workers (the latter case epitomized in the decidedly Continental countenances of the New York branch of the International Workingmen's Association).[47]

NEWSPAPER

NEW YORK, NOVEMBER 15, 1873. [PRICE, WITH SUPPLEMENT, 10 CENTS.

946—VOL. XXXVII.]

Figure 1.7. "Out of work. Saturday night at the iron mills during the crisis."
Wood engraving based on a sketch by Matthew Somerville Morgan, *Frank Leslie's Illustrated Newspaper,* November 15, 1873, cover. American Social History Project.

The alien signs registered in depictions of such gatherings easily transformed into more alarming scenes during the depression. The engraving that portrayed the January 13, 1874, Tompkins Square Riot relied on the representation of its participants to underscore that labor demonstration was illicit. "Last week," the accompanying editorial titled "'Bread or Blood'" ran,

> several thousands of the lower grades of workingmen of New York City, most of them Germans, Frenchmen and Poles, finding themselves out of work, and hungry, with no prospects of immediate employment, determined to parade through the streets in huge demonstration of numbers, as a sign of their sadness and despair. They were incited to enthusiasm by leaders who think radically about the antagonism of labor to capital; and many of them knew no alternative to getting bread by the fairest means but that of obtaining it by force, even to the shedding of blood.[48]

Though it acknowledged the justice of the demand for relief, the engraving legitimated the suppression of the Tompkins Square demonstration. The "lower grades of workingmen" fleeing toward the viewer defined the violence as the sorry product of foreign agitation, infecting labor republicanism and the streets of the city with a divisive class-conscious ideology.

Unlike other labor-related actions, the Tompkins Square riot elicited coverage in *Harper's Weekly* that was similar to *Leslie's* perspective—albeit in the form of one vituperative cartoon by Thomas Nast: "The emancipator of labor and the honest working-people" showed a death's-head communist offering his skeletal hand to a cringing working-class family. Meanwhile, the *New York Daily Graphic,* inaugurated in 1873, offered three days of pictorial coverage beginning with a January 13 cover cartoon by Frank Bellew. "The 'bread or blood' bugaboo" was consistent with the paper's view of the Internationalists as a minor influence on workers; but though the *Daily Graphic's* typically sketchy graphics did not provide discernible signs for deciphering the "quality" of the participants, a cut of "weapons found on the rioters" effectively carried its message.[49]

Though the depression and the depredations of the railroad and coal monopolies eventually prodded *Frank Leslie's* editorials to occasionally denounce capital as an agent of disorder and division, the representation of labor remained largely unchanged. With no visual social type for the urban or industrial worker, the preferred pictorial standard-bearer of American republican virtue became the midwestern farmer activist, the stalwart Granger. In a series of engravings published from September 1873 through February 1874, Grangers were shown at meetings and conventions that may have struck readers as oddly reminiscent of earlier cuts of labor meetings and strikes.

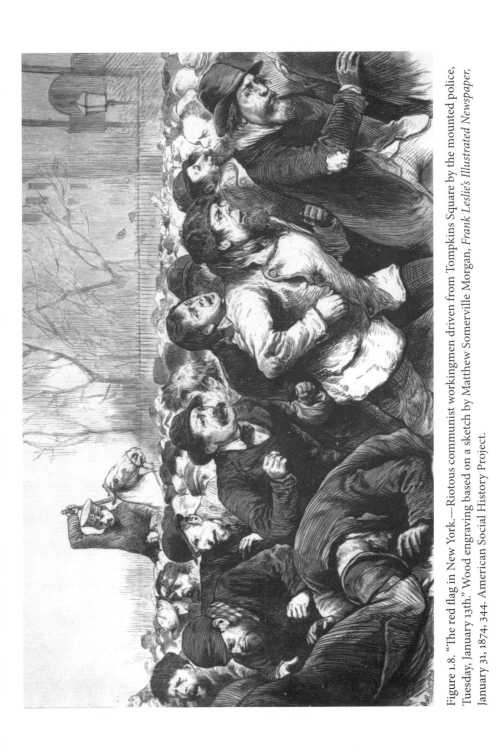

Figure 1.8. "The red flag in New York.—Riotous communist workingmen driven from Tompkins Square by the mounted police, Tuesday, January 13th." Wood engraving based on a sketch by Matthew Somerville Morgan, *Frank Leslie's Illustrated Newspaper*, January 31, 1874. 344. American Social History Project.

The similarity was hardly accidental, as a February 1874 editorial titled "The Farmers' Union" suggested: "The intellectual and social purposes of their organization are far in advance of anything ever before undertaken in America on a large scale; and while they cling honestly together social anarchy and un-American uprisings are impossible."[50] The heritage of genuine "labor" as crusader against the abuses of capital and corruption of government was now bestowed on the figure of the native-born noble yeoman, a development that the singular November 1873 engraving of the emblematic "Out of Work" ironworker only substantiated: he was an industrialized Yankee "Brother Jonathan," unemployed yet isolated from divisive, alien-inspired activism.[51]

Frank Leslie's Illustrated Newspaper would, over the course of the depression, acknowledge that strikes were sometimes an unavoidable (if probably ruinous) choice, and capital was sometimes provocative and unyielding. But these usually begrudging concessions (framed in laissez-faire reasoning) appeared solely in the publication's editorials.[52] In *Leslie's* engravings, militant workers and trade unionists continued to inhabit fairly rigid representational categories—usually exoticized, sometimes buffoonish, sometimes menacing.

The Great Uprising

The Great Uprising of July 1877 heralded the beginning of a new era of working-class protest and trade-union organization. Emanating from isolated railroad-worker protests over arbitrary wage reductions, the strike quickly spread along the nation's tracks to halt commerce for two weeks during July 1877. Extending over fourteen states and paralyzing most of the country's industrial cities, the railroad strike took on the character of a revolt against persistent hard times and railroad corporation abuses.[53]

Frank Leslie's diligently covered the Great Uprising for three weeks (including a sixteen-page "Railroad Riot Extra" supplement edition), its engravings showing halted trains, massive demonstrations, mobilized troops, street battles, flaming buildings, and smoldering ruins. In the strike's aftermath, the publication's August 11, 1877, editorial assessed the impact of the unprecedented event. Looking abroad, *Leslie's* bemoaned the damage to America's reputation, fearing the slowing of immigration and foreign investment as well as "the perpetuation of kingcraft" among European "advocates of monarchical impositions." Turning back home, *Leslie's* refrained from draconian solutions, favoring "pluckier men in civil authority, and a militia so organized and drilled and trusted as to be effective in emergencies" over reliance on "a powerful standing army." Moreover, *Leslie's* proposed, "What is more wanted . . . [is] a kindlier treatment of employees by capitalists and corporations. It should need no political economist to demonstrate to corporations the necessity of fostering labor instead of grinding it into the dust." If there was "one good result" in the "gigantic demonstration" of the railroad strikers, it was "in showing the existence of an element whose rights must be respected in common with the rights of the millionaire." Recognizing the necessity to correct the imbalance in economic and social power, *Leslie's* warned that, for the most part, "the element of disorganization and plunder, of incendiarism and murder, must not be confounded with the railroad strikers. This violent, revolutionary, and Communistic element is composed of the idle roughs and the vagabond tramps who infest the country and hasten to the centres of trouble."[54]

The distinction appeared to be reinforced in *Leslie's* images of railroad strikers. The engraving that depicted the July 17 incident at Martinsburg, West Virginia, that sparked the nationwide strike showed heavily armed "disaffected workmen dragging firemen and engineers" from a Baltimore & Ohio freight train; but the scene suggested a disciplined military action rather than a disorderly mob. Based on *Leslie's* editorial differentiation of railroad strikers and "rioters," however, one might assume that engravings of violence in the cities would resurrect the familiar physiognomic types of disorder and "foreign infusion." The editorials and descriptions accompanying such cuts certainly proposed that "we have among us an element as malicious, determined and desperate as ever appeared in Paris under the Commune"; the participants were characterized as "malcontents, loafers, and disreputable persons of both sexes." Yet in such illustrations as the Sixth Regiment of the Maryland National Guard "firing upon the mob" in the streets of Baltimore, *Leslie's* pictures generally defied the expectations raised in its text.[55]

Contradicting the "visual" typing suggested by its words, *Frank Leslie's* pictures reformulated the meaning of the Great Uprising. By their nature, the July events necessarily disrupted conventional categorizations. As the engravings showed, the strike placed unexpected types in the line of fire: in localities across the country, the broad "middle" came out to protest the abuses of the railroads. The illustration capping *Leslie's* "Railroad Riot Extra" supplement—a double-page panorama of the Philadelphia militia firing on the Pittsburgh crowd gathered near the Pennsylvania Railroad's Union Depot—was an extended visual performance demonstrating that potential readers had become "rioters."

To be sure, some engravings reverted to predictable social typing. Unlike in Pittsburgh, in Chicago the general strike split the city along class (and ethnic) lines, providing a ready frame within which the "traditional" agents of disorder could be persuasively rendered. *Leslie's* August 11 cover engraving, showing cavalry charging the rioters at the Halstead Street viaduct, closely

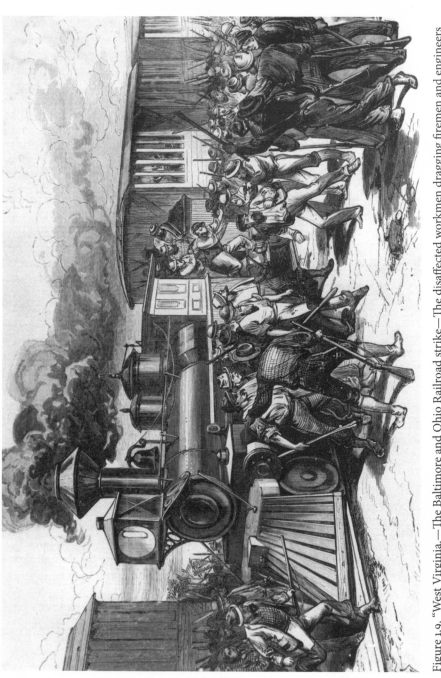

Figure 1.9. "West Virginia.—The Baltimore and Ohio Railroad strike—The disaffected workmen dragging firemen and engineers from a Baltimore freight train at Martinsburg, July 17th." Wood engraving based on a sketch by Fernando Miranda, *Frank Leslie's Illustrated Newspaper*, August 4, 1877, 373. American Social History Project.

Figure 1.10. "Maryland.—The Baltimore and Ohio Railroad strike—The Sixth Regiment, N.G.S.M., firing upon the mob, on the corner of Frederick and Baltimore Streets, July 20th." Wood engraving, *Frank Leslie's Illustrated Newspaper*, August 4, 1877, 372. American Social History Project.

Figure 1.11. "Pennsylvania.—The railroad riot in Pittsburgh—The Philadelphia militia firing on the mob, at the Twenty-eighth Street crossing, near the Union Depot of the Pennsylvania Railroad, on Saturday afternoon, July 21st." Wood engraving based on a sketch by John Donaghy, *Frank Leslie's Illustrated Newspaper* (supplement), August 4, 1877, 8–9. American Social History Project.

resembled in composition and characterization the rout of the disreputable in its earlier cut of the 1874 Tompkins Square Riot. But in most localities, the physiognomic signs denoting types no longer afforded readers an easy, useful guide to deciphering a news event. Just as physiognomy disappeared in depictions of the blameless victims of disasters, the signs of sedition and degradation formerly used to define the meaning of mayhem were now inoperable. The distancing function of social typing by facial appearance could not work in representing situations in which readers might, in effect, recognize themselves as participants and victims. Still framed in the conventions of history-painting narrative, the engravings of the strike depicted "anonymous Americans" without the predictable marks of moral character, social role, and motive.[56]

The Great Uprising thus marked a sea-change in *Frank Leslie's* representation of American labor and set it apart from the rest of the illustrated press.[57] In contrast, *Harper's Weekly* engravings largely opted for distant, panoramic views of mass destruction and milling crowds; the three engravings that vividly depicted battles between strikers and militia or police—one in Baltimore, two in Chicago—presented a more limited cast of male rioters.[58]

The *New York Daily Graphic's* many illustrations of the strike are harder to decipher. Its pictures, rendered quickly, showed little detail; nonetheless, the *Daily Graphic's* scenes of violence and looting (including a cover page containing picturesque and grotesque character studies of the Pittsburgh crowd's bacchanal after the destruction of the train yards) seemed to offer little change from previous representations of civil disorders.

Certainly, as one editorial declared, the subjects of the strike coverage would never be confused with those who read the *Daily Graphic:* "It is hardly worth while for the press of the leading cities to be giving advice to the rioters on the railroads, or to be propounding lessons in good conduct which they will not heed. Those who are now in revolt against the constituted authorities in five States of the Union, are not as a class newspaper readers[.]"[59]

The shift in *Frank Leslie's* treatment of American labor was not lost on contemporary readers. In its August 18 issue, *Leslie's* reprinted an editorial that had appeared in the July 31 *Pittsburgh Leader* complimenting the former's engravings, based on sketches by the local artist John Donaghy, of the July 21 clash between the Philadelphia militia and striking Pittsburgh railroad workers and sympathizers (e.g., Figure 1.11). The event culminated the following day in the burning of the Pennsylvania Railroad's train yards, the single most destructive incident in the nationwide strike. "The riots," the editorial began, "have given the illustrated newspapers an opportunity that they have availed themselves of to the fullest extent to curdle the blood of

Figure 1.12. "The great strike—The Sixth Maryland Regiment fighting its way through Baltimore." Wood engraving based on a photograph by D. Bendann, *Harper's Weekly*, August 11, 1877, cover. American Social History Project.

Figure 1.13. "Scenes and incidents of the railroad riots at Pittsburg, Pa." Top tier: "A dress full of sugar; A young pirate; Forming a vigilance committee; A baby thief; Smashing vases on the track." Middle tier: "A debauch on stolen whiskey; Plunder; Flour wasted; A captured gun of Hutchinson battery." Bottom tier: "Opening a whiskey car; A crazy citizen; Searching for valuables." Lithograph based on sketches by C. D. Weldon(?), *New York Daily Graphic,* Thursday, July 26, 1877, cover. American Social History Project.

the law-abiding citizen with representations of the wild scenes of last week." It was evident, however, that "with the single exception of John Donaghy, of this city, special artist for FRANK LESLIE'S ILLUSTRATED NEWSPAPER," no artist was "near enough to 'the mob' they assume to depict to know what it really looks like. They represent it as a wild and heterogeneous collection of rough men and virago women, in every variety of costume, some with blouses, some in open shirts and bare arms, some with bandannas around their brows and all with coarse, brutish features, exhibiting every phase of ignorance and malignity." This was a *French* mob, derived from cuts by English artists in old translated studies about the French Revolution. "The American mob," the *Leader* editorial chided,

> is a different sort of a body altogether. It has no varieties of costume except such as indicate the sex and social condition of the wearers. American work-men do not wear the Paris blouse at all, nor are they *sans-culottes*. Nor do they wear turbans or handkerchiefs around their heads. They dress in the ordi-nary male costume of coat, vest and pants, sometimes, however, going in their shirt-sleeves. They are generally very well-looking men. Railroad employees especially have the reputation of being quite fine-looking, and playing havoc with the hearts of country girls. The South-side delegation, which marched up to the Round-House to help the strikers on that fatal Saturday evening, was led by a man in a good frock-coat, with a white neck-tie, and the men generally were well clad, and many of them had their boots blacked.

An "American mob," the *Leader* concluded, "especially when, as was the case at Twenty-eighth Street, there were mingled with the malcontents large numbers of spectators and curiosity-seekers, is a pretty fair representation in appearance of the American people."[60]

* * *

What the *Leader* editorial observed—and the unpredictability of depiction, unmooring of types, and lessening of physiognomy in the representation of the poor and workers articulated—was a move toward realism. This call for the real may have had less to do with the much-vaunted hegemony of photographic practice than with the conflicting demands of a broad and increasingly diverse readership. The efficacy of physiognomic social typing relied on a widely shared cognitive map; as the Gilded Age progressed, a commonality of perceptions could not be assumed and, therefore, a reliance on pictorial social typing would undercut the very premise that made *Frank Leslie's Illustrated Newspaper* commercially viable.[61]

As its coverage of the Great Uprising starkly revealed, by the 1870s *Frank*

Leslie's found that its pictorial practice was inadequate. In a nation now seemingly locked in perpetual crisis, its middle readership had grown too broad and varied to accept representations rendered in exclusive codes derived from the antebellum period. Social typing would remain as a device for reading society and pictorially reporting the news; indeed, in the 1880s, physiognomic signs would locate new subjects in a new immigrant working class (as well as, persistently, in many images of African Americans). But while *Frank Leslie's* continued to frame its figures in familiar narratives and visual conventions, its need to address a range of readers opened the way for the newsweekly to experiment in capturing social reality without pictorial typing.

Notes

1. Joseph Becker, "An Artist's Interesting Recollections of *Leslie's Weekly*," *Leslie's Weekly*, December 14, 1905, 570. Becker, who was born in 1841, began his career with *Leslie's* in 1859 when he was hired as an errand boy; in 1863, he became one of the publication's special artists covering the Civil War. During 1869 and 1870, Becker traveled the West for *Leslie's*; his series of "Across the Continent" illustrations included pictures of San Francisco's Chinese population and Utah's Mormons. His tenure as supervisor of *Leslie's* art department lasted until 1900. For Becker's career, see ibid.; Robert Taft, *Artists and Illustrators of the Old West, 1850–1900* (New York: Charles Scribner's Sons, 1953), 89–93, 312–14; idem, "Joseph Becker's Sketch of the Gettysburg Ceremony, November 19, 1863," *Kansas Historical Quarterly* 21, no. 4 (winter 1954): 257–63.

2. *Frank Leslie's Illustrated Newspaper* (hereafter *FLIN*), March 25, 1871, cover (17); April 15, 1871, 76; April 22, 1871, 88; April 29, 1871, 108; May 6, 1871, cover (121); May 27, 1871, 177.

3. *FLIN*, July 19, 1873, 300 (drawn by John N. Hyde).

4. On the Long Strike, Gowen's plan to destroy the WBA, the organization of Irish miners' secret societies, and the prosecution of the Molly Maguires, see Kevin Kenny, *Making Sense of the Molly Maguires* (New York: Oxford University Press, 1997); Wayne G. Broehl Jr., *The Molly Maguires* (Cambridge, Mass.: Harvard University Press, 1964). Before Becker returned to Pennsylvania, Jonathan Lowe supplied one sketch for an engraving of a miners' faction fight, *FLIN*, October 24, 1874, 101 (see also Lowe's earlier cut of striking Ohio miners, September 5, 1874, 413).

5. *FLIN*, December 12, 1874, 232.

6. *FLIN*, February 6, 1875, 357, 364.

7. *FLIN*, March 13, 1875, 9, 11.

8. Becker, "An Artist's Interesting Recollections," 570. With the assistance of Kevin Kenny, author of the most recent and comprehensive study of the group, *Making Sense of the Molly Maguires*, I have ascertained that Becker's contribution to prosecuting the men accused of conspiracy has gone previously unrecorded in the annals of the case. If Becker's story is true, he joined forces with one of the five Pinkerton and Reading Railroad operatives who infiltrated the miners' ranks.

9. "Editorial Notes," *FLIN*, April 3, 1875, 51. I have been unable to locate more information about Hugh McGarvy. The standard histories of the Workingmen's Benevolent Association (officially known as the Miners' and Laborers' Benevolent Association after 1870)—including Andrew Roy, *A History of the Coal Mines of the United States . . .* (Columbus, Ohio: J. L. Trauger Printing Company, 1907) and Chris Evans, *History of the United Mine Workers of America from the Year 1860 to 1890*, 2 vols. (Indianapolis: United Mine Workers of America [1900])—do not mention McGarvy; Kevin Kenny graciously provided me with information from the WBA's newspaper, the *Anthracite Monitor*, for 1871 to 1872 (i.e., before the Long Strike), which did not name McGarvy but confirmed that the union's structure included a State General Council (composed of delegates from county-based district councils) with the office of president. The author of *Leslie's* editorial reply is difficult to determine. The two editors known to have worked for *Leslie's* in the early 1870s, Ephraim G. Squier and J. C. Goldsmith, had left the publication by 1875. For possible authors, see "A Tribute of Respect," *FLIN*, January 31, 1880, 403.

10. "Editorial Notes," *FLIN*, April 3, 1875, 51.

11. "Pennsylvania.—'A marked man.'—Scene in the coal regions during the miners' strike," *FLIN*, April 10, 1875, 77; "Pennsylvania.—Pay-day in the mining regions," September 4, 1875, 449 (quotation, 456). Compare Becker's latter treatment with Paul Frenzeny's more benign pictorial coverage in "The miners' pay-day," *Harper's Weekly* (hereafter *HW*), February 22, 1873, 157. But see also the editorial titled "Coal Trade," *FLIN*, June 12, 1875, 215, essentially a critique of the Reading Railroad's monopoly control of Pennsylvania coal.

12. The two-year hiatus in mining coverage was broken only by two engravings of coal region winter serenades and sledding in *FLIN*, March 25, 1876, 50, which were based on sketches Becker had made the year before.

13. *FLIN*, June 16, 1877, 253; June 30, 1877, 292; July 7, 1877, 305. An engraving showing four condemned prisoners, presumably also based on a sketch by Becker, appeared in the June 30, 1877, issue (189) of Leslie's *New York Illustrated Times* (formerly *The Days' Doings*).

14. Becker, "An Artist's Interesting Recollections," 570.

15. *HW*, January 31, 1874, 105. According to several commentators, the cut recalls Christ preaching to the twelve apostles; see Marianne Doezema, *American Realism and the Industrial Age* (Bloomington: Indiana University Press for the Cleveland Museum of Art, 1980), 38; John Gladstone, "Working-Class Imagery in *Harper's Weekly*, 1865–1895," *Labor's Heritage* 5, no. 1 (spring 1993): 47–49. On Frenzeny, see Taft, *Artists and Illustrators of the Old West*, 94–116.

16. Reports of the Molly Maguire trial and execution also appeared in the *Daily Graphic*: see *New York Daily Graphic* (hereafter *DG*), August 25, 1876; June 22, 1877.

17. Budd Leslie Gambee Jr., "Frank Leslie and His Illustrated Newspaper, 1855–1860: Artistic and Technical Operations of a Pioneer Pictorial News Weekly in America" (Ph.D. diss., University of Michigan, 1963); Madeleine Bettina Stern, *Purple Passage: The Life of Mrs. Frank Leslie* (Norman: University of Oklahoma Press, 1953); Frank Luther Mott, *A History of American Magazines, Volume 2: 1850–1865* (Cambridge, Mass.: Harvard University Press, 1938), 43–45, 437–41, 452–65; *Volume 3: 1865–1885*, 41–44; John Tebbel and Mary Ellen Zuckerman, *The Magazine in America, 1741–1990* (New York: Oxford University Press, 1991), 17–20 passim. For the vast expansion of the pictorial marketplace in

the 1850s, see Thomas C. Leonard, *The Power of the Press: The Birth of American Political Reporting* (New York: Oxford University Press, 1986), 57–59, 90–96.

18. When Leslie arrived in the United States, the closest publication to the *Illustrated London News* was *Gleason's Pictorial Drawing-Room Companion* (started in 1851, purchased and renamed *Ballou's Pictorial* from 1855 to 1859). Leslie worked for this weekly Boston "family miscellany," which included illustrations devoted to the news, from 1851 to 1852.

19. P. T. Barnum, *Struggles and Triumphs; or, Forty Years' Recollections* (1871; reprint, New York: Penguin, 1981), 234–35; A. H. Saxon, *P. T. Barnum: The Legend and the Man* (New York: Columbia University Press, 1989), 188–89. Barnum co-owned the short-lived *Illustrated News* with the *New York Sun*'s H. D. and A. E. Beach.

20. On *Frank Leslie's* broad readership, see Joshua Brown, *Beyond the Lines: Pictorial Reporting, Everyday Life, and the Crisis of Gilded Age America* (Berkeley: University of California Press, 2002), 40–46. My consideration of a "middle" reading public departs from recent historiography of popular culture in the nineteenth century that proposes a rapid bifurcation into "high" and "low" constituencies, most notably Lawrence W. Levine, *Highbrow/Lowbrow: The Emergence of Cultural Hierarchy in America* (Cambridge, Mass.: Harvard University Press, 1988).

21. Brown, *Beyond the Lines,* 34–40. This process, reputedly introduced by Leslie, was also used by *Harper's Weekly.* The *Daily Graphic,* in contrast, relied on a photolithographic process that transferred rough artist sketches.

22. *FLIN,* April 2, 1859; Brown, *Beyond the Lines,* 68–74.

23. Alan Trachtenberg, *Reading American Photographs: Images as History, from Mathew Brady to Walker Evans* (New York: Hill and Wang, 1989), 21–70.

24. Valerian Gribayedoff, "Pictorial Journalism," *The Cosmopolitan* 11, no. 4 (August 1891): 479; Leonard, *The Power of the Press,* 103–5. The above observation should not negate how readers derived a significant amount of information from such engravings. Aside from presenting a new range of "illustrious Americans"—including, significantly, African American legislators—pictorial information was often displayed with only cursory captions or brief descriptions in the expectation that readers could identify many of the unnamed assembled faces as well as gain a qualitative sense of the context of news events through the painfully detailed rendering of interiors, scenery, etc.

25. The political caricatures appearing in *Frank Leslie's* never achieved the impact of Thomas Nast's work in *Harper's Weekly.* Leslie imported the British cartoonist Matthew Somerville Morgan in 1870 to compete with Nast's acerbic and highly popular pro-Republican cartoons. Coming in a distant second in the publications' cartoon rivalry during the 1872 presidential campaign and the subsequent off-year election, Morgan had moved on by 1876. His replacement, Joseph Keppler, would himself soon leave *Leslie's* to start the satirical weekly *Puck;* Keppler was succeeded by James Albert Wales (later a prominent contributor to *Puck* and *Judge*). Thomas Milton Kemnitz, "The Cartoon as a Historical Source," *Journal of Interdisciplinary History,* 4 (summer 1973): 81–93; Leonard, *The Power of the Press,* 97–131, and Roger A. Fischer, *Them Damned Pictures: Explorations in American Political Cartoon Art* (North Haven, Conn.: Archon Books, 1996), 1–23, offer the most illuminating recent analyses of Nast's impact.

26. Elizabeth Johns, *American Genre Painting: The Politics of Everyday Life* (New Haven, Conn.: Yale University Press, 1991), 1–23; Joshua C. Taylor, *America as Art* (Washington,

D.C.: Smithsonian Institution Press, 1976), 37–94. For a self-conscious instance of typification, see "Citizens of the United States, According to Popular Impressions," *HW*, January 12, 1867.

27. Graeme Tytler, *Physiognomy in the European Novel: Faces and Fortunes* (Princeton, N.J.: Princeton University Press, 1982), 3–81; Mary Cowling, *The Artist as Anthropologist: The Representation of Type and Character in Victorian Art* (New York: Cambridge University Press, 1989), 87–120; L. Perry Curtis Jr., *Apes and Angels: The Irishman in Victorian Caricature* (Washington, D.C.: Smithsonian Institution Press, 1971), 1–15.

28. Karen Halttunen, *Confidence Men and Painted Women: A Study of Middle-Class Culture in America, 1830–1870* (New Haven, Conn.: Yale University Press, 1982); John F. Kasson, *Rudeness and Civility: Manners in Nineteenth-Century Urban America* (New York: Hill and Wang, 1990); Guy Szuberla, "Ladies, Gentlemen, Flirts, Mashers, Snoozers, and the Breaking of Etiquette's Code," *Prospects* 15 (1990): 169–96; David Scobey, "Anatomy of the Promenade: The Politics of Bourgeois Sociability in Nineteenth-Century New York," *Social History* 17, no. 2 (May 1992): 203–27. My interpretation of the role of the pictorial press departs from these authors' emphasis on the new bourgeoisie's anxiety over the unreliability of appearances; in this view the city ultimately remained unreadable for the uneasy middle class.

29. "The Cities of New York," *FLIN*, October 24, 1874, 98. On the segmented, polarized city as displayed in city guides in the period, see Stuart M. Blumin, "Explaining the New Metropolis: Perception, Depiction, and Analysis in Mid-Nineteenth-Century New York City," *Journal of Urban History* 11, no. 1 (November 1984): 9–38; idem, "Introduction: George G. Foster and the Emerging Metropolis," in George G. Foster, *New York by Gas-Light and Other Urban Sketches* (Berkeley: University of California Press, 1990), 1–61.

30. In contrast, the illustrated literary monthlies eschewed unpleasant urban themes, favoring the ideal and the picturesque; Robert J. Scholnick, "*Scribner's Monthly* and the 'Pictorial Representation of Life and Truth' in Post–Civil War America," *American Periodicals* 1, no. 1 (fall 1991): 59.

31. The twofold utility of the illustrated press both to shield and educate was espoused by the directors of the Association for the Improvement of the Condition of the Poor when they hired an artist to illustrate the 1884 *Annual Report* to show contributors how and where the poor lived without requiring them to suffer the hardship of personal exploration. Robert H. Bremner, *From the Depths: The Discovery of Poverty in the United States* (New York: New York University Press, 1956), 116.

32. *FLIN*, February 2, 1867, 309.

33. Brown, *Beyond the Lines*, 87–100.

34. Raymond Williams, *Culture* (Glasgow: Fontana, 1981), 99.

35. For the conditions of and responses to the depression, the most comprehensive work remains Herbert G. Gutman, "Social and Economic Structure and Depression: American Labor in 1873 and 1874" (Ph.D. diss., University of Wisconsin, 1959).

36. "The Tramp Nuisance," *FLIN*, August 5, 1876, 354–55. See also *FLIN*, July 21, 1877, 341; "The value of a pistol.—A villainous tramp repulsed by a plucky woman," *The Days' Doings* (hereafter *DD*), June 12, 1875, 9. As Michael Davis has shown, *Leslie's* view coincided with the labor movement's denunciation of the tramp in the 1870s; see Davis, "Forced to Tramp: The Perspective of the Labor Press, 1870–1900," in Eric H. Monkkonen, ed.,

Walking to Work: Tramps in America, 1790–1935 (Lincoln: University of Nebraska Press, 1984), 141–70.

37. For old types in markedly worse conditions: "Waiting for the second table.—Inmates of the poor-house on Randall's Island, East River, at New York City, forming in line for dinner," *FLIN*, February 13, 1875, 381. For new types in straitened circumstances: "Out of work.—Saturday night at the iron mills during the crisis," *FLIN*, November 15, 1873, cover (157); "The crisis—The dining hall of St. Barnabas Home, Nos. 304, 306 and 308 Mulberry Street, adjoining police headquarters, an institution for the relief of poor women," ibid., 164; "Hard times in New York.—The soup-house No. 110 Centre Street, one of the number instituted by Commodore James Gordon Bennett, and superintended by L. Delmonico," *FLIN*, March 7, 1874, 429 (its description noting the depiction of the presence of many children because their parents were too ashamed to appear in person). It should be mentioned that Frank Leslie himself felt the impact of hard times: although his publishing house weathered the depression, bad investments and ostentatious living led to his bankruptcy and the reorganization of his business in 1877.

38. *FLIN*, February 10, 1877, 379.

39. On the Lynn procession, see *FLIN*, March 17, 1860, 242, 251. See also May 5, 1866, 101; February 20, 1869, 360; May 8, 1869, 125; September 4, 1869, 392. *Leslie's* editorials against the eight-hour day include "Eight Hour Labor Movement," May 5, 1866, 97–98; "Labor Conventions," October 6, 1866, 34–35; "Eight Hours' Labor Bill," May 4, 1867, 98; "Town Gossip," May 11, 1867, 114–15; "The Eight Hour Humbug," July 11, 1868, 258; "Labor and Wages: The Eight Hour Humbug," December 26, 1868, 225–26; "Matters and Things," January 23, 1869, 231; "Creation and Recreation," July 15, 1871, 286; and editorial comments, January 27, 1872, 307; February 17, 1872, 355.

40. *FLIN*, September 30, 1871, cover (33); quotation, 37.

41. On the eight-hour movement and its press coverage, see Iver Bernstein, *The New York City Draft Riots: Their Significance for American Society and Politics in the Age of the Civil War* (New York: Oxford University Press, 1990), 237–57; Stanley Nadel, "Those Who Would Be Free: The Eight-Hour Day Strikes of 1872," *Labor's Heritage* 2, no. 2 (April 1990): 70–77.

42. *FLIN*, June 8, 1872, 199.

43. *Harper's Weekly* broke from its general neglect of labor issues to publish "Between the Strike and the Family," June 8, 1872, 444, a tableau by Paul Frenzeny showing strike organizers pressing a pensive worker to join their labor action.

44. *FLIN*, June 29, 1872, 252.

45. "The Great Strike—The Seed and Its Fruit. The Seed. The conclave of the strikers.— The beautiful International, Judith Marx, initiating a number of workmen as members of 'The Secret Order of the Sun,'" *DD*, June 29, 1872, 16; "The Great Strike and Its Heroine," ibid., 2.

46. On the "noble yeoman," see Sarah Burns, *Pastoral Inventions: Rural Life in Nineteenth-Century American Art and Culture* (Philadelphia: Temple University Press, 1989), 99–121. Thomas Nast's 1870s cartoons in *Harper's Weekly*, which were critical of the eight-hour movement and equated trade union organizing with communist agitation, tended to portray a nondescript, agrarian-like worker (usually encumbered by a dependent spouse and child); e.g., the anti-eight-hour "The workingman's mite," *HW*, May 20, 1871,

468 (supplement). Beginning in the 1870s, Nast began to articulate labor as an aproned and square-hatted artisan; e.g., "Inflation is 'as easy as lying,'" *HW,* May 23, 1874, 444. Ironically, the artisan symbol, purportedly Nast's invention, gained particular adherence during the 1880s (when Joseph Keppler borrowed the figure for cartoons in *Puck*).

47. While *Leslie's* consistently deplored the Internationalists' infusion of foreign ideologies into the relationship of American labor and capital, its coverage was surprisingly temperate, possibly in deference to the readers of the paper's German edition: an engraving of a January 1872 memorial procession for the Paris Commune showed a sober and unthreatening gathering (a view that, along with accompanying editorials and cartoons, challenged police suppression of the demonstration), and *Leslie's* supplied detailed coverage of the veteran Communard Henri de Rochefort in June 1874. For the Paris Commune memorial procession, see *FLIN,* January 6, 1872, 264–65; see also *DD,* January 6, 1872, 16. For criticism of the police suppression of the procession, see the editorial comment and cartoon, "Our municipal police bull becometh enraged at the display of the red flag," *FLIN,* December 30, 1871, 243 (comment), 256 (cartoon); see also January 6, 1872, 264–65. On de Rochefort's visit, see June 13, 1874, cover (209); June 20, 1874, 232.

48. "'Bread or Blood,'" *FLIN,* January 31, 1874, 338. See also the more panoramic and distinctively less sensational "Illinois.—The frustrated raid of Communists upon the Relief and Aid Society in Chicago," March 20, 1875, 21.

49. Thomas Nast, "The emancipator of labor and the honest working-people," *HW,* February 7, 1874, cover (121). *DG,* January 13, 1874, cover; January 14, 1874; January 15, 1874. Leslie's *The Days' Doings* characteristically reveled in the violence of the Tompkins Square demonstration: "The police prevent a demonstration by working-men on Tompkins' [*sic*] Square, N.Y. City, January 13," *DD,* January 24, 1874, 9. On the Tompkins Square Riot and its press coverage, see Herbert G. Gutman, "The Tompkins Square 'Riot' in New York City on January 13, 1874: A Re-examination of Its Causes and Its Aftermath," *Labor History* 6, no. 1 (winter 1965): 44–70.

50. "The Farmers' Union," *FLIN,* February 21, 1874, 386. For Granger cuts, see August 30, 1873, 397; September 13, 1873, 12; October 4, 1873, 56; October 18, 1873, 96; November 15, 1873, 168; January 31, 1874, 341 (also depicting women); February 21, 1874, 389.

51. Burns, *Pastoral Inventions,* 99–121.

52. See the following editorials: "The Great Labor Question," *FLIN,* March 15, 1873, 2; "The Labor Question," March 22, 1873, 18; "The Workingman," ibid.; "Lowell Mills," March 29, 1873, 37–38; "The Labor Question," April 26, 1873, 103; "American Labor," August 23, 1873, 375; "Wants of the Workingmen," February 14, 1874, 370; "Deterioration of Labor," May 2, 1874, 114; "Lessons Long Shore," December 26, 1874, 258; "Editorial Notices," March 27, 1875, 35 (an interesting contrast to earlier comments on the Tompkins Square Riot); "The Coal Trade," June 12, 1875, 215; "The Fall River Strikes," October 16, 1875, 83. See also the cartoon "Old King Coal—How his monopoly works," September 6, 1873, 420.

53. Robert V. Bruce, *1877: Year of Violence* (Indianapolis: Bobbs-Merrill, 1959), and Philip S. Foner, *The Great Labor Uprising of 1877* (New York: Monad Press, 1977), are the most comprehensive histories of the strike. In the last generation, numerous local studies have expanded our understanding of the Great Uprising's varied character and impact. For a valuable historiographic overview, see David O. Stowell, *Streets, Railroads, and the Great Strike of 1877* (Chicago: University of Chicago Press, 1999), 1–11.

54. "The Railroad Strike and Insurrection," *FLIN*, August 11, 1877. Subsequent editorials focused on recommendations for government regulation of the railroads (while defending the efficacy of previous subsidies) and, citing Indian resistance and contradicting its August 11 comments, expansion of the federal military: "A Lesson from the Riots," August 18, 1877, 398; "A Consideration for the Next Congress," August 25, 1877, 414; "The Strikes from an English Standpoint," September 29, 1877, 50.

55. *FLIN*, August 11, 1877, 385.

56. Other engravings of the strike include *FLIN*, August 4, 1877, cover (365), 373, and supplement; August 11, 1877, 385, 388–89, 393; August 18, 1877, cover (397), 401, 409.

57. The change also registered in the strike coverage of the *New York Illustrated Times*, the new name applied to Leslie's *The Days' Doings* after October 1876: over three issues (August 4, August 11, and August 25, 1877), the paper presented twenty-seven engravings that in many cases departed from its previous pictures of labor violence. On the 1877 railroad strike as treated in the contemporary press, see Richard Slotkin, *The Fatal Environment: The Myth of the Frontier in the Age of Industrialization, 1800–1890* (New York: Atheneum, 1985), 475–98. Consideration of *Leslie's* visual reportage revises Slotkin's interpretation that the militant worker was characterized as "savage" in the aftermath of the strike.

58. See also in *HW,* August 11, 1877, "The great strike—Blockade of engines at Martinsburg, West Virginia" (620); "The great strike—Burning of the Lebanon Valley railroad bridge by the rioters" (620); "The great strike—Destruction of the Union Depot and Hotel at Pittsburgh" (621); "The great strike—The work of destruction in Pittsburgh—The wall of fire and the scene of desolation" (624–25); "The great strike—Burning of the roundhouse at Pittsburgh" (628); "The great strike—A funeral among the ruins at Pittsburgh" (628); and "The great strike—Pittsburgh in the hands of the mob" (629); see also "The great strike—Scenes of riot in Chicago," *HW,* August 18, 1877, 640.

Michael L. Carlebach, *The Origins of Photojournalism in America* (Washington, D.C.: Smithsonian Institution Press, 1992), 159, cites the August 11 *Harper's Weekly* Baltimore engraving, based on a photograph by David Bendann, as an example of the broader range of news imagery that improvements in camera and film technology made accessible to the public by 1877. Like the Pittsburgh photographer S. V. Albee's celebrated stereograph series, "The Railroad War," the forty-four pictures of which depicted *only* the inert aftermath of the violence (e.g., twisted tracks, smoldering buildings, wrecked locomotives), it is more likely than not that Bendann's Baltimore photograph recorded the place but not the event itself.

59. "The Laborers' Revolt," *DG,* July 21, 1877. For other examples of the *Daily Graphic's* coverage, see "Scenes of the railroad riots in Baltimore, Md., last Friday and Saturday," July 24, 1877; "Scenes of the railroad riot in Pittsburg, Pa., last Saturday and Sunday"; "Scenes of the railroad riots at Pittsburg and Altoona, Pa., last Sunday," July 25, 1877; "Attack on the Philadelphia militia by the mob at Altoona," ibid.; "Endeavoring to move a train at the outer depot, Pittsburg," Ibid.; "Scenes of the communistic demonstration in Tompkins Square last Wednesday evening," July 27, 1877. A useful comparison between treatment in *Frank Leslie's* and the *Daily Graphic* may be found in respective depictions of the vigilance committees set up by the Pittsburgh strikers; see "Pennsylvania.—Robert M. Ammon, the leader of the Pittsburgh and Fort Wayne railroad strike, at his post, directing

the movements of the strikers," *FLIN,* August 11, 1877; "Forming a vigilance committee," *DG,* July 26, 1877 (the latter a vignette in the full page titled "Scenes and incidents of the railroad riots at Pittsburg, Pa.").

60. *Pittsburgh Leader,* July 31, 1877; quoted in "Notes and Comments: OUR RIOT PICTURES," *FLIN,* August 18, 1877, 399. On John Donaghy (1837–1931), see George C. Groce and David Wallace, *The New-York Historical Society's Dictionary of Artists in America, 1564–1860* (New Haven, Conn.: Yale University Press, 1957), 183; Jean McCullough, ed., *Art in Nineteenth-Century Pittsburgh: An Exhibition* (Pittsburgh: McCullough Communications, 1977), 16–17; Paul A. Chew, ed., *Southwestern Pennsylvania Painters, 1800–1945* (Greensburg, Pa.: Westmoreland County Museum of Art, 1981), 34, 37–38; Virginia Lewis, "Paintings by John Donaghy" (photocopy of a pamphlet that accompanied a Pittsburgh exhibition of Donaghy's paintings, n.d., in the files of the American Social History Project, New York).

61. Realism here denotes not any coherent school of art as much as, in Alan Trachtenberg's phrase, "a tendency . . . to depict contemporary life without moralistic condescension"; (Trachtenberg, *The Incorporation of America: Culture and Society in the Gilded Age* (New York: Hill and Wang, 1982), 182. A similar turn toward realism in British illustrated journalism can be seen in engravings published in the *Graphic* during the 1870s; see Julian Treuherz, *Hard Times: Social Realism and Victorian Art* (London: Lund Humphries, 1987), 53–64; see also Niamh O'Sullivan, "Through Irish Eyes: The Work of Aloysius O'Kelly in the *Illustrated London News*," *History Ireland* (autumn 1995): 10–16. On photography and realism, see Estelle Jussim, *Visual Communication and the Graphic Arts: Photographic Technologies in the Nineteenth Century,* new ed. (New York: R. R. Bowker, 1983); cf., Miles Orvell, *The Real Thing: Imitation and Authenticity in American Culture, 1880–1940* (Chapel Hill: University of North Carolina Press, 1989), 73–102, which discusses nineteenth-century photographic realism's balancing of mimesis and artifice. See also Dan Schiller, "Realism, Photography and Journalistic Objectivity in 19th Century America," *Studies in the Anthropology of Visual Communication* 4, no. 2 (winter 1977): 86–95; idem, *Objectivity and the News: The Public and the Rise of Commercial Journalism* (Philadelphia: University of Pennsylvania Press, 1981), 76–95. Although Schiller emphasizes the impact of photography on literary and journalistic realism, his critical evaluation of the culturally constructed limits of photographic representation suggest how *Leslie's* varied readership might undermine a unitary notion of "objectivity."

2. "Our Rights as Workingmen": Class Traditions and Collective Action in a Nineteenth-Century Railroad Town, Hornellsville, N.Y., 1869–82

SHELTON STROMQUIST

Just after the collapse of the 1877 railroad strikes, journalist J. A. Dacus began his timely book, *Annals of the Great Strikes,* with the observation: "Republican government in this country has just been subjected to a strain greater than any which our system has been before required to sustain."[1] Dacus was hardly alone in seeking the causes that underlay the unprecedented railroad strikes of the summer of 1877. A special commission appointed by the Pennsylvania legislature conducted extensive hearings into the causes of the "riots." A score of contemporary journals carried analyses. The strikes prompted Allan Pinkerton to add a second volume to what eventually became his celebrated series Great Detective Stories. Newspaper coverage during and after the strike had been so massive—in some dailies little other news was carried as the strikes unfolded—that public officials, businessmen, and subsequently historians found much fodder for analysis.

This spasm of self-reflection produced a litany of explanations from which most historians have hardly deviated. Contemporary observers generally concluded that the strikes had been spontaneous, spreading like wildfire from one center of discontent to the next. Depression conditions of low wages and deepening impoverishment had provided kindling, which in each instance easily ignited.[2] A number at the time assigned a critical role to tramps or other varieties of "outside agitators," particularly members of the Workingmen's Party, whose lineal descent from the Paris Commune was commonly noted. Finally, the railroad strikes have been portrayed by their chroniclers as unprecedented and highly exceptional events. The tale, as it has been told, began on July 16, 1877, or in secret organizing during the weeks immediately preceding. It concluded in the last days of July, with an afterglow reaching into the early fall of 1877. Such a story abstracts the strikes from the social context of railroad workers lives—the work experience and grievances acquired over many years, the traditions of collective organiza-tion and action the workers self-consciously built, the webs of culture and kinship that shaped their view of the world, the rhythms of the industry's growth and retrenchment, and the urban communities, small and large, that had grown to depend on it.[3]

One national pattern to the strikes is abundantly clear. Though news of the strikes did spread from one major rail center to another, the strike did not simply leap from Martinsburg, West Virginia, to Baltimore and thence to Pittsburgh, Chicago, and St. Louis. The strike had a morphology peculiar to locality and trunk line. Activity all along the Baltimore & Ohio, for instance, escalated almost simultaneously.[4] In Grafton, Keyser, Sir John's Run, Wheel-ing, and Cumberland, West Virginia, local committees met, recruited support from other workers—especially miners and boatmen—stopped freights, and intercepted troop trains. Some railroad workers moved between towns on the line as men collected at various strategic points to make a determined stand. Familiar with large sections of the trunk lines, they moved easily from one community to the next. As Herbert Gutman pointed out, support within par-ticular communities for railroad workers well known to them as parishioners, clients, or consumers was readily forthcoming and not without precedent. And towns along the same trunk line had clear and well-established com-mercial ties among them.[5]

Local Patterns: Hornellsville, N.Y.

For a span of several days in 1877, the name of a town in the southern tier of New York counties bordering on Pennsylvania made secondary headlines in most newspapers across the country. The events of the week in Hornellsville, though not taking on the proportions or the violence of the conflagrations in Baltimore or Pittsburgh or Chicago, were significant enough to warrant the dispatch of more than fifteen hundred members of the New York state militia. Erie Railroad officials knew Hornellsville all too well as a recurrent center of labor difficulties. And, once again, they found their road tied up by the actions of railroad men and their supporters in this small division town of several thousand souls.

Sparsely settled, and bypassed in the days of canal fever, the rolling, sometimes rugged hills of the southern tier New York counties reached an early, stable, and in places relatively prosperous level of agricultural development by the decades just before the Civil War. Steuben County lay roughly in the middle of the southern tier, buttressed to the south by Pennsylvania and to the north reaching virtually to the belt of commercial activity stimulated by the building of the Erie Canal. A town historian observed retrospectively, "The history of the growth of this village from a rural hamlet presents a long period of prosperity and general improvement. But the period of its rapid growth began with the construction of the New York and Erie Railroad."[6] From 1836, a quiet, relatively stagnant rural community began to be transformed into a prosperous "business" center. Few could have conceived the economic growth, let alone the social implications of industrial change that would follow in the wake of the "iron horse." But, even in 1870, despite rapid growth in its population to 5,837 and becoming the headquarters of three divisions on the Erie Railroad, Hornellsville remained smaller than two other Steuben County towns (Bath and Corning.) The decade of the 1870s, however, saw it grow by nearly 70 percent and leave the other towns in its wake.[7]

A new class of men had come with the railroad, swelling the town's population. A number of them, largely foreign and predominantly Irish, had done the initial construction and then sought livelihoods with the railroad they had built. Occupying shanties along the constructed route, they were not infrequently harassed by townspeople who feared and distrusted their presence in the area. Describing the hard physical work of railroad construction, John Reynolds, in his history of nearby Almond, wrote, "The horses were driven and pounded until they became exhausted, whereupon they were knocked in the head and rolled into the fill. The men were treated almost as badly."[8]

The foreign born predominated among some classes of railroad workmen, particularly laborers—in 1875, 72 percent of Hornellsville railroad laborers had been born in Ireland. But in the town generally in 1870, only 15 percent were foreign born, and of all railroad workers in 1875, only 31 percent were immigrants. The largest proportion of the community's swelling population had been born in the United States and had moved from other locales.[9]

Industrial change heralded by the coming of the railroad affected not only the size of the community and the composition of its population but the social organization of life within it. Artisan craftsmen of the earlier era, when the railroad was a mere dream in some people's minds, found their trades profoundly affected by the rise of an industrial economy. In 1855, there had been five local firms producing cabinets, furniture, or doors and sashes; they employed an average of four men, the largest employing five. By 1880, only two such manufacturers survived, but they employed fifty and sixty men, respectively. In 1855, four manufacturers producing shoes and boots employed an average of four men each, the largest having ten. In 1855, one boot and shoe manufacturer employed 150 men.[10] The largest "factory," of course, came to be the railroad itself. In 1855, the repair shop of the N.Y. & E.R.R. employed thirty-eight. In 1879, the shops and roundhouses of the Erie employed 172 men. The best accounting of total railroad employment in the town is for 1875, when 743 men found employment in all departments and levels of skill.[11]

The clearest evidence of changing social relations in this "railroad town" came from the level of union organization among its workers, particularly its railroad workers. The community experienced early strikes among locomotive engineers in June 1854 and October 1856, the last being a particularly bitter one over work rules established by the road's superintendent. But the decade of the 1870s witnessed the greatest upsurge in industrial conflict. Major strikes occurred among railroad workers beginning in June 1869 and followed by strikes in December 1870, June 1871, August 1873, February 1874, July 1877, and August 1881. In all except the last two, the railroad workers achieved their demands, wholly or partially. While the major brotherhoods had local lodges organized in 1864 (engineers), 1874 (conductors), and 1876 (firemen), committees dominated by the lesser-skilled trades, particularly brakemen, invariably led the strikes. The brakemen also had a more permanent, if some-what elusive, local organization, the Brakemen's Brotherhood.[12]

In the half-light of corporate capitalist development where expansion, fierce competition, and consolidation were the order of the day, railroads practiced the arts of survival in the highest form known. In 1885, Harvard economist Arthur Hadley described how railroads differed from other in-dustries in this respect: "And railroads have not the refuge, available in most other lines of business, either of contracting their capital or of driving their competitors out of business. A railroad once built is come to stay. It can neither retire from business voluntarily, nor be forced to do so by any other competitor. Drive it into bankruptcy, and it only fights the more strongly and recklessly."[13] Backed to the wall again and again during the decades from 1850 to 1900, railroad corporations refined the financial mechanisms for refunding debts and placating bondholders, ever continuing the process of expansion and consolidation. As indebtedness grew throughout this period, so too did the pressure to generate a surplus that could be used to reduce fixed costs (interest on debt). It is not surprising that problems of management formerly relegated to lower levels came increasingly to occupy the attention of higher officials. Foremost among those problems was labor costs and, more broadly, labor relations.[14]

"The great principle upon which we all joined to act was to earn more and to spend less," wrote John Garrett, president of the Baltimore & Ohio, to Junius Morgan following the March 1877 meetings of presidents of the four major trunk lines.[15] Concretely, the conference produced the first effective rate pool among eastern trunk lines, one that determined mutually acceptable freight rates as well as the share of the trade each was to have. More ominously for workers was the decision that all four lines—Baltimore & Ohio, Pennsylvania, Erie, and New York Central—would reduce wages by 10 percent across the board. That such an agreement had been reached was later denied by Tom Scott, president of the Pennsylvania Railroad, but historians have little doubt that the wave of wage cutting had been planned in March. For that matter, such coordinated wage cuts had appeared as early as 1873 when the depression had begun.[16]

Besides wage cuts, other options for increasing net earnings beckoned railroad managers in the 1870s. They might, for instance, raise labor productivity by increasing freight carried while holding costs steady. In the decade of the 1870s the rate of increase in freight hauled rose much faster than new mileage constructed.[17] Corporations operated more, larger, and faster trains. Indeed, the issue of "doubleheaders" (two engines pulling one, longer train) precipitated the 1877 strike on the Pennsylvania.[18] Doubleheaders had numerous advantages for management. Labor costs could be cut; half as many brakemen and conductors were required. Of equal importance, the load could be increased on uphill grades, for instance from Pittsburgh to Philadelphia. The *Hornell Daily Times* reported in 1879 that "[t]he Erie Road will lessen the number of freight trains by doubling the number of cars in each and stationing a pushing engine to help them over the grades east and west of Goshen. Each train will hereafter consist of fifty cars. The danger of collisions will be greatly reduced."[19] The report made no mention of the employees whose jobs would be eliminated and the increased danger in the work of those who remained. Of New England railroads during this period, historian Edward Kirkland has written, "Pay load increased more rapidly than dead weight, trains carried a greater tonnage without a proportionate multiplication of cars; maintenance and handling costs did not increase. Hazards to workers did."[20]

Brakemen on the major trunk lines faced constant pressure for the reduction of their crews. On the Erie, brakemen had successfully stopped an order reducing their number from four to three through timely strikes in 1869 and in 1874. On the Pennsylvania, they were not so successful in preventing the use of "doubleheaders," though in the course of the 1877 strike company officials may have asked themselves more than once whether their measures really cut costs (damage to company property during the strike totaled more than five million dollars).[21] The issue persisted. Just seven months after the strike in 1877, the Erie Railroad, after years of resistance, introduced the "Westinghouse Air Brake" on its trains, thereby reducing their need for brakemen.[22] In 1881, brakemen in Hornellsville again struck, along with other men, to restore the fourth man to crews of brakemen (among other demands); they were defeated. And, in 1884, brakemen on a western line acquired by the Erie struck against the reduction of brakemen on a train from three to two![23]

Trade organizations, or brotherhoods, had been founded in Hornellsville for all of the running trades by 1875. The engineers organized early in 1864, though some organization may have preceded even that date, as evidenced by the strikes of 1854 and 1856. They possessed a hall, met weekly, and provided for members' beneficial and social needs. The conductors appear to have organized formally in 1874 as Division No. 3 in the Order of Railway Conductors. Newspaper accounts mention semiweekly meetings and an annual ball among their activities. The firemen formed Lodge #2 of the Brotherhood of Locomotive Firemen in 1876 and apparently played a central role in organizing the national Brotherhood (Lodge #1 was in Port Jervis, New York, also on the Erie. Local firemen held major national offices for the first three years of the brotherhood's life; they possessed their own hall and met weekly.[24]

The Brakemen's Brotherhood became the most interesting and elusive organization of the running trades. Lodge #1 organized in Hornellsville in 1873. Evidence survives of an earlier "union" of brakemen dating from the summer of 1869.[25] The brotherhood held its "1st Annual Convention" at Hornellsville in January 1875 with representatives of three lodges attending—Hornellsville, Port Jervis, and a third, not identified. The brotherhood appears to have succeeded the earlier "union" of brakemen, which had existed in Hornellsville and Port Jervis as brakemen sought to extend their organization to other roads. In certain respects it followed the model of the Brotherhood of Locomotive Engineers; it possessed its own hall, met weekly, and provided the services of a beneficial society to its members. But in significant ways it diverged from the engineers' organizational style. Brakemen were central figures in all of the major strikes of the 1870s. Their brotherhood, once organized in 1873, provided an organizational vehicle for industrial action. Most important, the Brakemen's Brotherhood seems never wholly to have been confined to brakemen but rather from the outset assumed the form of a nascent industrial union of railroad workers.

A prominent conductor, W. L. Collins, served as first president and chief organizer. In January 1876, members of the brotherhood recognized him in a lighthearted, surprise ceremony for his valuable service to the brotherhood. A mock arrest by a local policeman as Collins stepped off his train brought him to the Brakemen's Hall. There, charges consisting of three parts were read: "did aid and assist in organizing the Brakemen's Brotherhood," "did take an active part in organizing a Grand Division of the Brotherhood," and "did travel through the West and Southern states as far as Florida during the fall of 1875 and at different times and in many places represent the organization known as the Brakemen's Brotherhood." As a "sentence," members and their wives presented him with "a magnificent tea set."[26]

An interview with a "veteran engineer" in 1878 revealed additional details about the breadth of this organization of "brakemen." He reported that "its members are not all brakemen as the name of the union would imply. There are many locomotive engineers among the members. . . ." In addition, he said, the brotherhood numbered "among its members thousands of track-men and workmen in the shops."[27] Its extreme secrecy left many observers puzzled as to the precise size of the organization, but in the aftermath of the strike of 1877, they believed its influence to be extensive indeed. The "veteran engineer" commented that, "The Brakemen's Union is strongest in the West. Its members are on nearly every railroad in Ohio, Indiana and Illinois. There are only a few members on the Erie Road east of Hornellsville. The Union has a strong membership on the N.Y. Central and on the Lake Shore."[28]

From a single lodge of roughly 150 men, the Brakemen's Brotherhood grew in a short space of time to be an extensive industrial union. As late as 1881, a *New York Times* reporter discovered "meetings of members of the Trainmen's Union" in communities all along the Erie.[29] "A prominent officer of this organization, whose membership includes nearly every department of railway service and whose influence extends to every state and territory in the Union, says the association was never in a better condition than at present to begin a strike."[30] The Hornellsville city directories for 1883 and 1887 list the Brakemen's Brotherhood without naming its officers, as had been done in 1875; "no regular place of meeting" is its only entry. The Great Strike of 1877 clearly marked a significant turning point, but the brotherhood's industrial character had already been shaped by forms of interunion cooperation that had emerged in Hornellsville in the context of conflict with Erie management.

Strikes of railroad workers at Hornellsville occurred with remarkable frequency over a period of slightly more than ten years, roughly coinciding with the decade of the 1870s. Though the particular issue varied, the strategy and style of organization showed continuity from one strike to the next. And generally the railroad workers were successful in achieving their demands.

Several features are apparent from the course of the strikes. Brakemen played a central role in nearly every one. Other trades showed an increasing tendency to act with the brakemen, initially in supporting roles, later adding

Table 2.1. Railroad Strikes, Hornellsville, New York, 1869–81

Date	Trades	Issues	Outcome
June 1869	Brakemen	regular payment; reduction in crews	Success
Oct. 1869	Machinists	back pay	Success
Dec. 1870	Brakemen, Engineers, Switchmen	resisting wage reduction	Part success
June 1871	Brakemen	resisting wage cut; new men	Unknown
Aug. 1873	Brakeman and others	free passes; same time as engineers on road	Success
Feb. 1874	Brakemen, others	crew reduction; wage increase; passes	Success
July 1877	general	discharge of grievance cmte.; and other	Defeat
Aug. 1881	Brakemen, Trackmen, Switchmen	restore 1877 wage cuts	Defeat

demands of their own. A broad range of demands characterized the later strikes in particular, and though they reflected the interests of particular trades, all of the trades stood behind all of the demands. The strike of 1874 illustrates the way in which the company initially conceded on all issues except a wage increase for trackmen, which they promised for later in the spring. The firemen, brakemen, and switchmen broke off negotiations and insisted that "now was the accepted time."[31] The company then conceded the trackmen's wage increase as well.

Finally, the strikes succeeded wholly or at least partially prior to 1877, and even in 1877 the strikers won on a few minor issues. But on the major point— the Erie's discharge of the grievance committee—they lost. That defeat and the strike of 1881, which also ended in defeat, produced severe consequences. The 1881 strike departed in significant ways from a tradition of handling grievances that had been forged in the conflicts of the previous decade.

What was that tradition and what values underlay it? In February 1874 the *Hornellsville Tribune* reported that the men had "declined to work and the *usual* strategic movement of removing coupling pins was resorted to."[32] A report of the strike of December 1870 had described the same activity early on the first morning of the strike: "[The strikers] commenced operations by uncoupling the cars and secreting the coupling pins, and as fast as a freight train entered the yard it was seized and uncoupled, the coupling irons were secretly and expeditiously disposed of, their brakemen joining the crowd."[33]

Operating in large groups, railroad workers in this manner stopped all movement of trains through the community and, because Hornellsville was the major switching point between the eastern and western divisions, all traffic on the Erie came to a virtual standstill. And in a similar manner four years later, "All of the first class cars of the company were stored on the side tracks in the yard at this place and together with the freight cars were in a disabled condition, owing to the removal of brake wheels."[34] Typically, the men allowed an engine and a postal car to pass, after the freight and passenger cars had been removed, "so as not to bring down the wrath of Uncle Sam." Local police were wholly unable to stop the action. In 1870, the sheriff and a posse of deputies deployed on the company grounds but were "unable to do anything as the men were quiet and orderly and claimed to be still in the service of the company. . . ."[35]

Company officials after a day or two invariably arrived and attempted, despite the strike, to move a train out of the yard. In 1870 and 1877 this was done with the assistance of state militia. Invariably at this point the solidarity of the trades received an important test. The extent of support given by the engineers, who were usually not an organized part of the strike, proved critical. They frequently claimed that the track was dangerous, rails having been removed (which was usually true), and refused to take out trains under those conditions. In 1881, when brakemen, still suffering the effects of 1877, did not initially join the strike led by switchmen, the company ordered a crew of brakemen to make up a train in the yard and run it out. As the *Hornell Daily Times* reported, "They refused to go out unless the train were made up for them. The next crew was called upon but declined to 'jump' the first. In this manner seven crews refused to make up the train. . . ."[36]

If company officials succeeded in mustering a crew to move a train, sometimes under the protection of militia, the strikers over the years consistently employed a number of strategies. The crews were heckled, cajoled, harassed, and persuaded to leave their trains. If a crew persisted, small bands of strikers kept ahead of the cautiously moving train as it left town, removing rails, leaving obstacles on the track, each time requiring the train to stop and repair the damage, and each stop creating an opportunity for the strikers to create further obstacles.

Trains leaving town heading west had to climb a steep grade just outside the town limits. In 1870, 1874, and 1877, railroad workers and their families and supporters carried buckets of soft soap to the steepest part of the grade and soaped the rails. There they waited in a large crowd—men, women, and children. As the train reached the soaped rails and lost speed, its wheels slipping, men mounted the train in large numbers, forcibly set the brakes,

and removed coupling pins, sending the cars careening back into the railroad yard. The militia did not pose an insurmountable obstacle to the men
as they carried out their strategy; in some cases, fraternization weakened
the militiamen's resolve; in others, the strikers and their supporters simply
outwitted the militia. "On Sunday an attempt was made to get out a freight
train going west, which was defeated several times, once by the old brakemen
coolly taking their places at the brakes, which was done so that the troops
guarding it supposed that they belonged there, and on reaching the steep
grade, the brakes were all tightly set, and as the track had been soaped it
came to a stand. . . ."[37]

The organization of the strikers extended beyond the direct action of
preventing the movement of trains. Strikers sought to maintain discipline
in their own ranks, to provide for the needs of passengers stranded by the
blockade, and to build support with occupying troops and the community.
Nearly every observer mentioned the remarkable discipline of the railroad
workers; their reports intimate that this was no accident but rather the result
of deliberate efforts on the part of "the committee." In 1874, the *Hornellsville
Tribune* reported, "There was one noticeable thing during the strike. Not a
drunken man was seen around the railway, all was orderly and a stranger
would scarcely have suspected that a serious strike was in progress. This was
due in great measure to the prosecutions of the committee, who visited every
saloon and barroom and requested that no liquor be sold to a railway man
during the progress of the strike, a request that was pretty generally granted
and observed."[38] Another reporter observed that they conducted themselves
with a seriousness reminiscent of Quakers.

The strikers sought to establish friendly relations with the occupying troops,
and the evidence suggests they succeeded. Reporters noted that they seemed
always to be well informed in advance of troop movements. The *New York
Tribune* said that the Fifty-fourth Regiment was "openly in sympathy with the
mob."[39] A sentry said he observed the strikers bringing cigars and whiskey at
3:00 A.M. for a sergeant to give the men on duty. In 1877, a group of strikers
intercepted a troop train several miles before it reached Hornellsville. "There
about twenty men approached the engine waving a red flag. At the same time
it was seen that a rail had been torn from the track a short distance ahead.
As the train stopped, several men sprang upon the engine, drew a pin from
one of the connecting rods and ordered the fireman to go with them. This
he did, and the gang passed along the train, assuring the troops that there
was no trouble and they wished to be on friendly terms with them."[40]

The strike of 1877 presented more formidable organizational problems for
the men on strike than had earlier strikes. Occupation of the town by more

than 1,500 state troops made it difficult to move in and around the railroad yard. The arrest of key leaders and the report that an additional fifty to one hundred warrants had been issued in New York City, as well as news of the $500 reward, forced the strikers to operate from camps outside of town. At night, on the hillsides around the town, "scores of moving lanterns gave evidence of [the strikers] vigilance and activity."[41] By day they surveyed the railway yard through field glasses to anticipate the movement of trains. They had a prearranged system of signals by flashing lights from one hill to the next. The *New York Tribune* reported that "in different portions of the woods, and not remote from the line of the Road, they had over half a dozen camps, subsisting mainly on raw pork, cracks, bread and water. Every preparation had been made for a long siege, and the camp had been provisioned by breaking open and plundering the freight cars in the yard." A reporter visiting the camps noted that nearly every man had a revolver, and in addition, "fully 200 had rifles or muskets, and two small cannon formed the artillery strength." One man in the camps, when interviewed after the strike, said, "When we started this strike two weeks ago, three hundred of us took a solemn oath not to drink a drop of intoxicating liquor until the matter was settled, and to use all means in our power to prevent the destruction of the company's property. We did not see any necessity for the militia being sent here, and had they provoked us by firing on any of our men, we would have never yielded until all were killed."[42] One reporter for the *New York Sun* concluded that "fighting the strikers is much like Indian warfare, so secret and quick are their movements."[43] Indeed, a rumor had it that one hundred Indians from the Salamanca reservation had joined the strikers.

A delegated committee of strikers, representing the various trades, carried on negotiations with some level of management, which varied from one strike to the next, depending on the seriousness of the issues. The strikers met frequently en masse to hear reports of their committees, and in some cases they delegated additional members, numbering as many as thirty, to participate in the negotiations.

Industrial Organization

A new form of organization emerged during the struggles of the 1870s based on a sustained ability of diverse trades to cooperate in collective action around common grievances. At some point, the Brakemen's Brotherhood, which had consistently played a critical role in bringing the various trades together when action was demanded, began to take on the character of an industrial union. It may have been only in the months after the 1877 strike, and with the failure of the Engineers' and Firemen's Brotherhoods to support their fellow railroad workers, that engineers and firemen formally joined the Brakemen's Brotherhood. But probably well before 1877, the Brakemen's Brotherhood functioned on behalf of less-skilled railroaders, particularly trackmen and switchmen.[44]

The important point is that industrial solidarity took shape long before its formal organization. Within the structure of separate brotherhoods lay the seeds of industrial organization. In some communities, like Hornellsville, they germinated into full-bloomed reality; in others, they may have been nipped in the bud. The Brotherhood of Locomotive Engineers reached a crisis point after the loss of the Boston & Maine and the Reading strikes in early 1877. By July, the BLE had moved away from any support of industrial militancy, purging those elements from its ranks, even if that meant in the short-run crippling locals such as Division #47 at Hornellsville.[45] In November 1878, P. M. Arthur, grand chief engineer of the BLE, wrote,

> I am aware that there is a strong prejudice existing in some sections of the country against our organization, which has been created to a great extent by the hasty, ill-advised, unwarranted actions of a portion of the members and the strikes. We have no desire to conceal or cover up the misdeeds of the members. Many of them have done wrong, and we have no apology to make or excuse to offer for them. They have disgraced themselves, their families, and the society of which they were members. It is mortifying to think that we had such characters in our midst, and I hope we are forever rid of them.[46]

An engineer at Port Jervis was asked several years later by a reporter, "Is there anything new in brotherhood circles?" He replied,

> I'm not a brotherhood man and can tell you nothing about them. [He was then asked why he was not one of the brotherhood.] Oh, I'm alright so far as being a sympathizer with labor organizations is concerned, but I don't like Pete Arthur for a cent, and I don't like the way the brotherhood has always had of holding itself aloof, when other departments of the service were in trouble. . . . None for me at present. But if the brotherhood went out to aid in a good cause, I'd never mount a footboard until we went back together.[47]

After 1877, the leadership narrowed and tightened up the structure of the brotherhoods, and industrial organization began to take formal shape at a new, more secretive, "subterranean" level. The Brakemen's Brotherhood held a ball in early 1878, its last public function reported in the local press of Hornellsville.[48] In June, the *Evening Tribune* reported, "There are wild rumors flying in the air that the communists are gathering in force on the outskirts of the village."[49] In October the papers reported that a notice mysteriously appeared in the Buffalo papers calling for a meeting of the Brakemen's Brotherhood, but when reporters investigated, they could find no room let for the occasion.[50] The veteran engineer previously quoted was interviewed in Jersey City that same month, and the papers quoted him affirming the Brakemen's Brotherhood's extreme secrecy and considerable growth since 1877, with membership reaching into the thousands.

Railroad workers were not alone in their movement toward industrial organization, and the Brakemen's Brotherhood was not the only industrial union of railroad workers. The Knights of Labor, still operating under the label * * * * *, underwent its first phase of rapid growth, particularly in the coal regions of eastern and western Pennsylvania.[51] Terence Powderly, who earlier in the decade had attempted to push the Machinists' and Blacksmiths' Union toward opening their ranks to other railroad shopmen, had organized a Knights Local Assembly of railroad machinists in Scranton.[52] By 1878 reports of the Knights appeared in the national press with some regularity. Although the numbers reported, with descriptions couched in hyperbole and allusions to "Molly Maguires," were undoubtedly exaggerated, the phenomenon of growth in industrial consciousness certainly was not. The *New York Times* referred in July 1878 to a report of a Philadelphia meeting of local "clans." "The report shows an increase of 800,000 members since July, 1877, the most numerous class being former members of different railroad organizations which have disbanded since the strike. This is the foundation of the new political party."[53] Although direct connections between the Knights of Labor and the Brakemen's Brotherhood cannot be proved in this period of secret organization, we can hardly imagine them as wholly unrelated. If not organizationally linked, they certainly sprang from common needs, and in 1878–79 found expression in a common political movement, which demonstrated particular strength in the southern tier of New York counties through which the Erie ran.[54]

The "Rights of Workingmen" and the Question of Control

"Riot, Revolution, Anarchy" blared the headlines of the *New York Tribune* in the midst of the Great Strike of 1877. "We only wanted our rights as workingmen" wrote Barney Donahue a few days later from the Ludlow Street jail in New York City. Both observations held some measure of truth.[55] At the time, many Americans would have agreed that the country had never been so close to fundamental social revolution. And yet the demands of the workingmen seemed humble indeed alongside the upheaval they had stirred.

Officers of the Erie and other major trunk lines operated under new pressures in the depression of the 1870s. Court-ordered reorganization demanded higher earnings in relation to fixed investment; operating costs had to be reduced. Competition between trunk lines had grown so destructive to their mutual interests that some degree of rationalization seemed required. If roads were to grow and prosper, the lines insisted on a free hand to increase productivity, and that implied new labor-saving measures and a more tractable labor force. Driven to the wall by overcapitalization, with the agitation and intrigue of foreign and domestic stockholders ever at their backs, railroad officers became ruthless in their pursuit of "greater economy."[56] In a joint letter to the Supreme Court of the State of New York in 1878, the officers of the Erie listed their accomplishments "in answer to allegations" made by a group of stockholders:

> The reductions in our rates of wages which took effect July 1st, 1877, in which month the almost national labor difficulties recurred, have resulted in an average monthly savings of $55,000. In addition to these gains in items readily specified, we believe the discipline of the employees is improved, more rigid systems of accountability are enforced, and the line of service is more harmonious and that these results have been accomplished, particularly during the past year, notwithstanding the efforts of opposing parties to create disaffection.[57]

Underlying the apparently simple issue of a fair wage lay fundamental questions of discipline and "the right of the company to operate its own property," as a vice president of the Erie had put it.[58] Indeed, persuaded that the company would not under any conditions rescind the 10 percent wage reduction, the committee of brakemen, firemen, switchmen, and trackmen that had been sent to New York to negotiate with President Jewett recommended that the wage reduction not be resisted at that time. The strike came not over the issue of wages, but over managerial authority and the right of a workers' organization to represent their interests, when the company discharged the entire grievance committee for absenting themselves from their duties. Mr. Taylor, a division superintendent, gave the following account of what happened. He noted,

> That these men asked leave of absence to visit New York and lay their grievances before Receiver Jewett, and he refused, supposing it was a private matter, and not the action of a regular meeting of the Brotherhood. They then informed him that they would go anyhow, and were informed by him that they did so at their peril, and he discharged them. This was made necessary in order to maintain discipline; and while he was free to admit that they were good railroad men, and efficient in their positions, rather than be forced to reinstate them by the strikers, he would resign his position.[59]

The higher officers of the Erie stood steadfastly behind the superintendent; compromise was apparently possible on all other, minor issues, but not this one. "The company will not make any concessions whatever [on this issue] to the men, and if it is necessary to close the road until the company's authority is re-established then the road will be closed," said assistant receiver Sherman on arrival in Hornellsville.[60]

The strikers perceived the company's objectives as part of a deliberate plan to dismantle the basis of their "control" over the conditions of their work, namely their organization and even the cultural foundations of their class. Hornellsville strike leader Barney Donahue wrote the *Irish World*:

> It seemed to me that the officers of the road were bound to break the spirit of the men, and any and all organizations they belonged to. The company had a fixed policy to pursue in common with other trunk lines, and they were making the experiment then and there—all of their movements were and are well understood. . . . They [the workers] also knew by bitter experience that all organizations among themselves, for mutual improvement, were opposed, as thousands of men on railroads in the United States can testify to. They were to be squeezed out of all organizations they belonged to. Many of the men belong to Masonic and Odd Fellowship societies and also various societies belonging to the Catholic Church, so if the men had not the money to pay their dues, of course they would have to withdraw from all those associations, from all fellowship for mutual aid with fellow men, *leaving them a heterogeneous mass, without civil or social aid.* [emphasis added][61]

The control that railroad employees in Hornellsville exercised was real. It formed the basis of what they regarded as their "rights." An examination of the issues that precipitated the strikes throughout the 1870s provides a sense of what those rights were: a fair wage, regularly paid; a job secure against reduction in crews; promotion according to some fair standard, such as length of service; the right to organize; and equitable treatment of the trades in such things as free passes and payment for time over the road.

Clearly, from the record of strikes, such rights were under fundamental challenge by railroad companies. Companies saw even mere wage demands as a challenge to their authority. As President Griswold of the Chicago, Burlington & Quincy said: "We should at once show that the row is not a question of money, but as to who shall manage the road."[62] It is also clear that until 1877 the railroad workers at Hornellsville defended their control with great success. The strike of 1877 became a showdown of the first magnitude. The discharge of the grievance committee was a direct attack on the collective organization of the workers, and their organization had become the basis of their control.[63]

It would be incorrect to paint a picture of railroadmen's sense of their own rights as wholly static in defense against the encroachments of capital. From one strike to the next, the solidarity among the trades grew, and the contentious issues multiplied. Industrial organization was rooted in an increasingly stable community, with proliferating "organizations for mutual benefit." Political solidarity in local elections grew gradually during the decade, ultimately taking the form of a "workingmen's party" (Greenback-Labor). We have little concrete evidence of where the railroad workers themselves saw class organization leading. We do not know what lay at the heart of their developing claims. But it is fair to assume that their social world and their aspirations changed significantly over the decade through their own organizational initiatives and in response to the increasing pressures of corporate capitalist growth. In the midst of negotiations in the strike of 1877, railroadmen not only fought to protect established "rights" but also raised new conditions to their acceptance of the 10 percent wage reduction. Switchmen would accept the reduction only if ten hours constituted a day. Firemen would accept it only if promotion were henceforth strictly according to age. Trackmen would not accept it at all, and in addition demanded overtime. Brakemen were prepared to accept a 10 percent cut, if they were paid overtime for time they were abandoned out on the line.[64] These and more became "rights of workingmen" as well.[65] Through their own collective organization and action, railroadmen built a tradition of control that allowed them to glimpse a future that might promise a still greater measure of security and dignity.

Notes

1. J. A. Dacus, *Annals of the Great Strikes* (Chicago: L. T. Palmer, 1877), 1.

2. General historical studies that reflect these interpretive trends include Robert V. Bruce, *1877: Year of Violence* (Indianapolis: Bobbs Merrill, 1959), and, to a lesser extent, Philip S. Foner, *The Great Labor Uprising of 1877* (New York: Monad Press, 1977), and Jeremy Brecher, *Strike!* (Cambridge, Mass.: South End Press, 1997). A more recent analysis that emphasizes the "spontaneous" character of the 1877 strikes is Glenn Stephens, "Remodeling Collective Violence: James Tong's Rational Choice Model and the Great Strikes of 1877," *Political Research Quarterly* 48, no. 2 (June 1995): 348–49.

3. Over the years we have been blessed by a generation of local studies, including new work represented in this collection, that examine particular community contexts and enlarge the interpretive canvas of the strikes and their causes: Nick Salvatore, "Railroad Workers and the Great Strike of 1877: The View from a Small Midwestern City," *Labor History* 21 (fall 1980): 522–45, on Terre Haute; David Roediger, "'Not Only the Ruling Classes to Overcome, but Also the So-Called Mob': Class, Skill and Community in the St. Louis General Strike of 1877," *Journal of Social History* 19, no. 2 (1985): 213–39, on St. Louis;

David O. Stowell, *Streets, Railroads, and the Great Strike of 1877* (Chicago: University of Chicago Press, 1999), on Albany, Buffalo, and Syracuse; Shelton Stromquist, *A Generation of Boomers: The Pattern of Railroad Labor Conflict in Nineteenth-Century America* (Urbana: University of Illinois Press, 1987); Richard Schneirov, "Chicago's Great Upheaval in 1877," *Chicago History* 9, no. 1 (1980): 2–17, on Chicago. For an instructive study that gets behind the supposed "spontaneity" of collective action to its social context, see Leopold Haimson, "The Problem of Social Stability in Urban Russia, 1905–1907," *Slavic Review* 23, no. 4 (December 1964): 619–42, and 24, no. 1 (March 1965), 1–22. See also Joan W. Scott, *The Glassworkers of Carmaux* (Cambridge, Mass.: Harvard University Press, 1974).

4. Bruce, *1877,* 74–92.

5. Herbert Gutman, "Trouble on the Railroads in 1873–74: Prelude to the 1877 Crisis?" *Labor History* 2, no. 2 (spring 1961): 215–35. Towns on the Erie Railroad in southern New York and northeastern Pennsylvania included Port Jervis, Susquehanna Depot (Pa.), Hornellsville, and Buffalo.

6. I. W. Near, *History of Steuben County and Its People* (Chicago: Lewis Publishing Co., 1911), 324.

7. Bureau of the Census, *Population Statistics* (Washington, D.C., 1850–90).

8. John F. Reynolds, *The Almond Story: The Early Years* (Hornell, N.Y.: J. F. Reynolds, 1962), 99. On canal and railroad construction workers in the antebellum period, see Peter Way, *Common Labour: Workers and the Digging of North American Canals, 1780–1860* (New York: Cambridge University Press, 1993).

9. Bureau of the Census, Manuscript Schedules (Washington, D.C., 1870). New York State, Secretary of State, *Census of the State of New York for 1875,* Manuscript Schedules, Steuben County, Hornellsville Township.

10. New York State, Census, Manufacturing Schedule, 1855. Bureau of the Census, Manufacturing Schedule, 1880.

11. W. W. Clayton, *History of Steuben County, N.Y.* (Philadelphia: Lewis Peck Co., 1879). New York State, Census, Population Schedules, 1875.

12. Edward H. Mott, *Between Ocean and Lakes: The Story of the Erie* (New York: J. S. Collins, 1901), 115, 119. For the strikes from 1869 to 1881, see the accounts primarily in the local press: *Hornellsville Tribune* and the *Evening Tribune.*

13. Arthur T. Hadley, *Railroad Transportation: Its History and Laws* (New York: G. P. Putnam and Sons, 1885), 19–20.

14. For a discussion of these problems of railroad expansion, financial crisis, and corporate reorganization, see Stromquist, *A Generation of Boomers,* 10–16; see also Alfred D. Chandler, *The Railroads: The Nation's First Big Business* (New York: Harcourt, 1965).

15. Peter Lyon, *To Hell in a Day Coach* (Philadelphia: Lippincott, 1968), 76.

16. State of Pennsylvania, General Assembly, Legislative Document, v. 5, Doc. 29, 1878 *Report of the Committee Appointed to Investigate the Railroad Riots in July, 1877* (Harrisburg, Pa.: Lane S. Hart, 1878). On the previous round of wage cuts, see Herbert Gutman, "Trouble on the Railroads in 1873–74: Prelude to the 1877 Crisis?" in Gutman, *Work, Culture and Society in Industrializing America* (New York: Vintage, 1977), 298–303.

17. Chandler, *The Railroads,* 13–14.

18. Bruce, *1877,* 115–16.

19. *Hornell Daily Times,* April 12, 1879.

20. Edward C. Kirkland, *Men, Cities, and Transportation: A Study in New England History, 1820–1900* (Cambridge, Mass.: Harvard University Press, 1948), 369.

21. Philip Slaner, "The Railroad Strikes of 1877," *Marxist Quarterly* 1 (April–June 1937): 227.

22. The saga of the delayed introduction of air brakes, which had been invented by George Westinghouse in 1868, is recounted in Emory R. Johnson and Truman W. Van Metre, *Principles of Railroad Transportation* (New York: D. Appleton and Co., 1902), 64; Henry G. Prout, *A Life of George Westinghouse* (New York: American Society of Mechanical Engineers, 1921), 32; and John F. Stover, *The Life and Decline of the American Railroad* (New York: Oxford University Press, 1970), 72.

23. *Evening Tribune* (Hornellsville), February 18, 1878; Stuart Daggett, *Railroad Reorganization* (New York: Houghton Mifflin, 1908), 54.

24. Information on the Brotherhoods in Hornellsville has been drawn from the lists of organizations in the city directories for 1875, 1877, and 1880, and from scattered references in the *Hornellsville Tribune*. On the organization of the BLF and Eugene V. Debs's early leadership, see Nick Salvatore, *Eugene V. Debs: Citizen and Socialist* (Urbana: University of Illinois Press, 1982).

25. *New York Times,* November 26, 1869.

26. Clipping from James P. Hogan Scrapbook, January 1876. The source is a scrapbook belonging to a former engineer with the Erie, James Hogan, who worked from the late 1870s until he was killed in the early twentieth century. Most of the clippings are not dated, but many describe events that can be approximately dated from other sources. (The scrapbook is in the possession of Rosemary Hogan of Hornell, N.Y.)

27. James P. Hogan Scrapbook; *New York World,* October 1878.

28. Ibid.

29. The names "Trainmen's Union" and "Brakemen's Brotherhood" were used interchangeably by the press in discussing the organization of railroadmen on the Erie. A "Trainmen Union" founded in Allegheny City, Pennsylvania, in late May 1877 became the leading force behind the strikes in Pittsburgh that summer and has received considerable attention from historians. Known largely through testimony before the Pennsylvania state legislative committee, which investigated the "riots" in Pennsylvania, it has consistently been assumed to have been a local and transitory phenomenon. I believe it was plausibly a local branch of the earlier Brakemen's Brotherhood that organized first on the Erie; there certainly were links of some sort between the two. Besides the evidence of the far-flung organizational efforts of Hornellsville brakemen earlier in the decade, there was direct telegraphic communication between the leadership of the strike on the Erie in Hornellsville and Pittsburgh. Barney Donahue, a leader of the strike on the Erie, was released from jail in New York City late in August 1877. Accompanied by the sheriff of Steuben County back to the county seat of Bath, Donahue made a point of refusing to take rail transportation—which would have forced him to travel through the northeast corner of Pennsylvania—because he feared additional charges in that state, though he had committed no illegal acts in other states; the Brotherhood of Railroad Trainmen (BRT) organized in 1886 and appears to have no direct lineage with the earlier efforts of brakemen to organize.

30. *New York Times,* August 21, 1881.

31. *Hornellsville Tribune*, March 6, 1874.

32. Ibid., February 27, 1874.

33. Ibid., December 23, 1870.

34. Ibid., March 6, 1874.

35. Ibid., December 23, 1870.

36. *Hornell Daily Times*, August 18, 1881.

37. *Hornellsville Tribune*, December 23, 1870.

38. Ibid., March 6, 1874.

39. *New York Tribune*, July 30, 1877.

40. *New York Sun*, July 24, 1877.

41. *New York Tribune*, July 27, 1877.

42. Ibid.

43. *New York Sun*, July 24, 1877.

44. The impulse toward industrial organization clearly rose and subsided from time to time with changing conditions on the railroads, in the economy, and in the wider world of labor. In addition to the role played by the Knights of Labor in the mid-1880s, western railroad workers following the Great Burlington Strike of 1888 crafted a trades' federation and ultimately the American Railway Union in the early 1890s to provide a vehicle for such aspirations. See Stromquist, *A Generation of Boomers*, 54–99.

45. The columns of the *Engineers' Monthly Journal* in 1878 had long lists of engineers expelled for "violating obligations," many of them from the Erie and at least fifty-nine from Division #47 at Hornellsville. See the monthly issues, March–May 1878. These, without question, appear to be engineers who directly participated in the 1877 strike.

46. *Engineers' Monthly Journal*, November 1878, 498.

47. Hogan scrapbook. Precise date of clipping is not known.

48. *Hornell Daily Times*, January 7, 1879 (a review of the major events of 1878).

49. *Evening Tribune* (Hornellsville), June 7, 1878.

50. Ibid., October 9, 1878.

51. On the Knights of Labor and secrecy, see Robert E. Weir, *Beyond Labor's Veil: The Culture of the Knights of Labor* (State College: Pennsylvania State University Press, 1996), and his *Knights Unhorsed: Internal Conflict in a Gilded Age Social Movement* (Detroit: Wayne State University Press, 2000); see also Jonathan Garlock, "A Structural Analysis of the Knights of Labor: Prolegomena to the History of the Producing Classes" (Ph.D. diss., University of Rochester, 1974).

52. Powderly, in his autobiography *The Path I Trod* (New York: Columbia University Press, 1940), 41–42, recalled how at the Louisville convention of the Machinists' and Black-smiths' Union in 1874, he had pushed for a resolution to admit boilermakers, a resolution that was resoundingly defeated amid comments from the chair about the boilermakers' "untidy habits and lack of neatness in dress." Powderly angrily rushed up to the secretary's desk and inscribed the following poem to be presented as new business.

Aristocrats of Labor we,	The Carpenter and the molder, too
Are up on airs and graces.	The Mason and the miner,
We wear clean collars, cuffs and shirts	Must stand aside as we pass by,
Likewise, we wash our faces.	Than we there's nothing finer.

There's no one quite so good as we	But some day, some how things will change
In all the ranks of labor.	Throughout this glorious nation,
The boilermaker we despise,	And men of toil will surely meet
Although he is our neighbor.	In one great combination.

Like machinists and blacksmiths, so too among engineers and firemen, internal divisions over broader industrial sympathies ran deep.

53. Following the collapse of the strike in 1877, the Greenback-Labor Party showed surprising strength for the next year or two in local elections in many former hotbeds of railroad strike activity. This was certainly true of the southern tier of New York counties through which the Erie ran. On the Greenback-Labor Party, see John D. French, "'Reaping the Whirlwind': The Origins of the Allegheny County Greenback Labor Party in 1877," *Western Pennsylvania Historical Magazine* 64, no. 2 (April 1981): 97–119; Elizabeth Sanders, *Roots of Reform: Farmers, Workers, and the American State, 1877–1917* (Chicago: University of Chicago Press, 1999); and Gretchen Ritter, *Goldbugs and Greenbacks: The Antimonopoly Traditions and the Politics of Finance in America* (New York: Cambridge University Press, 1997).

54. Selig Perlman, "Upheaval and Reorganization (since 1876)," in J. R. Commons, *History of Labour in the United States,* vol. 2 (New York: MacMillan, 1918), 242.

55. *New York World,* July 31, 1877.

56. For a discussion of the general climate of railroad investment in these years, see Julius Gordinsky, *Transcontinental Railway Strategy, 1869–1893: A Study of Businessmen* (Philadelphia: University of Pennsylvania Press, 1962), 226–55, 319–32; Albert Fishlow, "Productivity and Technological Change in the Railroad Sector, 1840–1910," in *Output, Employment, and Productivity in the United States after 1800,* Conference on Research in Income and Wealth, Studies in Income and Wealth, vol. 30 (New York: National Bureau of Economic Research, 1966), 628–29; see also Stromquist, *A Generation of Boomers,* 10–12, 100–103.

57. "Joint Letter (G. R. Blanchard & others) to Hon. H. J. Jewett in answer to allegations made in complaint of Charles Potter and others in the Supreme Court of New York," 12878, Miscellaneous Papers of the Erie Railroad Company, New York Public Library.

58. Gutman, "Trouble on the Railroads," 233.

59. *New York Tribune,* July 27, 1877.

60. *New York World,* July 22, 1877.

61. *Irish World,* August 18, 1877.

62. Thomas Cochran, *Railroad Leaders, 1845–1890* (Cambridge, Mass.: Harvard University Press, 1953), 180.

63. For a discussion of the place of control issues in railroad strikes for the remainder of the nineteenth century, see Stromquist, *A Generation of Boomers,* 34–40; see also David Montgomery, "Strikes in Nineteenth-Century America," *Social Science History* 4, no. 1 (February 1980): 81–100.

64. *Buffalo Commercial Advertiser,* July 26, 1877.

65. Samuel Gompers may have put this expansive idea of workers' rights most forcefully when he spoke of "practical improvement" and "final emancipation," or when he told the World Labor Congress in 1893: "We want more school houses and less jails; more books

and less arsenals; more learning and less vice; more constant work and less crime; more leisure and less greed; more justice and less revenge; in fact, more of the opportunities to cultivate our better natures, to make manhood more noble, womanhood more beautiful and childhood more happy and bright," in Samuel Gompers, "What does labor want?" a paper read before the International Labor Congress, Chicago, September 1893, 4–5, Chicago Historical Society. See also David Montgomery, "Labor and the Republic in Industrializing America," *Le Mouvement Social,* 1980.

3. Chicago's Great Upheaval of 1877: Class Polarization and Democratic Politics

RICHARD SCHNEIROV

The raw violence and widespread bitterness of feeling attending the great upheaval that shook Chicago during the late July days of 1877 were not only part of the nationwide railroad strike but were integral to the turbulent socioeconomic and political change that was transforming Chicago in the 1860s and 1870s. The strike and riot brought to a crisis point the increasing polarization of two emerging industrial classes: on the one hand, large-scale employers and allied property owners, and on the other, a new immigrant, industrial working class. That polarization, in turn, created a major problem for democratic politics: could majority rule exercised by professional politicians, who were responsive to those who had no income-producing property to protect, be reconciled with the existence of an industrial capitalist order?

On the eve of the Civil War, Chicago was an outpost of the East, a "gateway city" in which finished goods from the East were transshipped to the city's hinterlands in exchange for primary products, including grain, lumber, coal, and ore. The city's economy emphasized wholesaling, transportation, banking, and insurance to the detriment of manufacturing; and real estate speculators and promoters of trade known as "boosters" ran the government. The making of Chicago into the nation's railroad hub, the explosive population growth of the city and its Midwest hinterland, and the trade disruptions occasioned by the war, which led large numbers of eastern manufacturers to relocate in Chicago, changed that. Between 1860 and 1870, Chicago's population increased 2.7-fold to 299,000 (the city increased another 67 percent in the following decade), and the dollar amount invested in manufacturing grew sevenfold. The scale of the city's manufacturing establishments grew accordingly, reaching the average level of Philadelphia's by 1870. Chicago's largest industry was meatpacking, which produced about one-quarter of the city's entire manufacturing output. The hothouse development of this period swamped the old booster elite, generating a modern capitalist class, whose profits derived as much from the employment of labor as from mercantile activities.[1]

By 1870, Chicago was also a working-class city, with 38 percent of its population employed on the basis of wage-labor, about the same percentage as in eastern cities. The city's workforce was 69 percent foreign born. Approximately one-quarter of all workers were of German parentage, 19 percent were Irish, 8 percent British, and 17 percent other nationalities. Despite workers' ethnic diversity and the divergence in views between Irish and Germans regarding slavery, the Civil War era witnessed Chicago's first great labor upheaval. Nineteen different unions emerged during or immediately after the war, all of them multiethnic associations governed by skilled craftsmen and oriented toward striking. In 1865, twenty-four local unions were affiliated with the city's new Trades Assembly, representing 8,500 workers, about 28 percent of the city's workforce. The most well-known labor leader, Andrew Cameron, published a local labor newspaper of national repute, *The Workingman's Advocate*. In 1867, at the height of labor's influence, Chicago's unions, with the support or acquiescence of the city's political establishment, mounted a general strike for the eight-hour day. In a foretaste of the future, Chicago's unskilled factory hands, helpers, and general laborers joined the conflict in a series of riotous crowd actions that police ultimately suppressed.[2]

The emergence of new classes functional to the city's industrial economy created new social and economic requirements in the great city of the West, which could not be effectively served by the city's existing political and governmental apparatus, then in the hands of "ring" politicians of ill-repute. By the early 1870s, a series of dramatic events precipitated this clash of need and structure, setting the stage for the great collision of 1877.

The Great Chicago Fire of 1871 and the subsequent rebuilding effort inaugurated a three-year crisis in class relations. Reflecting the lack of confidence of the city's "best men" in local government, the mayor transferred city policing immediately after the fire to the U.S. Army under Gen. Phillip Sheridan. Acceding to widespread fears that "indiscriminate" distribution of relief aid would exacerbate the city's existing labor shortage and raise the cost of rebuilding, he also turned over the collection and disbursement of relief money to the Relief and Aid Society, a private body run by members of the city's Yankee establishment. Meanwhile, under threat that eastern insurance companies would withdraw their coverage, which, together with high wages, might precipitate a flight of eastern and European capital, the city's upper classes united to help place in the mayor's seat the *Chicago Tribune's* editor, the Republican Joseph Medill. To appease the New York–based insurance companies, the new mayor attempted to institute and then enforce an ordinance eliminating flammable wood-built structures from the commercial center of the city.[3]

Disaster struck these efforts to restore and firm up economic ties with the outside capital when Medill decided to enforce the law mandating Sunday closing for saloons, an ordinance that had lain dormant for almost two decades. Though popular among native-born pietistic Protestants as a way of restoring social stability, it infuriated the Germans, most of whom had voted Republican, and therefore splintered the Republican Party coalition that had ruled the city since 1857. By 1873, a coalition of ex–German Republican and ex–Irish Democratic ethnic politicians had joined forces to form the anti-temperance People's Party, which swept to power in the November elections. The new party declined to enforce the new fire limits and soon repealed the odious temperance law. More significantly, when the Depression of 1873–78 arrived, the People's Party governed the city in ways that undermined the business confidence of the Yankee Protestant upper class.[4]

With approximately 20 percent of the manufacturing workforce unemployed, many of them single male immigrants attracted to the city by the rebuilding effort, a new group of German-speaking labor leaders, the city's first self-proclaimed socialists, stepped into the breech. The *Sozial Politischer Arbeiterverein* (Social Political Workers' Society), loosely affiliated with Karl Marx's First International, mobilized thousands of unemployed men in a series of marches to demand either municipally supplied jobs or relief in the form of disbursement of the remaining fire relief funds held by the Relief and Aid Society. In other cities impromptu coalitions of labor reformers, trade unionists, and socialists raised similar demands, but in Chicago, where socialist leadership of the movement was uncontested, it raised the specter in the press of another Paris Commune and opened a deep rift in the labor movement between labor reformers and German-speaking socialists. With its political base threatened, the People's Party moved left. People's Party Mayor Harvey Colvin voiced support for the "mob's" demand that the Society turn over its funds, which led to four times the amount of relief being paid out that winter to the indigent. The People's Party–controlled city council also tried to launch a job-creating public works program in the form of a new courthouse.[5]

At this critical juncture the political pendulum swung back in the other direction. Another large fire hit the city in July 1874. Though not as catastrophic as the one of 1871, it had a more profound impact on local politics. Faced with the prospect, as Horace White of the *Chicago Tribune* put it, of "the withdrawal of capital from the city, the departure of our most energetic citizens, the diversion of population, trade, and wealth away from us, and the dwarfing of Chicago to the dimension of a second or third-rate town," leading Chicagoans of property united, including the German, former Republican, now People's Party leader, Anton Hesing. A week later one hundred of the city's top business leaders formed the Citizens Association. The new association sought to lead the city into compliance with the Fire Insurance Underwriters' Association's demands for an extension of the fire limits, the professionalization and depoliticization of the city's police and fire departments, and a centralization in the hands of the mayor of the entire fragmented municipal administration, with its township governments and independent boards.[6]

The Citizens Association was the first social organization of the new capitalist class that frankly articulated that stratum's pressing needs and fears and sought to harness municipal government to the requirements of the new economy. The most urgent requirement of the day was to restore the investor confidence of eastern and foreign sources of capital accumulation by establishing a centralized and professionalized city administration where it touched on such industry affairs as fire protection. Its primary fear was that machine politicians like those in the People's Party would use government to redistribute wealth downward by taxing the holders of large-scale property to pay for job programs, and undermine pecuniary incentives in the labor market by disbursing relief funds indiscriminately.

The Citizens Association was frankly distrustful of the masses of new immigrant workers, whose democratic participation it blamed for the professional politicians. As Franklin MacVeagh, the Association's first president, put it, "the immoderate fancy for the freedom of all human males above the age of twenty-one years . . . [has] pretty much succeeded, in our great cities at least, in binding hand and foot the best part of the community, and placing political power in the hands of the baser elements of the people." Echoing an older discourse that linked the preservation of a republic with property holding, MacVeagh wondered aloud in his address how the "protection of property" was possible with a government of men with "no property to protect." These antidemocratic, anti–working class sentiments closely paralleled the national-level retreat of Republican "liberals" from support of Reconstruction governments in the South whose corruption was blamed on the voting power of the newly enfranchised freedmen.[7]

The Citizens Association sought to unify holders of capitalist property under its wing in new ways. It transcended partisan political loyalties by remaining aloof from party identification and electoral politics. In contrast to the old boosters, its leaders eschewed direct office holding and the established leadership of evangelical Protestant churches. It displaced and pushed into abeyance many of the issues and concerns that had structured politics in the Civil War–Reconstruction era, notably, sectional divisions with regard to the conduct of Reconstruction, soft money versus hard money, high tariff versus free trade, and temperance and nativism versus personal liberty. Not least, it was a politics unapologetically based on the existing class polarization and hostility to the sort of democracy embodied in "ring" or machine politics.[8]

By 1877, the reform liberals were largely triumphant in the city and in Republican Party state counsels. Under pressure from the Citizens Association, the city administration professionalized the fire department, the police began enforcing the new fire limits, and Chicago's electorate supported a new charter that abolished independent boards and centralized the powers of appointment and removal in the hands of the mayor. The Citizens Association also collected funds to recruit and pay white-collar clerks and bookkeepers to man the first "businessman's militia." When the militia, together with local police, intimidated socialists into staying home from a planned demonstration on the Relief and Aid Society in April 1875, the socialists formed their own militia, the *Lehr- und Wehr-Verein*. In response, the Citizens Association urged state legislators to formulate legislation establishing a comprehensive military code, which passed in May 1877. Two years later the Association successfully lobbied legislators to prohibit private militia companies and ban public drilling without the governor's permission, provisions aimed at the socialists and their foreign-born constituency.[9]

In 1876 the upper-class assault on machine politics reached a crescendo. In the wake of further spectacular revelations of local corruption, Chicago's "better sort" fielded a bipartisan slate of candidates for mayor and the city council in April. The People's Party mayor suffered a convincing defeat, and the *Chicago Tribune* estimated that twenty-eight of the thirty-six new aldermen elected were "respectable." Though a new election had to be called because of a court suit, a hastily called special polling resulted in the victory of an anti-ring candidate, Republican Monroe Heath.[10]

On the eve of the 1877 strikes, the array of political opportunities for the formation of organized movements among workers was highly unfavorable. Unlike 1867, when Republicans supported the eight-hour day, or the 1872–74 period, when an administration friendly to immigrant workers and unions had controlled city hall, in 1877 the liberal forces in power feared that any labor organizing or political initiative favorable to workers would either stymie needed political reforms or feed the socialist menace to property and order. The inability of mainstream politicians to offer viable appeals to workers during the long depression created an opening for the socialists to take leadership of the labor movement. The particular constellation of circumstances in Chicago contrasted with many eastern cities, where machine politicians were able to offer inducements to workers to "immunize" them from socialist appeals.[11]

The intransigence of the local establishment only reinforced the impact of the 1873–78 depression on the labor movement. Even at the height of the labor upsurge of 1864–72, only two unions—the typographers and stonecutters—were powerful enough to control wages and working conditions in their trade. Among other unions, membership and bargaining strength and ability to enforce a closed shop fluctuated wildly according to seasonal and business cycles. Following the 1867 eight-hour day strike, the Trades Assembly declined into insignificance and by 1870 had been displaced by the German Trades Assembly. With the coming of the depression and widespread wage-cutting in response to falling prices, organized labor activity of all types almost came to a halt. Nonetheless, among German-speaking central Europeans—Germans, Poles, Czechs, and Hungarians—the level of organization and morale remained high. Already a thriving community-based movement culture was emerging among Chicago socialists that paralleled that of the socialists in imperial Germany, one that included a party press, periodic parades, picnics, meetings, militia drills, and yearly celebrations of the Paris Commune. Given the decline of multiethnic labor unions, this culture, together with the rump organizations among German-speaking workers, would play a major mobilizing role in the 1877 strikes and riots.[12]

Less than a month before the great strike was to begin, the great depression of the 1870s seemed to have reached its nadir. Seeking to avoid bankruptcy, employers ran their businesses at a loss, wages fell to their lowest point, and unemployed workingmen tramped the country. In Chicago as elsewhere the sight or prospect of unemployed workers wandering the countryside or thronging city streets became visible reminders of spreading crime, bomb-throwing "Mollie McGuires," or foreign-born communists. On July 2, a new Illinois vagrant law went into effect that allowed police for the first time to arrest without warrant "any one who goes about begging; . . . persons who do not support themselves or their families; and those who take lodgings in the open air or unoccupied houses or barns and give no accounts of themselves."[13]

On the railroads, the nation's largest industry, court-appointed receivers ran bankrupt rail lines to get business in any way possible; these lines set the standard for fratricidal rate-cutting wars that pushed the country's railroads to the brink of insolvency. In spring 1877, the large railroads decided to pass along their losses to their employees in wages cuts starting at 10 percent—on top of earlier cuts of approximately 20 percent. In April the only viable railroad union, the Brotherhood of Locomotive Engineers, balked at the cuts but suffered defeat at the hands of the Philadelphia & Reading Railroad. Nonetheless, on July 16 a virtually spontaneous strike began among brakemen of the Baltimore & Ohio Railroad at Camden Junction, Maryland. The strike, marked by the stopping of trains, seizing and destruction of railroad property, and violent clashes with police and militia, spread rapidly into New York state along the New York Central lines and into Baltimore, Reading, and Pittsburgh, Pennsylvania, along the Pennsylvania and Reading Railroad lines. Louisville, Cincinnati, Chicago, and St. Louis, plus a host of smaller cities such as Terre Haute, Indiana, would also experience strikes. In many cities, the rail strike quickly spread to workers in other industries, and the dispatch of the militia by authorities sparked widespread rioting and violence. In Pittsburgh on July 21, the militia sent from Philadelphia to protect strikebreakers fired into a crowd of railroaders, killing at least twenty workers and prompting a crowd swelled with sympathizers to burn the rail yard.[14]

Leading Chicagoans, still embroiled in debates over reform of municipal governance, suffered through the fourth year of depression, with somewhere between fifteen and thirty thousand unemployed. Leaders felt anxious about immigrant workers' simmering restiveness, and were ill disposed to take a sober-minded view of events in Baltimore and Pittsburgh. The *Tribune* termed the great strike "Civil War," and "Fever," and described a country "surging with suppressed excitement," while the *Inter Ocean* dubbed it "America's First Great Revolution." Though the local press expressed sympathy for the real grievances of railroad workers and offered various remedies for the unrestrained cutthroat competition that had precipitated the wage cutting, only the upstart tabloid, *Chicago Daily News,* backed workers' right to assemble and strike once mob action mushroomed out of control in Pittsburgh.[15]

The most ominous development for authorities was the aggressive role taken by the socialists, now part of the Workingmen's Party of the United States (WPUS). Founded the previous year in Pittsburgh, but headquartered in Chicago, the WPUS, 4,500 members strong, had temporarily settled its internal division between electorally oriented Lassalleans and trade union– and strike-oriented Marxists—which boded well for relating to the strike once begun. In Chicago, its largely foreign-born and German-speaking constituency could for the first time present an English-speaking face. Chicago-based national president chairman Philip Van Patten was native born and a fluent speaker. Three other effective leaders had recently been "converted" to socialism by Peter J. McGuire, the socialist founder of the carpenters' union, when he visited the city in 1876. Now representing the party before the public were George Schilling, a bilingual German-born cooper, who would later become an influential Knights of Labor and (nonphysical-force) anarchist; Thomas J. Morgan, a British-born machinist, poised to become the city's leading advocate of independent socialist involvement in electoral politics; and the charismatic Albert Parsons, a tramping printer of old American stock, recently arrived in Chicago, with his African American wife Lucy, from Texas, where they had been Radical Republicans. The new English speakers, however, were close to the Lassallean wing of the party in their favoring of the ballot over trade union action.[16]

On Saturday, July 21, all eyes were on the railroad workers. While skilled and semiskilled workers averaged $2.00 a day, unskilled laborers received a full dollar less, making it difficult to impossible to support a family. Talk circulated among employees of the Rock Island & Pacific, Lake Shore & Michigan Southern, and Illinois Central railroads of a strike against recent wage cuts. Since Friday, WPUS leaders had been agitating for a strike, assuring railroaders of support. That night the party held a packed solidarity rally in Sacks Hall, decorated with large banners displaying slogans, including "Down with Wages-Slavery," "Why Does Our Production Causes Starvation?" and "We Want Work, Not Charity." Though the main speaker, Albert Parsons, did not advocate violence or revolution, portentous talk emanated from the working-class audience of applying the "Pittsburgh solution" to the Chicago problem.[17]

That same day, the party's Chicago-based national executive committee met to ask its members to "render all possible moral and substantial assistance to our brethren" now on strike. It promulgated the party's program of nationalization of the railroads and telegraph lines and establishment of the eight-hour day as a solution to unemployment and falling wages. Still, it was only in Chicago and St. Louis that the attempt to offer leadership to the great strike would meet with any success. Those cities had workforces dominated by German-speaking immigrants and small but significant numbers of party members based among them.[18]

At the newspaper offices downtown on Sunday, large crowds gathered for the latest word on the strike. All the newspapers came out with extra editions. For the *Chicago Tribune* it was the first since the Civil War. Again, Albert Parsons addressed a crowd packed "almost to suffocation" into Sacks Hall. That night Parsons spoke to a smaller audience of unionized railroad switchmen while mounted on a fireplug. He counseled them to "strike while the anvil is hot," and promised support.[19]

On Monday, July 23, it seemed only a matter of time before events similar to Pittsburgh overtook the rail center of the nation. Railroad workers from different lines gathered in small knots throughout the rail yards to discuss grievances and plan action. Meanwhile, fearing property damage like that which had befallen Pittsburgh and seeking to forestall or contain a strike, many railroad officials in the city indicated they would cancel their freight runs, leaving their rolling stock on tracks outside the city. The North Western & Chicago, Danville & Vincennes Railroads restored the pay cut of some or all of their workers; other lines discussed doing the same. In secret conclave with police chief Michael Hickey and militia commanders, Mayor Heath decided to assemble the militia in readiness for action, but reportedly decided not to board trains, escort strikebreakers, or "do anything to precipitate violence." Later reports indicated that the mayor instructed police either to use blanks in their pistols or fire over the heads of rioters if provoked. Though that decision probably forestalled property damage to the railroads, it would be widely questioned by leading citizens once the strikes and riots had begun in earnest.[20]

All day, socialists leafleted the working-class districts advertising an evening mass meeting for the third consecutive day. The republican rhetoric of the leaflet reflected the influence of the new English-speaking leadership of the party. It asked workingmen, "Have You No Rights?—No Ambition? No Manhood?" The circular went on to accuse the dominant liberals, whom it referred to as "money lords," of conspiring to restrict the vote to property holders and return to a monarchy. Obviously this fear originated in the agitation of the Chicago Citizens Association three years earlier, but concern about the vote may have been intensified by a controversial New York state constitutional amendment then at issue that would have barred almost 70 percent of all voters from participating in fiscal decision making in cities. Drawing on the nineteenth century's equal rights tradition, the leaflet contrasted the new tramp law and the state law against workers' combinations to the uncontrolled combining by their employers to reduce wages. "These aristocrats refuse to pay their taxes! HOW LONG WILL YOU BE MADE FOOLS OF?"[21]

That night one of the largest gatherings the city had known crowded into the intersection of Market and Madison streets downtown. The size of the gathering, somewhere between ten and thirty thousand, made it necessary for six speaker rostrums to be erected.[22] John McAuliffe, the only Socialist to sanction forcible resistance, warned that "if capital fired on their Fort Sumter," the newspaper report ran, "he swore by the yet warm bodies and radiant spirits of their martyred dead who had been brutally murdered at Pittsburgh . . . his thought and voice would be raised for Bloody War (cheering)." The eloquent Parsons was the main attraction, and he did not disappoint. In an ironic allusion to the Grand Army of the Republic (the post–Civil War veterans' organization and mainstay of the Republican Party) that any of his listeners would have understood, Parsons addressed his listeners as the "Grand Army of Starvation." He continued:

> Fellow workers, let us recollect that in this Great Republic that has been handed down to us by our forefathers from 1776, that while we have the Republic, we still have hope. A mighty spirit is animating the hearts of the American people today. When I say the American people I mean the backbone of the country—the men who till the soil, guide the machine, who weave the material and cover the backs of civilized men. We are a portion of that people. Our brothers . . . have demanded of those in possession of the means of production . . . that they be permitted to live and that those men do not appropriate the life to themselves, and that they be not allowed to turn us upon the earth as vagrants and tramps. . . . We have come together this evening, if it is possible, to find the means by which the great gloom that now hangs over our Republic can be lifted and once more the rays of happiness can be shed on the face of this broad land.[23]

As the throng swelled beyond the point where any single speaker could be heard, additional rostrums were improvised at different locations. Speakers arose spontaneously to address the audience. One of the few whose words were recorded was an Irish Union Army veteran who had fought at Shiloh: "The Black man has been fought for; and we have given him the ballot; the people have shown an interest in him, and have done all they can to bring him up to the point where he could compete with the white man. Now why not do something for the workingman? . . . I was through the war. I fought for the big bugs—the capitalists—and many of you have done the same. And what is our reward now? What have the capitalists done for us?"[24]

The theme of corruption of the republic by an oligarchy of wealth, and the veteran's complaint of betrayal and disinheritance would echo in the actions of strikers and rioters in the days to come.

The strike, inaugurated formally on Monday by the railroaders, was prosecuted in earnest on Tuesday, July 24. Mobile crowds—what the *Inter Ocean* called "roaming committees of strikers"—traveled from workplace to workplace calling out employees on strike. To the bulk of the press this manner of striking made participants into a dangerous mob, in part because it attracted sympathizers and hangers-on not directly interested in the strike, in part because it extralegally appropriated public thoroughfares as its theater of action, and in part because it involved coercion of proprietors and other workers. Thus, while occasionally referring to crowds as strikers aided by sympathizers both wanted and unwanted, for the most part the press characterized them as composed of, according to one account, "hordes of ragamuffins, vagrants, saloon bummers, and generally speaking the dregs of the population." This was almost certainly a distortion.[25]

Indeed, the method of striking did not differ much from that of existing unions. Early unions, before they were able to sustain membership loyalty, employ paid, full-time leadership, or rely on bargaining relations with employers, were usually makeshift operations that coalesced members only in times of strike. Typically they resorted to crowd actions and the enthusiasm of the moment, often supplied by brass bands—the "bandwagon effect." This was especially the case with unions that enrolled significant number of unskilled workers. In the early to mid-1870s Chicago had boasted a number of unions that enrolled these types of workers, including the carpenters, painters, sailors, and coopers; the largest unions, the Laborer's Benevolent Society (dockhands) and the Knights of Saint Crispin (boot- and shoemakers), each had more than five hundred members when the depression started. The organizational experience of these workers may help explain the ease with which large numbers of workers, unskilled as well as skilled, became involved in strike actions in 1877.[26]

A more complex explanation is required to understand why crowds almost immediately thought to broaden strikes at their places of employment, their particular trades, or their industries into industrial strikes and a general strike of all industries. Certainly, part of the reason was the example afforded by strikes in other cities, which, while originating in the grievances of railroaders, quickly drew in workers in other industries because the issue of wage cutting was generalized across the working class. Indeed, on Sunday and Monday, mass meetings in St. Louis and Kansas City had declared general strikes, which, with the acquiescence or support of authorities, lasted through the rest of the week. Another part of the explanation may lie in the precedent of the 1867 Chicago general strike for the eight-hour day. Though begun by organized skilled tradesmen, it had quickly mushroomed into a strike of the unskilled relying on mobile crowd actions. But, the larger part of the explanation lies in the mid-1870s defeat of machine politicians by the Citizens Association and the subsequent prominence of the socialists in the early stages of the Chicago events. Before crowd actions became general, the socialists alone had offered the railroad workers support and encouragement, had suggested a program of the eight-hour day that spoke to the interests of all workers, including the unemployed, and unlike English-speaking labor reformers, still maintained an organizational base among an important segment of Chicago's workers.[27]

The initiators of the crowd action on Tuesday were a small group of Michigan Central switchmen, soon joined by freight hands and teenage apprentices. The crowd of several hundred was led by a handful of railroaders, the acknowledged chief of which was a discharged railroad hand named John Hanlon, a "dark complexioned man with chinwhiskers and a pipe in his mouth." Carrying pine sticks, the men marched south along the tracks stopping at the Baltimore & Ohio, Rock Island & Chicago, and Alton freight shops. There was no opposition from police. At each stop Hanlon, attempting to persuade rather than intimidate, led a small delegation inside the shop. Not all employees suspended work voluntarily, but railroad officials, evidently instructed to avoid property damage at all costs, generally told all hands to go home when confronted with the crowd. At one yard, employees didn't want to quit, saying that their pay cut had been restored. Hanlon asked if the restoration applied to all employees on the line. When told that it didn't, he responded that "they were working for the rights of all" and that work must cease until wages had been restored to all employees.[28]

An offshoot of the crowd boarded a train to the Southside, where it tried to spread the strike to the packinghouses. The men visited each establishment and after securing a verbal agreement to restore wage cuts, raised a cheer for the employers.[29]

During this time, Bohemian lumbershovers, at least some of whom were socialists or socialist influenced, commenced a strike for the third year in a row. It was the first time the strike had spread beyond the railroads. The crowd of about two thousand roamed throughout the lumber district driving out the few men remaining on the job, and then moved on to close the brickyards and stove works.

By the late afternoon, the strike was no longer confined to the railroads. Not only had the lumbershovers joined spontaneously, but the strike had spread to the heavily industrialized area just west of the Chicago River. Bands of workers and teenagers roamed up and down Canal, Clinton, and Jefferson streets shutting shops and factories. One group, led by a tall brawny man named Flinn, attempted to convince workers to strike of their own volition. Many did, but in other cases, as the crowd approached, proprietors closed their shops and factories and sent their employees home before they could call a strike. At least one group of employees in this region, German and Bohemian furniture workers, many of whom were socialists, joined the crowd.

As yet there had been no interference by police, and the mood of the crowd was exuberant, like being "out on holiday," a disapproving reporter noted. Every instance of shutdown was lustily cheered and buoyed the crowd's enthusiasm. Occasionally, there were shouts of "Vive la Liberté" and "Down with the Thieving Monopolies." One Bohemian, with the assent of his Irish companion, attempted to start up "The Marseillaise," the anthem of the French Revolution, now sung as well by socialists and free thinkers.

Later that day, Tom Littleton, a discharged railroad hand, led one section of the West Side crowd to his former place of employment, where it shut down the freight depot. Another portion stopped at Fortune's Brewery for free beer dispensed by an anxious owner. At Monroe and Franklin, two hundred shoemakers, led by a small delegation, closed two factories before being dispersed by police. Late in the afternoon, a self-described "committee of sailors" distributed a circular calling for a wage raise, but few sailors were in port, and the strike had to wait.

At least half of most crowds were young men between the ages of twelve and nineteen. "It seems strange," remarked a *Tribune* reporter, "that full grown men should at the bidding of half-grown men and boys quit their work, but so it was." In fact, the phenomenon should not have seemed so strange. In an era before effective compulsory education, half-grown men and boys were important elements of the city's growing industrial workforce, working as apprentices, helpers, and more generally in the sweated trades. Though, no doubt, many were attracted for thrills, others understood the crowd actions as being in their interest. Thus, one boy, on being asked by a reporter why he was striking, replied, "No man ought to work for less'n a dollar 'n a half" [a day].[30]

The WPUS continued to try to organize a general strike for a 20 percent wage increase and the eight-hour day. A socialist circular called on workers to appoint delegates to a provisional strike committee. Though a minority of the committee wanted the party to support the crowd actions, the Lassallean-tending majority opinion, as expressed in the circular, urged strikers to "keep quiet" until an orderly strike could be planned. The city's business leaders, however, accused the socialists of inciting the strikes and crowd actions and were fearful of future consequences. That afternoon, they took matters into their own hands. Albert Parsons, the most influential socialist, found himself fired from his job as printer at the *Chicago Times,* and detectives escorted him to city hall. There, in the company of the police chief and more than thirty Board of Trade businessmen and aldermen, he and WPUS chairman Van Patten were browbeaten and threatened with lynching. They were saved from arrest only because the authorities feared creating martyrs, and they released the men on the promise to absent themselves from strike activity for twenty-four hours. "Parsons, your life is in danger," said Police Chief Hickey, before he was freed. "Everything you say or do is made known to me.... Do you know you are liable to be assassinated any moment on the street? Why, those board of trade men would as leave hang you to a lamp post as not." Meanwhile, the mayor issued a proclamation calling for citizen patrols in local neighborhoods and for closing all saloons.[31]

In spite of the WPUS circular, a crowd of about three thousand gathered Tuesday evening at the spot of the previous night's rally. The socialists, their leaders intimidated into silence and inaction, were absent, but the police were not. A phalanx of bluecoats charged the peaceable gathering, clubbing indiscriminately and firing over the heads of the panic-stricken crowd. The police ignored a rival meeting of labor reformers and twenty trade union delegates, who met to endorse the railroad strike, but whose emphasis was on currency reform as a solution to the depression.

The police attack on the WPUS meeting was the first during the strike in which widespread clubbing and shooting had been used to disperse a peaceful crowd. It set a precedent for a pattern of police violence against working-class crowd actions that would transform them into an armed confrontation; it also further intimidated the socialists and precluded them from organizing a more effective general strike. That such a strike was possible was evident from the Kansas City and St. Louis general strikes that same week.

The next day, Wednesday, July 25, with no attempt being made to run freight trains or provide police escorts to strikebreakers, the center of the strike's gravity shifted to the city's main industrial areas. The composition of the crowds also changed. Teenagers composed a large portion of Tuesday's crowds; adult workingmen dominated Wednesday's crowds.

Now that the strike had developed into crowd actions, the policy of local authorities toward the crowd changed. The *Chicago Tribune* described a debate going on among city and business leaders. One faction, consisting of "the mayor and his advisors," counseled police restraint to avoid bloodshed and property damage. The other, led by the city's press and business leaders, argued that "by allowing the crowds to run wild through the streets, the riot was but abetted, because ... persons who had no idea of joining the innumerable gangs would, by the exercise of a little persuasion, be led in and gradually changed in mind. ...." By Wednesday this latter faction was in the ascendance.[32]

A delegation of Board of Trade businessmen asked the mayor to call a citizen's meeting in the afternoon. Perhaps sensing the tide of opinion, the mayor opened the gathering at the Moody and Sankey Tabernacle by issuing a proclamation calling on five thousand citizens, composed as much as possible of ex-soldiers, to organize themselves as auxiliaries to the police. The gathering, attended by the city's notables, passed a resolution backing the mayor's call, and the city council followed suit. Only Alderman Frank Lawler, ex–ship carpenter union president from the 1860s and author of the state eight-hour-day law, supported strikers by calling in vain for a public works program to provide employment.[33]

The action resumed early, when between six hundred and eight hundred Bohemian and a number of Polish lumbershovers gathered in the lumber district again. Armed with clubs taken from lumber scrap, they scattered the few employees remaining at work, closed the Union Rolling Stock Company, and advanced on McCormick's Reaper Plant. The crowd, now having grown to about 1,500, was met by a squad of fifty bluecoats. The commander ordered the crowd to disperse, but his words were met with jeers and curses. The lumbershovers were the most combative group of workers in the city, and the Bohemians among them were known as strong socialists. When the police attempted to arrest their leaders, the lumbershovers responded with a shower of stones. The police, who had begun to feel acutely their lack of numbers, fired into the crowd, wounding two and causing a wild retreat. When part of the crowd reassembled on the prairie west of the city, a few of the participants, apparently officers in the Bohemian militia company, talked of calling this unit out to protect their strike. News of such a possibility reached authorities, for on that same day, General Torrence, commander of the National Guard, signed an order disarming the "Bohemian Rifles."[34]

By early afternoon, the entire city was in ferment. A group of South Siders had carried the strike to the North Side by shutting the Chicago Rolling Mills and precipitating a strike of the unskilled tanners along Goose Island on the north branch of the river. On the West Side, crowds patrolled Canal Street to ensure that all factories remained shut. A large contingent of South Side Bridgeport youths and Canal Street "toughs" closed the South Side Street Railway. At the Union Stock Yard in the Town of Lake south of the city, a more organized group of packinghouse workers expelled a group of boys—they wanted to appear respectable—and made their own tour of the packinghouses, forcing the proprietors to sign agreements that raised wages to two dollars a day.[35]

With so many discontented people lining the streets and excitement at such high pitch, any small group of workers with purpose and a target could get up a crowd. Conversely, a large crowd often would melt away just as quickly as it had formed. Many police literally bloodied their feet marching back and forth dispersing crowds that seemed to rise up, disappear, and reappear at random. One notable small crowd of unemployed dockworkers and laborers gathered near the lake. Finding nearly everything shut down, an Irish boat hand climbed up on an abandoned flatcar to make a speech:

"Look at me, . . . do I look like a loafer or a laboring man?" [in apparent response to press characterizations of the crowd] The crowd yelled and cheered and assured him that was one of them. "Of course I am," he said; "I am as honest a workingman as ever worked in a shop. Look at my hands. . . . These hands show what I am. We know what we're fighting for and what we're doing. We're fighting those God d—d capitalists. That is what we're doing. Ain't we? . . . Let us kill those damned aristocrats." He had been a railroad worker himself once, he said, and knew what he was talking about. They had the thing started, and they were going to keep it going until those big bugs had been put down.[36]

The city was now preparing itself for a full-scale insurrection, even though the violent confrontations were rooted in police attacks on nonviolent crowds. Two companies of the U.S. Army arrived in the city at the request of the governor, who had responded to the mayor's request the day before. They had lately been battling Sioux in the Dakotas. In a revealing metaphor, the *Tribune* headlined "Red War" the next day, conjuring up at once images of insurrectionary Communists, Indian savages, and the spilling of blood. While the bronzed and grizzled veterans won cheers from businessmen and clerks downtown, they fielded jeers and catcalls from Canal Street crowds as they marched west along Madison Street to the Exposition Building.[37]

In response to the mayor's proclamation the previous day, the city's propertied middle classes had begun to arm themselves. Field, Leiter & Co. and J. V. Farwell dry goods stores organized companies of armed clerks, as did the Illinois Central Railroad. In the heavily Republican Fourth Ward, three hundred Civil War veterans organized. Citizen patrols formed in a host of wards, but reports of patrols were notably absent in the wards of the foreign born. Despite the feeling conveyed by the press that the city was in the midst of civil war, with a few minor exceptions, neither the armed citizen patrols, the special police, the state militia, nor the U.S. Army saw action; only the Chicago police engaged in battle.

After dinner, a crowd of about 1,500 gathered at the Burlington yards. Upon satisfying themselves that the rail lines were not in use, they were about to disperse when a squad of sixteen policemen under Lieutenant Callahan pulled up. Called "peelers" by Irish workers—after the hated Irish constabulary of Sir Robert Peel, manned by native-born Irishmen viewed as turncoats—the police rode headlong into a volley of stones and shouts of defiance. Though the police fired at the crowd with their revolvers, the crowd did not flee. A *Chicago Times* reporter wrote in language reminiscent of the Civil War, "They faltered not in the least but stood up under fire like war-scarred veterans or men resolved to perish for their cause rather than abandon it." Some of the crowd replied to the police fusillade with stones and sporadic fire from their own weapons. Shots were exchanged for fully two minutes until the police ran out of ammunition and fled for their lives. Part of the crowd followed in close pursuit. The roles of the past two days had been reversed, and for the first time the crowd had taken the offensive.[38]

The strike, which had turned into an armed confrontation Wednesday night, continued along these lines Thursday morning. Now the scene of crowd activity shifted to the residential communities. By 9 A.M., a crowd of three thousand men, women, and teenagers from surrounding neighborhoods had gathered along Halsted Street between 12th Street and the viaduct at 16th Street. This area of Halsted was narrow, skirted with frame buildings, and could easily be blockaded.[39]

The battle of Halsted Street began when a squad of police attempted to break up the crowd by chasing it south. At 16th Street, confronted by an angry crowd of approximately five thousand, the police emptied their revolvers into the masses of humanity. "Although men were seen to drop away at every minute the mob dragged or carried them away at the instant. . . ." When they almost expended their last round of ammunition, the police turned into headlong retreat north over the viaduct. They were closely followed by the crowd, which pelted them with stones. One officer later admitted, "I was never in such close quarters in my life before."[40] One block later, the police picked up reinforcements and again turned on the crowd, firing and clubbing mercilessly. One member of the crowd that had been shooting at police fell mortally wounded; this had a "sobering effect," and the tide turned once again. But, after the officers had chased the rioters across the river, a "gang of toughs" raised the bridge and isolated a small band of police on the South Side. The police might have suffered grievously had not a small boy turned a lever to lower the bridge and allow a squad of volunteer cavalry to ride to the rescue of the beleaguered peelers.

South Halsted Street, the scene of battle, straddled two working-class communities, whose residents made up the single largest group of rioters. Of the eighty-eight casualties reported in the press, 45 percent were boys, nineteen and under. Virtually all those whose addresses were listed lived in the Fifth, Sixth, and Seventh wards. Of the total number of all riot victims identifiable by residence, 42 percent came from the Sixth Ward and 22 percent lived in the Sixth Ward's largely Bohemian Fourth Precinct adjoining the lumberyards.[41] According to the 1880 manuscript census schedules the fourth precinct was 57 percent Bohemian, and half of all heads of families were laborers.[42] The precinct lay in the heart of the Bohemian community known as Pilsen. About half of the community consisted of free thinkers, recently alienated from the Catholic Church, with strong sympathies for socialism. During the 1877 strikes and riots almost the entire Pilsen community rose up against the police. One disapproving Republican wrote in a letter to the *Tribune*: "I was perhaps the only Bohemian in Chicago who opposed the powerful current of the aroused public feeling of my countrymen."[43]

The other major source of crowd casualties was the Fifth Ward Irish community of Bridgeport. Bridgeport originated as a settlement of Irish and German canal laborers, but by the 1870s was the site of three fast-growing industries: brick making, iron and steel making, and slaughtering and meat packing, the latter of which employed upward of twenty thousand at its seasonal peak. In 1875 a reporter commented, "There is probably as much real poverty in Bridgeport as anywhere in the town. It is also the haunt of the roughest characters." A slight majority of all those arrested had Irish surnames, and teenagers with Irish names were two and a half times as likely to be killed as German and Bohemian teenagers.[44]

On Thursday in the midst of the "Battle of Halsted Street," a contingent of five hundred stockyard workers from Bridgeport set out along Archer Avenue to join the Bohemian lumbershovers on Halsted. Many of them were butchers, still wearing their aprons and carrying butcher knives and gambrels for clubs. At the front of the procession two boys carried a banner bearing the words WORKINGMEN'S RIGHTS. The crowd, now swollen to 1,500, was a "determined one," conceded the *Tribune*, composed of "men in every sense of the word . . . brave and daring in the extreme. . . . When the police called on them to disperse, they vowed they would rather die than return." A desperate battle for possession of the Halsted Street bridge ensued, lasting nearly an hour. "Every inch gained was warmly contested by both sides. If there was a coward in the battle, he could not be detected." Only the arrival of a squad of police reinforcements shooting into the crowd decided the contest, and the stockyard workers retreated to Bridgeport.[45]

Despite the mayor's ordering out of the militia's Second Regiment to the Halsted Street viaduct, the crowd was neither beaten nor overawed. About ten thousand people packed Halsted, mainly on the sidewalks and alleys. The majority were onlookers, but seemingly all were sympathetic to the strike and angry at the police. When the police or cavalry approached, the crowd would part and then close behind them, many chucking stones and pieces of wood. When the police turned on their tormentors, the crowd would melt away into the alleys. Police arrested Mollie Cook and her two sons for firing at them from their Halsted Street home; in the afternoon police ordered shut every window along the street.

When the crowd actions shifted to the neighborhoods, large numbers of women joined the fray. According to the *Times,* they constituted at least one-fifth of every gathering. On Halsted Street, Bohemian women brought stones in their aprons to the men, encouraging them to "clean out and kill the soldiers." Not only did they incite the men, but they engaged in their own resistance. Police detectives roaming the crowd sought out women wearing one stocking on the assumption they had used the other to fill with stones for use as a swinging weapon. In Pilsen on 22nd Street between Fisk and May, Bohemian women gathered in the afternoon at a door and sash manufactory. The reporters' descriptions of the ensuing altercation reflected their dismay at behavior that blatantly violated the norms of middle-class womanhood. "Dresses were tucked up around the waists," and "brawny, sunburnt arms brandished clubs" torn from the fence surrounding the factory. When the police arrived to protect the factory from what the *Chicago Inter Ocean* styled an "Outbreak of Bohemian Amazons," they remained firm and stoned the hated bluecoats until they left. The *Tribune* concluded that these immigrant working-class women were "a great deal worse than the men."[46]

Up until Thursday, the organized trade unions had stayed aloof from the crowd actions. On Thursday, a number of trades began holding meetings to discuss striking. But by this time, the police were making no distinction between the proverbial "honest workingman" and the rioters. The coopers, cigarmakers, stonecutters, and tailors all had their meetings proscribed or attacked by police. The most blatant abridgment of the right to free assembly occurred at South Side Turner Hall on Halsted, where three hundred journeymen cabinetmakers had gathered to negotiate with their employers. With no provocation a band of police rushed into the hall, clubbing and shooting indiscriminately. One carpenter, Carl Tessman, was killed, and dozens wounded. Two years later the Harmonia Joiners Society won a suit against the policemen involved, the judge terming their actions a "criminal riot." The Turner Hall incident was remembered by labor for years afterward, and Governor John Peter Altgeld referred to it in his pardon message justifying the freeing of the imprisoned Haymarket anarchists in 1893.[47]

As evening approached, the Battle of Halsted Street subsided. Here and there police exchanged shots with snipers and occasionally cleared out homes, but the high tide of the upheaval had passed. The city was an armed camp, and mobile crowd actions were impossible without immediate opposition. But as street action dwindled, hitherto sporadic attempts of workers to call strikes began producing results. The West Division Street railway stockmen, stonecutters, West Side gas workers, South Side glass workers, and lime-kiln workers all went on strike. The majority of railroads, as well as the city's rolling mills, lumberyards, and stockyards, remained closed into the next week.

By then, a significant minority of those involved, notably railroad workers, had won restoration of wage cuts.

Throughout the city's West and South Sides, Irish, Bohemian, German, and Polish families mourned their dead relatives and neighbors, tended the wounded, or attempted to raise bond for the almost two hundred men who had been arrested. Approximately thirty men and boys had been killed—many buried anonymously in lime pits—and another two hundred wounded. Chicago's casualties exceeded that of any other city in the great railroad strike of 1877. No police had been killed and eighteen had been wounded, none seriously.[48]

That Sunday's *Chicago Tribune* contained an editorial by Joseph Medill, entitled "The Dangerous Classes," that offered a rethinking of America's mid-century free-labor faith. Medill argued the thesis that mass immigration, the Civil War, widespread tramping, and the rise of labor union intimidation of employers and strikebreakers had created something hitherto unknown in America: the dangerous classes. "They are governed by their passions; they are coarse in tastes and vicious in habits; they are ignorant and revengeful; they are readily influenced by the worst class of demagogues and revolutionists, and are easily maddened by liquor." Medill advocated enforcing laws against interference with the railroads "at whatever cost. A few lives taken at the first saves human life in the end. . . . A little powder, used to teach the dangerous classes a needful lesson, is well burned, provided there are bullets in front of it." The idea that labor was a dangerous class was far from new. Classical republican doctrine warned against the interested actions of an ungovernable mob as much as it did the tyrannies of oligarchy and monarchy. By the mid-1870s, respectable public opinion endorsed an updated version of this concern in the fear that the new industrial working class was incompatible with the progress of civilization, and that drastic steps might be necessary.[49]

But, far from seeking to destroy modern civilization, labor leaders were busy in the aftermath of 1877 building new, more inclusive institutions of civil society. The aggressive crowd actions—and even more, the myriad instances of unity across lines of skill, trade, ethnicity, religion, and sex—made it clear to many labor leaders that new forms of organization and action for incorporating the unskilled laborers and factory hands were both necessary and possible. The dean of Chicago's Civil War–era labor movement and editor of the *Workingmen's Advocate*, Andrew Cameron, admitted that "our unions are isolated and consequently are weak and inefficient. They have no common ties, no sympathy in common with each other and are indifferent to each others' success and elevation." Responding to this widespread perception, in August 1877 former Knights of Saint Crispin's leader Richard Griffiths called the city's first (secret) meeting of the Knights of Labor, a gathering of fifty trade union leaders. A local Knights' historian recalled that the "principal feature" of the new order that "aroused the curiosity of all laboring men was that it embraced all who earned an honest living without distinction of trade. In comparison to the old English system of trade unions, this was a new departure."[50]

The Knights were not the only organization to offer an all-embracing organizational vision to the city's workers. The WPUS socialists, now dominated by Lassalleans, sought to reorganize all trade unions "on socialist principles." At a pivotal December meeting, Chicago labor delegates voted narrowly to reject the secret Knights of Labor and establish a Trade and Labor Assembly (TLA)—with the word "labor" being added to the pre-1877 name "Trades Council"—and elected the now famous Albert Parsons as its first president. As unions sought to revive and reorganize in 1878 and 1879, most ended up joining the socialist-led TLA. Unlike the shadowy Knights, the TLA could offer concrete assistance in the shape of sponsorship of citywide mass meetings and the collection of strike support funds. Not only did German-led unions like the cigarmakers, coopers, furniture workers, silver gilders, clothing cutters, and wood carvers join the TLA, but so did the reviving union of boot- and shoemakers, the KOSC.[51]

During this same period, Irish workers, many of them participants in the 1877 upheaval, formed or revived organizations with a Bridgeport base. In spring 1878, brickmakers founded a protective organization, and sailors revived their union under the leadership of Richard Powers. According to Powers, the 1877 strikes, "although detrimental to some, gave stability and backbone to others. . . . It was then that many of the unions now existing . . . were organized." The most important union to emerge from the 1877 experience was the Butchers and Packinghouse Workers Benevolent Society, the city's first industrial union of the post-1877 era. Fearful that unemployed sailors would cross their picket lines, the skilled butchers decided to expand their organization to laborers with the help of Powers. Initially backed by the local Catholic church, the five-thousand-man-strong union mounted a large but ultimately unsuccessful strike of the packinghouses in 1879. When church support faltered, the union turned to socialist-run labor institutions for support.[52]

The WPUS—renamed the Socialist Labor Party (SLP) in December 1877 and under the control of the Lassalleans again—also began to exercise a loose hegemony over the labor movement in electoral politics. The Greenback-oriented Labor League and the WPUS each held mass meetings in August 1877 hoping to attract support from aroused labor voters for the upcoming county elections. Both organizations frankly sought to don the mantle of 1877, but the largest part of the Labor League's leadership at the last minute fused with the Democrats. Though a remnant of the Labor Leaguers joined with the national Greenback-Labor Party, it won only 1,673 votes that fall, far fewer than the WPUS total of 6,592. About half of the socialist vote came from the largely German-speaking Fifth, Sixth, and Fourteenth wards. The Sixth Ward's Bohemian precinct adjoining the lumberyards, the core local-ity of riot victims, delivered the highest socialist vote of any precinct in the city and continued to do so in two of the next three elections. The socialist hegemony in Chicago contrasted with the situation in most other American cities, where Greenback-Labor coalitions came forward as the representatives of discontented labor.[53]

Though the SLP finished a distant third to triumphant Republicans in the 1877 election, its newfound strength made it the center of public attention. The police exaggerated local SLP membership by a factor of ten. Even more menacing, the socialist armed groups assumed public visibility. The *Lehr- und Wehr-Verein* and the smaller Bohemian Sharpshooters drilled in public and regularly assembled to protect socialist picnics from roughs. The Socialists viewed them as an answer to the armed forces arrayed against them in 1877. "If the police try to break up our meetings as they did at Turner Hall," asserted Albert Parsons, "they will meet foes worthy of their steel." The alarmed Citi-zens Association raised $30,000 to fund the First and Second Regiments of the militia and lobbied for a state law effectively banning public drilling.[54]

SLP strength reached its zenith in spring 1879, when it nominated German doctor Ernst Schmidt for mayor. Schmidt's respectability and presumed in-corruptibility almost doubled the SLP vote total to twelve thousand, about 19 percent of the total. The bulk of the new voters were the same liberal Germans who had become accustomed to bolting the Republican Party over ethno-class issues beginning in 1873. The resulting diminution of the Republican total allowed a surprise Democratic winner, Carter Harrison I, to claim the mayor's seat. Indeed, the increase in the SLP vote almost precisely equaled Harrison's margin of victory.[55]

Because of his narrow victory and the fact that the SLP had mobilized significant numbers of German Republicans in a Republican city, Harrison recognized that maintaining his majority required either bringing the Social-ists directly into the Democratic Party or fostering a strong Socialist vote as a third force in upcoming elections. He also needed the support of four SLP aldermen in the closely divided city council. Accordingly, Harrison began almost immediately to openly court Socialist voters. In his inaugural address he defended their rights "to peaceably assemble," to "speak," and "to keep and bear arms." "Some persons fear an organized resistance to authority in Chicago," observed Harrison, "I do not."[56]

Under Harrison the Democrats rebuilt the patronage and policy ties to the Socialist-led immigrant working class that had been severed earlier as a result of the rise of the Citizens Association. During his first term as mayor, Harrison appointed the defeated Schmidt to the Library Board, German Socialist politico Joe Gruenhut to the city's health department, and gave the city's printing to the SLP paper, *Arbeiter Zeitung.* When members of the Bohemian militia were arrested for firing at Irish toughs who had invaded their picnic, Harrison arranged for their immediate release and defused public clamor for retaliation. In June 1879, the SLP supported the reelection of Judge William McAllister, a Democrat, who had just declared the Vagrant Act unconstitutional. Large numbers of SLP voters split their tickets in the ensuing city elections of 1881. In the party's Fourteenth Ward stronghold, the SLP aldermanic candidate received 837 votes, while its mayoral rival to Harrison won only 231 votes. In the companion Sixteenth Ward, only 75 of 1,359 SLP voters cast ballots for the Socialist candidate for mayor. With the accession of the Socialist vote to Democratic totals, the city experienced an electoral realignment. Between 1857 and 1877, Republicans dominated all but two city elections; but from Harrison's election in 1879 through 1897, Democrats won seven of the ten mayoral elections, and two of the three Republican victories owed to a split in the Democratic vote.[57]

Harrison also mended his ties with Irish Bridgeport by appointing police officials sympathetic with the community. In one notable example, the Irish-born policeman John Byrne, who had resigned from the force in 1877, was reinstated by Harrison and elevated to a lieutenancy. In the Bridgeport strikes of brickmakers, blast furnacemen, and iron ore shovelers during the early 1880s, Byrne's local police stayed neutral, allowing strikers to overawe and physically intimidate strikebreakers, much as they had done during the first two days of the 1877 strike. According to a biographical sketch of Byrne, during "many serious strikes among rolling mill employees and . . . other large strikes and threatened riots, [he] could accomplish better results with masses of determined and excited men by reasoning and persuasion than could be gained by any show of force." By 1885, the unwillingness of Harrison's police to protect strikebreakers had become notorious. A Citizens Association report observed that politicians found it advantageous "to calculate the probable effect of a prompt, bold, and determined attitude against a large body of defiant rioters who have ballots to cast."[58]

But Harrison could not have accumulated the political capital to renew major party ties with socialist-led workers had he not also satisfied the requirements of the city's business leaders and wealthy property holders for efficient administration and relative immunity from taxation. In the same inaugural address that he defended socialist civil rights, he accepted the need to keep property taxes low by retrenching on city spending. Moreover, once in office, he appointed honest professionals rather than patronage hacks to head the fire department, the departments of public works and health, and, most important, the post of city comptroller, Chicago's financial czar. As a result, despite continued opposition from Citizen Association liberal reformers, whose solution to 1877 was an increase in the police force to be paid for by license fees on saloons, Harrison was able to garner the tolerance if not the support of most businessmen.[59]

In accommodating the needs of the propertied middle class, employers, the new immigrant working class, organized labor, and the city's diverse ethnic and religious groups, Carter Harrison forged a new kind of municipal politics in the city. In some ways it relied on the old "machine" approach to contentious issues. Thus, Harrison dealt with workers' strikes in the same way the old machine had dealt with the saloon and fire limit issues: by granting violators immunity from police enforcement of the law. But, Harrison also pioneered overt appeals to organized interest groups, including those hitherto excluded from respectability and power.[60] Thus, when multiethnic trade unions revived and grew during the 1880s prosperity, Harrison bargained with them. He also met the minimal reform needs of businessmen without acceding to the program of the Citizens Association. In that way his administration advanced the practice of democracy and marginalized the sort of antidemocratic ideology espoused by the liberals in the Citizens Association and practiced by the city's business establishment during the 1877 great upheaval. Harrison's regime thus demonstrated for the first time that rather than being locked in an irreconcilable conflict for supremacy, workers and capitalists, and Socialists and the Citizens Association, could coexist within the political system without either vanquishing the other.

Harrison's political solution to the crisis of the 1870s was at first precarious and vulnerable to conservative counterattack. In 1885, a renewed outrage at corruption, a revitalized antisaloon movement, and concern about the social costs of Harrison's tolerant policies toward the strikes of organized labor and the open meetings of the anarchists, revived class polarization and created the preconditions for the Haymarket Affair and another great upheaval. Nonetheless, after a short interval, Harrisonian accommodationist policies reasserted themselves in the mayor's office. The vote of the so-called dangerous classes, and the growing participation in government of its representatives along with that of organized labor, would prove enduring, setting the stage for the more well-known reforms of the Progressive Era.[61]

This account of the Chicago 1877 great upheaval argues for the necessity of studying actions of workers in the context of developing class relations and shifting political ideologies and governing coalitions over an extended time period. Viewing it in this context has implications for the study of Gilded Age political as well as labor history. There has been a curious disjuncture between Gilded Age political history and Gilded Age labor history. On the one hand, many labor historians argue that a powerful coalition of anti-labor employers and a repressive state apparatus repeatedly defeated important strikes and labor upheavals and steered the emerging labor movement away from radical challenges to capitalism.[62] On the other hand, recent historians of Gilded Age politics have questioned older characterizations of its politics as corrupt, superficial, and out of touch with the "real" issues facing Americans. Instead, they have portrayed this political era as a "complex and portentous time" and even as an "unheralded triumph."[63] The emergence of a socialist-led labor movement in Chicago, and the subsequent ascendancy of Carter Harrison and his approach to governance following the 1877 strikes, helps reconcile these divergent interpretations because it shows how the new labor movement not only retained but also expanded its power to reshape and revitalize democratic politics even as it faced its own limitations in the course of class conflict.

Notes

1. Carl Abbott, *Boosters and Businessmen: Popular Economic Thought and Urban Growth in the Antebellum Middle West* (Westport, Conn.: Greenwood, 1981), 19, 20, 65; David R. Meyer, "Midwestern Industrialization and the American Manufacturing Belt in the Nineteenth Century," *Journal of Economic History* 59 (December 1989): 921–35; William Cronon, *Nature's Metropolis: Chicago and the Great West* (New York: W. W. Norton, 1991), 60–61, 207–59, 307–8; figures on manufacturing scale compiled by the Chicago Working-Class History Project from the 1850, 1860, and 1870 federal manuscript manufacturing censuses; Bruce Laurie and Mark Schmitz, "Manufacturing and Productivity: The Making of an Industrial Base, Philadelphia, 1850–1880," in *Philadelphia: Work, Space, Family, and Group Experience in the Nineteenth Century; Essays toward an Interdisciplinary History of the City*, ed. Theodore Hershberg (New York: Oxford University Press, 1981), 43–92.

2. Figures on nationality from Chicago Working Class History Project; figures on Trades Assembly from *Chicago City Directory, 1864–65* (Chicago: John C. W. Bailey, 1865); *workforce* is defined as the same percentage of the population in 1865 as the workforce was in 1870; see Bessie Louis Pierce, *A History of Chicago, vol. 2: From Town to City, 1848–1871* (New York: Alfred A. Knopf, 1940), 151n4.

3. *Chicago Tribune*, October 12, 1871, October 14, 1871; October 15, 1871, October 18, 1871, October 20, 1871, January 16, 1872, January 17, 1872; Karen Sawislak, *Smoldering City: Chicagoans and the Great Fire, 1871–1874* (Chicago: University of Chicago Press, 1995), chaps. 1–3.

4. *Chicago Tribune*, October 5, 1873, November 6, 1873; Michael L. Ahern, *The Great Revolution: A History of the Rise and Progress of the People's Party in the City of Chicago and County of Cook* (Chicago: Lakeside Publishing, 1874); Sawislak, *Smoldering City*, chap. 5.

5. *Der Deutsche Arbeiter*, August 28, 1869, July 25, 1870, August 1, 1870; John B. Jentz, "Class and Politics in an Emerging Industrial City: Chicago in the 1860s and 1870s," *Journal of Urban History* 17 (May 1991): 227–63; *Chicago Tribune*, December 23–28, 1873; January 1–7, 1874.

6. *Chicago Tribune*, July 16, 1874 (quote); Richard Schneirov, "Class Conflict, Municipal Politics, and Governmental Reform in Gilded Age Chicago, 1871–1875," in *German Workers in Industrial Chicago, 1850–1910: A Comparative Perspective*, ed. Hartmut Keil and John B. Jentz (De Kalb: Northern Illinois University Press, 1983), 183–205.

7. "Address by Franklin MacVeagh, Sept. 11, 1874," in *Citizens Association of Chicago, Annual Reports, 1874–1901*, 1874 report (Chicago: Citizens Association of Chicago, 1901), 6; Eric Foner, *Reconstruction: America's Unfinished Revolution, 1863–1877* (New York: Harper and Row, 1988); Sven Beckert, *The Monied Metropolis: New York City and the Consolidation of the American Bourgeoisie, 1850–1896* (Cambridge: Cambridge University Press, 2001); Heather Cox Richardson, *The Death of Reconstruction: Race, Labor, and Politics in the Post–Civil War North, 1865–1901* (Cambridge, Mass.: Harvard University Press, 2001).

8. Richard Schneirov, *Labor and Urban Politics: Class Conflict and the Origins of Modern Liberalism in Chicago, 1864–97* (Urbana: University of Illinois Press, 1998), chaps. 1 and 2.

9. *Chicago Tribune*, October 7, 1874, November 4, 1874; January 3, 1875, March 17, 1875; April 24, 1875, June 29, 1875; Schneirov, "Class Conflict and Governmental Reform in Chicago," 196–98; Pierce, *History of Chicago*, 2:300–304.

10. *Chicago Tribune*, April 20, 1876; June 6, 1876; July 13, 1876.

11. Martin Shefter, "Regional Receptivity to Reform: The Legacy of the Progressive Era," *Political Science Quarterly* 98 (autumn 1983): 459–83.

12. On the typographers, see *Workingman's Advocate*, January 30, 1869; February 18, 1871, September 5, 1874; on the stonecutters, see February 27, 1869, May 10, 1870, September 7, 1872, May 10, 1872, January 16, 1876; on the decline of Trade Assembly, see September 19, 1868, April 17, 1869, May 1, 1869, June 19, 1869; on movement culture, see *Workingman's Advocate*, January 8, 1876; *Chicago Tribune*, June 17, 1878; Bruce C. Nelson, *Beyond the Martyrs: A Social History of Chicago's Anarchists, 1870–1900* (New Brunswick, N.J.: Rutgers University Press, 1988), 146–52; Vernon Lidtke, *The Alternative Culture: Socialist Labor in Imperial Germany* (New York: Oxford University Press, 1985).

13. *Chicago Tribune*, July 1, 1877.

14. Robert V. Bruce, *1877: Year of Violence* (Chicago: Quadrangle, 1970), 33–42; Philip S. Foner, *The Great Labor Uprising of 1877* (New York: Monad Press, 1977), Prologue.

15. *Chicago Tribune*, July 23, 1877; *Chicago Inter Ocean*, July 23, 1877.

16. Foner, *The Great Labor Uprising of 1877*, 106–14; George A. Schilling, "A History of the Labor Movement in Chicago," in *Life of Albert R. Parsons with Brief History of the Labor Movement in America: Also Sketches of the Lives of A. Spies, Geo. Engel, A. Fischer and Louis Lingg*, ed. Lucy E. Parsons (Chicago: Lucy E. Parsons, 1903), xxii.

17. *Chicago Tribune*, July 22, 1877.

18. Ibid., July 23, 1877; Foner, *The Great Labor Uprising of 1877*, 115–17.

19. *Chicago Tribune*, July 23, 1877; *Chicago Inter Ocean*, July 23, 1877.

20. *Chicago Tribune*, July 24, 1874.

21. Ibid.; Beckert, *Monied Metropolis*, 218–24.

22. John J. Flinn, *History of the Chicago Police from the Settlement of the Community to the Present Time* (Chicago: Police Book Fund, 1887), 162; There were widely varying estimates of the crowd. The *Chicago Tribune*, July 24, 1877, mentioned six thousand; the *Chicago Inter Ocean*, July 24, 1877, claimed thirty thousand; Schilling, in "A History of the Labor Movement in Chicago," xxvi, claimed forty thousand.

23. A text of part of the speech was reprinted in the *Chicago Inter Ocean*, July 26, 1877.

24. *Chicago Tribune*, July 24, 1877.

25. *Chicago Inter Ocean*, July 25, 1875; *Chicago Tribune*, July 25, 1877; a similar description of the crowd was given by Chicago historian Bessie Louis Pierce in her *A History of Chicago, vol. 3: The Rise of a Modern City, 1871–1893* (Chicago: University of Chicago Press, 1957), 248. However, the *Chicago Inter Ocean*, July 28, 1877, reported: "It must be admitted that when the mob was attacked, except in one or two instances, they were attacked for assembling in crowds and not for any unlawful acts they were committing."

26. Schneirov, *Labor and Urban Politics*, 32–33, 38–39; Richard Schneirov and Thomas J. Suhrbur, *Union Brotherhood, Union Town: The History of the Carpenters' Union of Chicago, 1863–1987* (Carbondale: Southern Illinois University Press, 1988), 9–10, 13–14, 15, 16, 17.

27. Foner, *The Great Labor Uprising of 1877*, 157–87.

28. *Chicago Tribune*, July 25, 1877; *Chicago Times*, July 25, 1877.

29. Unless otherwise noted, the descriptions of the crowd on this day are composites based on the July 25, 1877, editions of the *Chicago Tribune*, *Chicago Inter Ocean*, *Chicago Times*, and *Chicago Evening Journal*.

30. *Chicago Tribune*, July 25, 1877 (quote); *Chicago Times*, July 25, 1877 (quote).

31. *Chicago Tribune*, July 25, 1877; "Autobiography of Albert Parsons" in Parsons, *Life of Albert Parsons*, 18–19.

32. *Chicago Tribune*, July 26, 1877.

33. Ibid.

34. Ibid., July 25, 1877, July 26, 1877, July 27, 1877.

35. Unless otherwise noted, the descriptions of the crowd on this day are composites based on the July 26, 1877, editions of the *Chicago Tribune*, *Chicago Inter Ocean*, *Chicago Times*, and *Chicago Evening Journal*.

36. *Chicago Tribune*, July 26, 1877.

37. Ibid.

38. *Chicago Times*, July 26, 1877.

39. Unless otherwise noted, the descriptions of the crowd on this day are composites based on the July 27, 1877, editions of the *Chicago Tribune*, *Chicago Inter Ocean*, *Chicago Times*, and *Chicago Evening Journal*.

40. *Chicago Times*, July 27, 1877.

41. Of the total of thirty-five whose addresses could be ascertained, eleven riot victims came from the Fifth Ward, thirteen from the Sixth Ward, eight from the Seventh Ward, two from the Eighth Ward, and one from the Thirteenth Ward.

42. Figures are based on a sample of one in five heads of family, yielding 2,089 heads of family; see Federal Manuscript Census Schedules, Chicago, Sixth Ward, Roll 89.

43. Letter published in *Chicago Inter Ocean,* July 28, 1877, from J. Oliverius, editor of Bohemian newspaper, *Vestnck;* Richard Schneirov, "Free Thought and Socialism in the Czech Community in Chicago, 1875–1887," in *"Struggle a Hard Battle": Essays on Working-Class Immigrants,* ed. Dirk Hoerder (De Kalb: Northern Illinois University Press, 1986), 121–42.

44. Schneirov, *Labor and Urban Politics,* chap. 4; *Chicago Tribune,* February 14, 1875; a list of 132 arrestees was checked for birthplace in Richard Edwards, *Chicago Census Report and Statistical Review* (Chicago: Edwards and Co., 1871).

45. *Chicago Tribune,* July 27, 1877 (quote); see also descriptions in the *Chicago Times* and *Chicago Inter Ocean.*

46. *Chicago Tribune,* July 27, 1877; *Chicago Times,* July 27, 1877; *Chicago Tribune,* July 29, 1877.

47. *Illinois Staats Zeitung,* April 25, 1879; April 26, 1879; *Chicago Tribune,* July 27, 1877; July 29, 1877; *Chicago Inter Ocean,* May 6, 1879; John Peter Altgeld, "Reasons for Pardoning Fielden, Neebe, and Schwab, the So-Called Anarchists," in *The Mind and Spirit of John Peter Altgeld, Selected Writings and Addresses,* ed. Henry M. Christman (Urbana: University of Illinois Press, 1965), 58–59.

48. A figure of twenty-eight deaths was compiled from lists in the *Chicago Tribune, Chicago Times,* and *Chicago Inter Ocean.* Flinn, *Chicago Police,* 199, listed thirty-five dead; the figure of two hundred wounded is from Howard Myers, "The Policing of Labor Disputes in Chicago: A Case Study" (Ph.D. diss., University of Chicago, 1929), 117, 118.

49. *Chicago Tribune,* July 29, 1877; Beckert, *Monied Metropolis,* 183–92, 211–36; Larry Isaac, "To Counter 'The Very Devil' and More: The Making of Independent Capitalist Militia in the Gilded Age," *American Journal of Sociology* 108 (September 2002): 353–405.

50. *Workingman's Advocate,* May 19, 1877; *Knights of Labor,* January 29, 1887. For a national survey of the emergence of a working-class presence in the 1870s, see Sean Wilentz in "The Rise of the American Working Class, 1776–1877" in *Perspectives on American Labor History: The Problems of Synthesis,* eds. J Carroll Moody and Alice Kessler-Harris (De Kalb: Northern Illinois University Press, 1989), 83–151, esp. 118–34.

51. Foner, *The Great Labor Uprising of 1877,* 227; *Chicago Inter Ocean,* December 2, 1877; *Chicago Tribune,* December 2, 1877, December 16, 1877; Schneirov, *Labor and Urban Politics,* 84–86.

52. *Irish World and American Industrial Liberator,* October 4, 1879; *Progressive Age,* October 18, 1879, January 3, 1880, November 12, 1881 (quote); Schneirov, *Labor and Urban Politics,* 106–10.

53. Schneirov, *Labor and Urban Politics,* 81–84.

54. *Chicago Tribune,* April 25, 1878, April 26, 1878 (quote), April 28, 1878, May 12, 1878; Pierce, *History of Chicago,* 3:252–55.

55. *Chicago Tribune,* April 3, 1879; on Harrison and the Germans, see the translated interview with editor of the *Neus Freie-Press,* July 2, 1879.

56. Ibid., April 29, 1879.

57. Ernst Schmidt, *He Chose: The Other Was a Treadmill Thing,* ed. and trans. Frederick R. Schmidt (Santa Fe, N.M.: Vegara, 1968), 122–23; *Chicago Tribune,* June 7, 1879, June 25,

1879, July 7, 1879, October 28, 1879, April 18, 1879, September 3, 1880, April 5, 1881, April 6, 1881, April 7, 1881, September 8, 1885; *Chicago Times,* August 28, 1884; Pierce, *History of Chicago,* 3:352–54, 356, 379–80, 539. The presence of a large number of German voters able to swing between the two parties over labor issues seems to have been a major factor in the Democratic Party's receptivity to labor demands in many Gilded Age cities, not just Chicago. See David Montgomery, *Citizen Worker: The Experience of Workers in the United State with Democracy and the Free Market during the Nineteenth Century* (Cambridge: Cambridge University Press, 1993), 152–53.

58. Schneirov, *Labor and Urban Politics,* 110–13; Charles French, *Biographical History of the American Irish in Chicago* (Chicago: American Biographical Publishing, 1897), 790–92; Citizens Association, *Annual Reports,* 1885, 21.

59. *Chicago Tribune,* May 14, 1879, April 5, 1883; Pierce, *History of Chicago,* 3:360; Jon C. Teaford, *Unheralded Triumph: City Government in America, 1870–1900* (Baltimore: Johns Hopkins University Press, 1984), 56, 60–64; Schneirov, *Labor and Urban Politics,* 60–63; 162–68.

60. Claudius O. Johnson, *Carter Harrison I: A Political Leader* (Chicago: University of Chicago Press, 1928), 150.

61. Schneirov, *Labor and Urban Politics,* 162–79, 275–84, 287–88, and 366–70.

62. See, notably, Gerald Friedman, "The State and the Making of the Working Class: France and the United States, 1880–1914," *Theory and Society* 17 (1988): 403–30; Leon Fink, "The New Labor History and the Powers of Historical Pessimism: Consensus, Hegemony, and the Case of the Knights of Labor," *Journal of American History* 75 (June 1988): 115–36; Kim Voss, *The Making of American Exceptionalism: The Knights of Labor and Class Formation in the Nineteenth Century* (Ithaca, N.Y.: Cornell University Press, 1993); and Victoria Hattam, *Labor Visions and State Power: The Origins of Business Unionism in the United States* (Princeton, N.J.: Princeton University Press, 1993). Beckert's *Monied Metropolis* also argues that New York workers were locked out of power in the Gilded Age.

63. Teaford, *Unheralded Triumph;* Vincent De Santis, "The Gilded Age in American History," *Hayes Historical Journal* 7 (1988): 38–41; Philip J. Ethington, *The Public City: The Political Construction of Urban Life in San Francisco, 1850–1900* (Cambridge: Cambridge University Press, 1994); Charles W. Calhoun," The Political Culture: Public Life and the Conduct of Politics" in *The Gilded Age: Essays on the Origins of Modern America,* ed. Charles W. Calhoun (Wilmington, Del.: Scholarly Resources, 1996), 185–213; Schneirov, *Labor and Urban Politics.*

4. Looking North: A Mid-South Perspective on the Great Strike

STEVEN J. HOFFMAN

Although they deplored the violence accompanying the Great Strike, the newspapers of the Mid-South were generally supportive of the rights of laborers and suspicious of the power of the federal government. Sympathetic to the plight of the workers, if not to the behavior of the rebellious crowds, the *Memphis Daily Appeal,* the *Nashville Daily American,* and the *Louisville Courier-Journal* used the strike and its associated violence to contrast the virtues of the South with the failings of northern industrial society, interpreting events through the lens of southern sectionalism. In much the same way, workers throughout the Mid-South also used the specter of the Great Strike for their own purposes, seeking where they could opportunities to advance their own economic interests.[1]

Much has been written about the end of Reconstruction in the South, the redemption of southern state governments by conservative Democrats, and the abandonment of the cause of African Americans by the national Republican Party.[2] 1877 was a critical year for sectionalism in national politics, as northern Republicans traded an end to political interference in the South and a withdrawal of the last federal troops from Louisiana and South Carolina for control of the presidency and the national economy. The Compromise of 1877, brokered in February of that year, averted a national crisis and gave both northern white Republicans and southern white Democrats much of what they desired, but did little to change the general public's perceptions of sectional differences held since the end of the war. Many southern whites continued to resent the interference, both real and perceived, of northern

Republicans during Reconstruction, and took the opportunities presented by widespread violence across the North in July 1877 to proclaim the superiority and rightness of their own region. Most southern newspapers, and not a few politicians, found the issue particularly sweet as the strike focused attention on the relationship between labor and capital, an area in which southerners felt they had suffered an unfair number of indignities since before the war.[3] In many ways, the Great Strike was tailor-made for use by the southern press in its rhetorical campaign highlighting the injustice and abuse inflicted by the national government and its use of troops to enforce its will against an honorable people, as well as the basic rightness of the South's labor relations and the oppressive labor conditions existing in the North. But it could only serve that propaganda function well if southern workers would not join the strike, a prospect that was not as assured as many newspaper pundits initially believed.

Although southern workers did not participate in the Great Strike to the same extent as their northeastern counterparts, they did their best to capitalize on the opportunities it offered.[4] In the Mid-South cities of Memphis, Nashville, and Louisville, railroad workers, following the lead of railroad workers in Baltimore, Pittsburgh, and elsewhere, threatened to strike unless their wages were restored to their former levels. In general, these workers were successful, and only in Nashville, where the workers on one line were unsuccessful in achieving their demands, did the railroad workers actually participate in the strike. Other workers in the three cities also took advantage of the turmoil presented by the national strike—and the fear it generated—to press their own demands for higher wages or better working conditions. Thus, much of the labor peace that prevailed among southern workers in July 1877, at least in the Mid-South, did so not because southern workers were content with their lot but because most would-be strikers' demands were met without needing to resort to an actual strike.

Although in a region acutely hostile to unions, in 1877 southern workers had a long history of using strikes in an attempt to achieve higher pay and better working conditions.[5] Workers in the South, both black and white, sought to improve their lives by developing community-building organizations and engaging in various protest actions in the workplace and the community.[6] In 1871 Louisville blacks protested successfully against segregation of streetcars, and black dock workers in New Orleans struck, without a union, successfully for higher wages in 1865 and 1867.[7] Complicated by issues of race, the relationship between labor and capital was frequently a contested one. Southern workers were never the contented and accommodating labor force the newspapers claimed, as their actions in Memphis, Nashville, and Louisville in July 1877 demonstrate well.

The Great Strike in the Mid-South

In line with its sectional perspective, when news of the Great Strike reached Memphis, the editors of the *Daily Appeal* presented the strike in terms of a rebellion pitting labor against capital.[8] Expressing sympathy with the workers, the *Appeal* led with headlines suggesting workers could choose "Starvation Wages and Hard Work or Co-operative Opposition."[9] The headline further indicated the *Appeal*'s sympathy for the strikers by proclaiming that "In Presence of the Troops of the United States the Unfortunate Working Men Succumb to the Capitalists." With headlines like these, a reader might mistakenly assume the *Memphis Daily Appeal* was a radical paper published by a workingmen's press and not the typically conservative southern Democratic newspaper that it was.[10] Even as the strike became more general and spread throughout the northern states, the *Appeal* remained unabashedly sympathetic to the strikers. Pronouncing in bold, large block letters "Starving Strikers!" the *Appeal* continued to lead with headlines such as "Labor Confronting Capital, Impelled by Desperation-'Give us Bread,' is the Cry which Goes Up in Answer to the Soldiers' Appeal."[11]

But the *Appeal*'s stance had as much to do with the fact that the strike portrayed a negative aspect of the urban industrial society of the North as it did with any evident sympathy for the plight of American workers. It seems likely that if the strike were to come closer to home, the imagery used to portray the participants would be dramatically changed.[12] But with the strike initially confined to the North, the *Appeal* saw an opportunity to call attention to the shortcomings of northern society, recently victorious in the Civil War and a constant irritant during Reconstruction. In its coverage of July 20, just its second day of reporting on the strike, the *Appeal* gleefully noted that "In the Name of Law and Order the White Slaves of the North are Compelled to Yield to their Masters—No Emancipation for Them."[13] The use of this kind of rhetoric, complete with references to "The Enslaved Workingmen," visibly cast the labor conflict in sectional terms its readers could understand.[14]

The *Appeal*'s editorial on the twenty-fourth presented the dilemma faced by the strikers. Given the economic downturn, work was not always available and workers might only work half or one-quarter time. This did not mean that the worker stayed home, however. A worker would make a run from Baltimore to Martinsburg but be kept there three or four days before being able to work a run back. The Baltimore-Martinsburg run paid two days' wages, even though workers would have to pay their own room and board in Martinsburg waiting for a return run. One worker complained he had only worked five days in the previous month, and that "nearly half of the seventeen days of July he had spent at Wheeling, waiting for his turn."[15] The reduced pay, minus the cost of room and board away from home, would leave little left for support of families. This situation repeated itself up and down the line. The imposed pay cut in July only made a bad situation worse.[16]

Not willing to cast this economic injustice purely in terms of labor versus capital, the *Appeal* tried to place the situation in its sectional context. "What man at the south, who reads this and recalls the vindictiveness with which our planters were pursued before and since the war on the labor question, but will admit that the curses of our northern brethren have gone home to roost." After discussing the wage rates of the railroad workers, the *Appeal* continued its sectional analysis: "compare these prices with what is paid to the negro plantation laborers, and it will be seen that slavery is now a northern institution." Disingenuously, the *Appeal* remarked that "we care not to gloat over the misfortunes of those who fattened upon our misfortunes, and who have held us up to the gaze of a too credulous world as examples of all that was vile and base."[17] The North may have won the war, the *Appeal* seems to remind its readers, but the South remains the superior civilization. We do not want to gloat, the editors say, but we will:

> Yet we cannot keep back the feeling of exultation which the dread occasion gives rise to, that here in the vilified south peace reigns supreme under the direction of governments of the people, that the poor, ignorant negro finds employment at a rate of wages that shames the pittance which has made madmen of the strikers of Pittsburg and Baltimore. We congratulate ourselves that, though feeling the pinching necessities of these times, no attempt has been made by our planters to reduce the wages of the negro laborers, and that no attempt has been made to force the white laborer down to starvation rates.[18]

To the editors of the *Appeal,* the Great Strike, perceived as a conflict between labor and capital in the urban North, provided strong evidence of the virtue of the South.

The editors of the *Nashville Daily American* similarly cast the Great Strike in sectional terms, although they tended to focus more on the issue of states' rights in the face of growing national power. After the first few days of reporting on the strike, but before realizing there would be any local manifestations of it, the *Daily American* noted under the headline "Federal Interference in Local Troubles" that "One of the most dangerous signs of our time is the readiness to call for military aid from the Federal Government."[19] Casting responsibility for the strike on the corruption and extravagance of the Republican Party, the *Daily American* called for "a complete and thorough change of system . . . untrammeled by corrupt politics, false financial policies, and a radically wrong economic system."[20] As long as the strikers remained in the

North, the strike could usefully provide ammunition in an ongoing partisan, sectional fight. Despite what might have been going on in boardrooms and in the upper echelons of Democratic and Republican Party organizations that would ultimately give rise to a new national economic and political order, viewing current events through the lens of sectionalism was still a powerful way to achieve high rates of newspaper sales in the South.[21]

Like their counterparts in Memphis, the editors of the *Daily American* repeatedly used the strike to condemn the northern intervention in southern affairs following the Civil War, pushing for an acknowledged end to Reconstruction in the South.[22] The strike, the *Daily American* argued, "will compel those busy people who are always so capable of taking care of their own business and that of their neighbors, to spend more thought upon their own affairs." Acknowledging that there was already "a growing disposition to leave Southern affairs to Southern people," the *Daily American* argued that "the imminent danger at home is likely to compel, not only the lately-grown wise, but also all others, the implacables and mischief-makers and Bourbons to attend strictly to their own business." With perhaps more insight than they realized, the *Daily American* proclaimed, "This sounds the death knell of Radicalism and all memory of the past and its sectional trouble."[23]

Not surprisingly, the *Louisville Courier-Journal* shared the perspective that the strike was emblematic of northern problems that did not exist in the Mid-South. While acknowledging that the strike owed to "universal conditions" affecting workers, the *Courier-Journal* proudly proclaimed that, "these conditions do not exist in Louisville or in Kentucky." The editors assured their readers that "our work people . . . are, as a rule, measurably prosperous and happy," a conclusion reached, no doubt, without actually speaking to any of the workers.[24] In telling their tale of northern violence and the Great Strike, the *Courier-Journal* happily noted that "the 'law-abiding North' presents a somewhat mixed aspect at the present moment."[25]

In Memphis, the *Appeal's* sympathy for the strikers was aided by the confidence the editors had that the labor troubles would be confined to the North and would not spread southward to Memphis, a confidence that was not entirely well founded. A week into the strike, the *Appeal* wrote that although it was the major topic of discussion in the city, "the strike has not reached Memphis, and no fears are entertained that it will extend this far."[26] In recounting for its readers the situation of the five railroads coming into Memphis, the *Appeal* claimed that "Nothing whatever justifies the belief that there will be a strike on any of the local roads named above." The Mississippi & Tennessee Road was, according to the *Appeal,* "in good working order, all the employes being satisfied with what they are now receiving in the way of wages." Puffed up with pride, the *Appeal* commented on "the cheerful disposition and feelings of the employes," noting that "anything like a strike is impossible." The paper pronounced the Memphis & Little Rock Railroad "also in a safe condition, and nothing in the nature of a strike is anticipated." A third railroad, the Memphis & Paducah, was only thirty miles long and employed few men, making it "almost too short to be affected by any strike." The *Appeal* happily proclaimed the line "safe from the effects of a railroad strike."[27]

Labor peace on these three lines was helped by the fact that the Mississippi & Tennessee Road and the Memphis & Little Rock Railroad had not reduced the wages of their employees, nor had they given any indication that they would do so.[28] Given the smallness of the Memphis & Paducah operation, it is unlikely that they had reduced wages yet either, but were waiting to follow the lead of the other lines into the city. The situation on the other two major railroads coming into the city, though, was less certain.

As the national strike progressed, employees of the Louisville & Nashville & Great Southern Railroad received decidedly mixed news about what would happen to their wage rates. In Memphis, the railroad workers heard on Monday, July 23, that the president of the company, E. D. Standiford, announced that "no reduction of wages or salaries would be made on the Louisville and Nashville and Great Southern railroad."[29] This good news was attributed to the effect of the national strike, and the *Appeal* noted that "it was rumored yesterday that this road contemplated a reduction of wages the first of August, and the belief obtains that such determination was changed because of the influence of the strike and its probable effect upon this company."[30] According to the *Appeal,* workers held an informal meeting in the roundhouse of the Louisville & Nashville & Great Southern Railroad on Monday night (the 23rd), and "the situation was discussed, but no definite action was had. The employes are doubtless satisfied, inasmuch as assurances have been made that the wages and salaries of employes would not be reduced, but restored to the sums which prevailed in June."[31]

This victory without a fight and the goodwill the company earned thereby, however, was cast into doubt by reports in Memphis indicating that the *Nashville Daily American* had earlier reported that an order had been "received from Louisville, Friday night, announcing that on the first of next month the wages of all the employes on the Louisville and Nashville and Great Southern road, from superintendents on down, would be reduced ten percent." "The order," the *American* noted, "was countermanded, however, shortly after it was bulletined, yesterday [Saturday] morning."[32] Newspapers were the chief means by which the public received its information, and the rapid transmission of news via telegraph, and railroad delivery of newspapers, permitted neighboring cities and towns to get up-to-the-minute reports, and if needed, to act on them.[33] Having heard Monday there would be no reduction in wages, then hearing Tuesday that such an order had, in fact, been issued and then countermanded the previous Saturday, created a great deal of excitement among the employees. The *Appeal* reported Tuesday that "The opinion prevails that this company will execute the intention of reducing wages the first of August, or as soon thereafter as the threatening aspect of the present strike is over."[34] The paper further noted that "it was rumored that there is somewhat of a discontent among the employes . . . because of the late changes and threatened ten per cent reduction of wages," concluding that "should the company attempt to execute the ten-per-cent reduction, there may be no little trouble and a determined opposition on the part of its employes." Despite these concerns, the *Appeal* reported that the officers of the company remained "confident that there cannot be a strike on this line, as all the employes are contented and satisfied." Fear that a possible strike on the Louisville & Cincinnati Short-Line, which had received a notice of reduction in pay, would spill over into the operations of the Louisville & Nashville dissolved when that order was rescinded, making company officials even more confident in their pronouncements of labor peace in Memphis.[35]

But things were not as peaceful in Memphis as they might have seemed on the surface. The workers on the Memphis & Charleston Railroad, who had already endured a pay cut in March, saw an opportunity in the Great Strike to redress their grievances. Although the vice president and general manager, Charles M. M'Ghee, was in Memphis and expressed "no fear of a strike" on the twenty-fourth, the workers of the Memphis & Charleston had met secretly the night before to discuss their situation.[36] Although in reporting on that meeting, the *Appeal* claimed that "the employes of the road are reticent upon the subject, and refuse to impart any information respecting the meeting," the editors remained confident and proclaimed on the twenty-fifth that "a strike is not likely to occur on this road."[37]

Despite the confidence of the *Appeal's* editors, however, the workers of the Memphis & Charleston Railroad met that very afternoon to pass resolutions demanding that their pay be raised to the level of the other railroads serving Memphis. Meeting in the roundhouse late in the afternoon on Wednesday the twenty-fifth, about 170 workers of the Memphis & Charleston Railroad appointed a committee to meet with the general manager of the railroad and "request him to advance the wages of the employes, so that they would be paid the same wages as are now paid the employes of the Mississippi and Tennessee and Memphis and Little Rock railroads." Choosing to peg their wages to these lines, instead of to the recently reduced then restored wages of the Louisville & Nashville & Great Southern, was probably just common sense, but could also have been related to the workers' general feelings of unease about the actual status of their future wages. Rumors abounded that the Louisville & Nashville & Great Southern workers were going to demand a written statement from the president of the line pledging himself "to abide by the terms of the contract," although the *Appeal* did its best to suggest those rumors were false.[38] The threat to public order, however, was real enough that the governor issued an order on the twenty-fifth authorizing Robert Duncan to take command of the local militia "in case of disturbance." Duncan assured the governor, writing "I do *not* [emphasis in original] anticipate any trouble, but should there be, will act promptly as you direct."[39]

With the hope of avoiding a strike in Memphis truly threatened by action on the Memphis & Charleston, the editors of the *Appeal* were quick to caution Memphis workers. Reacting to the threats expressed by "a few idle and inconsiderate persons, having no connection whatever with the working men," the *Appeal,* proclaiming itself the "true and tried friend of the laboring and working classes," warned that "the people of Memphis will not for a moment tolerate anything like riot or violence, and that any attempt at either will be promptly met and severely punished."[40] The newspaper gave clear notice that the image of labor presented by the *Appeal* could and would change on a moment's notice if the situation warranted it. The *Appeal* further noted the sectional image of peaceful labor relations that needed to be maintained if the South was to consolidate the victories achieved in the Compromise of 1877, remarking that "[w]e have hitherto prided ourselves on our capacity for self-government, and we mean to continue on that line at any sacrifice. . . . Property, which represents industry, should be only less sacred than life, both will be protected in Memphis, cost what it may."[41] Hope for a peaceful resolution, however, remained high, and the *Appeal* repeatedly remarked that the workers' demands were "so reasonable and couched in such language as to make it a subject for quick consideration," and clearly suggested that the request to be paid at the same rate as the other Memphis railroads was "neither unreasonable nor unnatural."[42]

The feared strike, and the stain upon southern honor it would entail, never came to pass. Vice President M'Ghee, general manager of the Memphis & Charleston, "consented to restore the wages as they existed previous to the reduction in March, the same to take effect August 1." The *Appeal* also reported that "he also agreed to advance the rates of all employes by the fifteenth of August, so as to make them equal to the wages paid by the Mississippi and Tennessee railroad."[43] The *Appeal* noted in its editorial that, by acceding to the demands of the workers, M'Ghee avoided "not only a strike on his own, but probably on all the other roads centering in Memphis."[44] By the weekend, the *Appeal* was able to proclaim "Peace Here" in its headlines: "All Possibility or Probability of a Strike Passed Away—Our Workingmen Content and Happy."[45]

Although labor peace among railroad workers held in Memphis during the Great Strike, it was not because management and labor "understood" each other, or because labor was truly "content and happy," but because they were successful in using the strike as it occurred elsewhere to their own advantage. The workers on the Louisville & Nashville & Great Southern Railroad benefited from action taken by others which led to their pay cut being rescinded even before it was issued to them. The workers on the Memphis & Charleston used the specter of the national strike to not only restore the wage cuts they had endured earlier in the Spring, but also to, in essence, give themselves a raise. In celebrating a successful resolution of any differences between the railroads in Memphis and their workers, the *Appeal* repeated its observations as to the sectional nature of the strike. "In common with our brethren of the southern press, we have many times the past two weeks congratulated our readers upon the fact that while the north was a prey to lawlessness more violent and disastrous than has ever befallen any people in the same time, the south was free from excitement and her people were engaged in attention to their business, intent on nothing so much as making good crops and increasing the wealth of our section by permanent and valuable improvements."[46] In Memphis, the events in July concluded in a classic win-win scenario: newspaper editors could claim the absence of a strike as evidence of a contented and happy workforce, while workers proved once again that the realistic threat of a strike could bring about significant improvements in wages.

Although the editors of the Nashville *Daily American* shared the *Appeal*'s sectional perspective regarding the status of labor, their city did not share Memphis' good fortune in avoiding a local outbreak of the railroad strike. Prospects for averting the strike initially seemed favorable, particularly after the Louisville & Nashville & Great Southern road rescinded its 10 percent pay cut on the twenty-first.[47] The lines coming into the city from Louisville were of particular concern, and as prospects for labor peace in that city increased, confidence in Nashville followed. Activity on the part of workers on the Louisville & Cincinnati Short-Line Railroad had led to fears that a strike would spill over into Nashville, and perhaps even Memphis. According to the *Daily American,* on Sunday the twenty-second, a committee of railroad men petitioned the court in Louisville to rescind "the order for a reduction of wages, to take effect Aug. 1." The men petitioned the court directly, through the railroad's lawyers, because the line was in receivership and the receiver, McLeod, was out of the city and could not be reached by telegraph. Judge Bruce complied with the request, rescinding the order reducing wages, thereby adding a second Louisville railroad to the ranks of roads restoring wages to their previous levels without the need for a strike.[48]

Despite the confidence that prevailed in both Louisville and Nashville, things would not remain calm for long. On Tuesday the twenty-fourth, the *Daily American* noted "a feverish anxiety for news concerning the railroad troubles" and reported not only on what it called unfounded rumors that "the men on the Southeastern road had resolved upon a strike," but that several workingmen's meetings and gatherings had taken place. Apparently, a meeting had been called Monday night at the courthouse to discuss railroad wages, but was subsequently postponed. Nonetheless, about two hundred people showed up to see what would happen, only about one-quarter of them reportedly from the railroad. That same night, however, around forty men from the Decatur Division of the Louisville & Nashville & Great Southern Railroad, who had seen their wages reduced 10 percent on June 1, held a meeting "in the hall above Haley's drug store," passed resolutions calling for a reinstatement of their wages to the level prior to the June 1 reduction, and "then marched down to the Public Square."[49] Clearly, not all workers in Nashville were satisfied with the way things were.

Up the road in Louisville, things were rapidly getting worse. Although the railroadmen on the Louisville & Nashville & Great Southern Railroad had their wages restored to their June levels, the specter of the Great Strike allowed other workers to voice their grievances. The *Daily American* reported that in Louisville on Tuesday, "a gang of negro sewer-men stopped work, and with picks, shovels, etc, on their shoulders, marched through the streets, stopping all other laborers. Before night there were seven hundred, including some whites."[50] In the midst of the disorder, at around 3 P.M., the superintendent of the Clarksville Division of the Louisville & Nashville, headquartered in Louisville, sent a dispatch to Superintendent Geddes in Nashville informing him that the president of the company had issued an order restoring wages to their earlier levels.[51]

Although the men of the Decatur depot greeted the news with applause and were reported as "saying they felt like working harder than ever and would increase their efforts in behalf of the company, which should lose nothing by its prompt concession," there were still other issues to resolve. Emboldened by their success, and capitalizing on the generalized fear created by the national strike, that evening the men met to sign a resolution "requesting the management of the road to send around the pay car a little earlier than heretofore, so that the company shall not be in arrears with them more than one month at a time."[52] It seems clear that the events associated with the Great Strike gave workers in Nashville, Louisville, and elsewhere opportunities to advance their own interests in ways both small and large, whether they worked for the railroads or not.

In the Mid-South as elsewhere, the events associated with the Great Strike grew well beyond the boundaries of a labor-management dispute.[53] In Nashville, on the evening the Decatur Division's wages were restored to their pre-June levels, a large crowd gathered on the public square. The *Daily American* reported that between three hundred and four hundred people "were on the ground waiting for something to turn up."[54] When it became clear that a meeting had not actually been called by the railroadmen, and that nothing was going on inside the courthouse, the crowd became boisterous and decided to make its own fun. Calling forward a local drunk, Jeems Cameron, and helping him sit up on the gate post, the crowd called out, "Do you want a drink, Jeems?" "No, sir; I've got a bottle in my pocket." The *Daily American* reported that after some "facetious remarks" by Cameron, "which were enjoyed immensely by the crowd, he slid down off the post and engaged in the rush of the crowd through the dark hallway toward the third story of the Court house." The paper noted that "no lights had been provided, and the noise and confusion were indescribable." Describing the scene further, the *Daily American* reported:

> At last some one appeared with candles, and calls were made upon various persons to occupy the chair, into which Charles Heuser was finally forced. He said he was no railroad man, but a beer agent. [Applause]. After stating he sympathized with the railroad men, he remarked if they wished to ask a railroad for a favor they should not have a mob of loafers, idlers and thieves with them to destroy property. Every good citizen ought to be opposed to such outrages.
>
> Marcus B. Toney, having been called upon, said that if a resolution was adopted it should set forth that the South did not countenance any such violence as that displayed north of the Ohio river. The South strongly condemned these mobs. [Applause.]
>
> Morris Moran thought that if any railroad man had a grievance he could have it righted by applying to the proper authority.
>
> Some man then yelled "Let's all go home!"—and they went.[55]

Having stormed the courthouse for their own purpose, and finding none, the crowd dispersed without any reported violence or further disturbance.[56] The meeting, as the *Memphis Appeal* suggested, "had no head nor tail," but was "a promiscuous assemblage" that "shouted and made fun until their lungs had been well-nigh exhausted."[57] Although the meeting ultimately did not result in any specific outcome directly related to advancing workers' interests, the potential for mob violence would not have gone unnoticed by the citizens of Nashville, particularly after the reports from Louisville started coming in.

The crowds that gathered in Louisville that night were not as playful as the one in Nashville turned out to be.[58] Beginning around 10 A.M., and then continuing through the afternoon, striking sewer workers had gone from one sewer construction site in the city to another, eventually reaching the new waterworks being constructed on the edge of the city, forcing or persuading the workers to strike for higher wages. At noon, all the laborers working on installing new gutters throughout the city also went on strike. The *Courier-Journal* described a gathering crowd of around "200 persons" with "very few white men," and that "the negroes were mostly half-dressed, dirty looking persons, evidently belonging to the worst class of colored men, and were armed with picks, shovels, and some with pieces of wood and sticks." When the strikers passed by the Knickerbocker saloon, a fight broke out, and when one of the young men involved in the fight fled the scene, police gave chase. According to the *Courier-Journal,* the pursuit "created excitement, and in less than five minutes probably a thousand persons, men and boys, white and black, were congregating around." The crowd did not interfere with the policemen, who successfully arrested Thomas Higgins on charges of assault and battery. When asked why he had not earlier tried "dispersing the negro mob before it commenced," the police chief, Col. Isaac Edwards, said "he feared that any effort of his to disperse them might have caused trouble and brought on a riot." Luckily, by late afternoon the crowd "dispersed of its own accord." Recognizing the threat to the city, however, a number of Louisville's notable citizens organized as a special militia, and the mayor called for reinforcements from the armory in Frankfort.[59]

That night, in a courthouse scene remarkably similar to the one that had occurred at the same time in Nashville, "people came together in response to no special call, but by some mutual consent or other. There was no head man to the affair, and consequently nobody seemed to know the exact reason for the assemblage." The *Courier-Journal* described a crowd of more than two thousand, but observed that there "was no indication of anything contemplated of a serious nature." Instead, the editors noted that a positive good humor seemed to prevail. Similar to events in Nashville, "yelling and cat-calls were indulged in, and different men were called upon to speak, but no one seemed disposed to gratify the crowd."[60] Eventually, the crowd called for the mayor to speak, and he came over from his office in city hall. Proclaiming himself the "friend of the workingmen," the mayor reiterated the sentiments he had expressed earlier in a printed proclamation to the workingmen of Louisville calling for order and moderation in pressing their claims. The mayor closed his remarks "by asking the crowd to disperse and retire quietly to their respective homes." But even before he had finished speaking, the crowd began shouting and the mayor "left amid an uproar."[61] In Nashville, the *Daily American* put a different spin on the event, claiming that Louisville officials had called a meeting that evening to attempt "to pacify the working men," but everyone agreed the meeting was a failure, and the *Daily American* wrote that when the mayor tried to speak, he was "hooted down."[62]

At this point, events in Louisville took a dramatically different turn than in Nashville. Instead of reaffirming the cause of order and moderation and closing with a call of "let's go home," as happened in Nashville, the speakers in the Louisville crowd took a more "inflammatory tone" and called for a march of protest. The *Courier-Journal* estimated that about five or six hundred people followed the leaders into the street and responded to the call, "Let's go to the Nashville depot."[63] Although the Louisville & Nashville & Great Southern Railroad had earlier rescinded its pay cut for mechanics and engineers, it refused to advance the wages of its lowest paid laborers.[64] The crowd, described as consisting of mostly "boys and negroes," quickly became violent, throwing stones through the windows of the Home sewing-machine company, breaking out street lamps, and smashing all the windows in the depot. When the police arrived, the crowd rushed up Broadway and stoned two policemen who had fired their pistols at the crowd, and "the officers escaped with their lives by beating a rapid retreat." The crowd, although dwindling down to around one hundred, continued down the street, smashing windows and looting stores. The mob forced the doors at a local saloon, demanded liquor, and freely raided the confectionary, grocery, and drug stores along the route. On their way to the Short-Line depot, the rioters stoned all the stores and residences they passed. After turning onto Third Avenue, the mob attacked the mayor's house, breaking several of the windows, and continued up the street, almost reaching Green Street, when they realized they had bypassed the residence of Dr. Standiford, president of the Louisville & Nashville & Great Southern Railroad. The *Courier-Journal* reported that "as soon as this became known, the mob turned in its tracks, and with stones assailed the house, and the stores and residences within throwing range. Every window in the house of Dr. Standiford was demolished and the furniture seriously damaged." The mob continued in this fashion, with "stones whizzing into all the residences on both sides of the street," until it reached the Short-Line depot, where about fifty policemen had formed a line across the street to protect the building. When someone in the crowd shouted out to "attack the police" so they could torch the depot, the officers fired on the crowd. The *Courier-Journal* initially reported that the police fired blank cartridges and that no one was hurt.[65] In Nashville, the *Daily American* reported that police fired over the heads of the rioters.[66] In a separate article written in the morning, the *Courier-Journal* confirmed that "there were several persons shot by the police at the Short-Line depot" and that "the shots fired by the police . . . were not blank cartridges."[67] In any event, the shots scattered the mob, and the police let them go.[68]

Back at the Louisville & Nashville depot, when police tried to arrest two whites and an African American they believed to be among the leaders of the mob, they found they had to fight their way through the angry crowd. The newspaper reported they were successful but were "compelled to beat up the prisoners somewhat on account of their resistance."[69] Shortly after midnight, the weapons from the armory in Frankfort arrived and several hundred more citizens were armed. Issuing a proclamation around midnight, the mayor noted, "With pleasure I announce that I now have fully armed and equipped a sufficient force to command and compel quiet and a due observance of the law." Commanding "all persons for the present not to assemble in crowds on the streets or in public places," he forcefully declared that "the spirit of law and order pervades the people of Louisville, and they are determined that mobocracy shall not obtain or rule in this city."[70] There were no further reports of mob violence that night, although someone tried and failed to burn down the building housing the main office of the Louisville & Nashville Railroad.[71]

The next day saw a semblance of order return to the streets of Louisville, accompanied by increased demands from the city's workers. According to press reports, more than 1,600 armed citizens and police patrolled the city, including a number on horseback.[72] To coordinate the spontaneous militia that had formed in response to Tuesday night's mob, in the early morning hours of Wednesday the twenty-fifth, Mayor Jacob directed the former police chief, Basil W. Duke, to organize and take command of "a volunteer corps to be used as Special Police."[73] Duke reported that the force "under arms and on duty during the nights of the 25th and 26th, was little less than twenty five hundred men." The commander of city forces, as Duke was called, expressed confidence that had enough arms been available and the need greater, he could easily have recruited five thousand men.[74] The *Courier-Journal* noted that morning that at "half-past 8 o'clock, the City Hall was alive with soldiers," and by nine A.M., Duke had partially distributed the arms from Frankfort and sent his three strongest companies out to patrol the principal streets of the city.[75] The mayor issued a proclamation at ten o'clock that morning closing until further notice all places where liquor was sold, with loss of license and a $10 penalty for any violations, and the police began the task of arresting the known leaders of the mob.[76]

The armed and mounted city forces were an effective counterweight to the demonstrations of the city's workers. Duke reported that on Wednesday, between seven and eight hundred men "were parading various parts of the city in gangs of from twenty to one hundred and fifty, creating much disturbance and more apprehension among peaceable and orderly people." Duke observed that "they were visiting the various establishments where large numbers of hands are employed, inviting, and in some instances forcing the operatives to quit work." The city forces were able to effectively deal with the crowds, and Duke noted that "this rabble was readily dispersed; in most cases the gangs dissolved upon learning of the approach of the troops. Many of them were arrested and lodged in jail; but as they in no instance attempted resistance, none of them were shot or in any way injured."[77] By bringing overwhelming force to bear against the demonstrating workers, order was restored to the streets. By Wednesday night the worst of the violence seemed to be over. By Thursday morning the *Courier-Journal* could claim that "the city of Louisville is as completely possessed by her citizen soldiery at this moment as ever a fortress was possessed by a triumphant army."[78] By Friday morning Joshua F. Speed, noted attorney and Republican leader in Louisville, was confident enough in the restoration of order to write to Norvin Green that it was now "as quiet as a Sabbath—the danger of a mob is over."[79]

But the mob action, and the sewer workers' strike that preceded it, had set in motion a series of strikes and job actions throughout the city. Railroad workers' involvement in the strikes was relatively short lived. The mechanics on the Louisville & Nashville Railroad had gone on strike in support of the line's unskilled laborers, who were demanding an increase in their wages. Although President Standiford had agreed to roll back the wage cuts for the engineers and other skilled workers on the line, he steadfastly refused to advance the pay of those laborers who wages were so low they were not included in the initial reduction.[80] After a lengthy discussion in which Standiford remained firm, the mechanics "went away satisfied" and returned that night "enthusiastically performing guard duty for the protection of the company's property."[81] In his report to shareholders at the end of the year, President Standiford praised the line's workers, noting that although "attempts to destroy your property were incited by the very worst elements of society, the idler and the restless labor agitator, who will not work under any consideration; but I am proud to say that our employes held to wiser counsel, and, when the crisis came, flew to our assistance, and, with arms in their hands, were day and night most vigilant in the protection of your property."[82] The support of the railroad workers, combined with large detachments of Duke's city forces that "picketed and guarded very closely" both the Short-Line and Louisville & Nashville depots, kept the destruction of railroad property in Louisville at a minimum.[83]

But the Great Strike in Louisville, as elsewhere, quickly expanded beyond the railroads and their workers.[84] On Wednesday, Louisville was in the midst of what could only be called a general strike. Despite the presence of thousands of armed citizen-soldiers, the workers at the metal shops and foundries downtown struck for higher wages. The *Courier-Journal* also reported strikes at the Kentucky lead and oil works, all the downtown furniture factories, woolen mills, horse collar makers, and tobacco factories, as well as by many of the city's coopers, brickmakers, and African American levee workers. Many of the demands of these workers, which tended to focus on wages and hours, were met and they returned to work quickly. Some, however, were not. The foundry workers, for example, were still holding out for higher wages at the end of the month.[85]

In part because of its sensationalism, and in part because of its proximity, the violence in Louisville attracted a great deal of attention in Nashville and added to an already growing sense of unease in that city. The *Nashville Daily American* reported extensively on the strikes in Louisville, indicating that there were more than a thousand strikers in the city on Wednesday, including "many car drivers, coopers, moulders and all classes of workmen." The editors noted that these strikers "were not in Tuesday's rabble, but quit work this morning and asked for higher wages." In addition, the *Daily American* noted that despite the presence of more than 1,600 armed guards and police, a mob burned down a contractor's stable.[86]

The effect on Nashville of the events in Louisville was immediate. Rumors spread "that a crowd of roughs had taken a 'wild train' at Louisville and was coming to Nashville to 'take the town.'"[87] It would turn out that trouble had indeed ridden the rails into Nashville, but it would not take the form of a train full of toughs invading the town. Nashville workers had grievances of their own, and would not be slow in using the disturbances in Louisville and elsewhere to press their case. Rumors began to circulate that workers on the Nashville, Chattanooga & St. Louis Railroad had called upon J. W. Thomas, the general superintendent, to make some sort of demands, but "he said that only a few men had called, but with no definite purpose in view."[88] Knowing the workers on his line had already endured a pay cut back in June, and not wanting to take any chances, the court-appointed receiver for the St. Louis & Southeastern Railway, Jas. H. Wilson, issued a warning to all Nashville residents: "All persons take notice that the property of the St. Louis and Southeastern railway is in the custody of the United States Courts, and injury to it or its employes is injury to the Federal Government."[89] Amid the worry and concern, the *Daily American* continued to dismiss fears of a strike on the Southeastern even though a mob in Evansville, Indiana, had prevented the company from sending anything more than a mail car down the line to Nashville. The paper noted that "the Southeastern pay car arrived yesterday on its regular tour, which doubtless had the effect to put the men employed by that road in a good humor."[90] But when everyone around them was using the strike to win back their lost wages, payday at their reduced wages would not keep the Southeastern workers in good humor for long.

By noon on Thursday the twenty-sixth, the Great Strike had arrived in Nashville. That morning, workers on the Southeastern telegraphed a petition to the general manager, Gen. J. H. Wilson, in St. Louis indicating that because "the Louisville & Great Southern railroad has restored the wages paid their employes before June 1, we, the engineers and firemen of this company, think that it is nothing but right that a like courtesy should be extended to us." In addition to the restoration of their wages, the workers requested the abolition of a classification scheme that had been enacted at the time of the wage cuts whereby engineers were paid different rates based upon their length of service and type of equipment they operated. When receiver Wilson replied that "this railway is in the custody of the United States Court, and that I, in the capacity of receiver, am an agent of that tribunal . . . the matter rests with the judges and I decline to take any action," the workers decided to go out on strike. As the *Daily American* noted, "the men claim that if General Wilson had the power to reduce their salaries they could not see why he could not increase them as well."[91] The mere threat of a strike had already won back the wages for the men on the Louisville & Cincinnati Short-Line, as well as the Louisville & Nashville & Great Southern, and reports from Memphis indicated that on the night before, the men of the Memphis & Charleston had asked for a restoration of their wages, a request that was granted on the twenty-sixth.[92] Under cover of the turmoil of the Great Strike nationally, and of the violence closer to home in Louisville, the men of the Southeastern struck to achieve what they saw others around them receiving.

Telegraphing his responses from St. Louis, a city gripped by its own set of problems in relation to the Great Strike, Wilson, the receiver for the Southeastern, refused to act to increase the strikers' wages.[93] In support of Wilson, on Friday the twenty-seventh, the U.S. District Court judge for the Middle District of Tennessee, Connelly F. Trigg, issued an order to the U.S. marshall in Nashville, E. S. Wheat, to take immediate action to protect the property of

the Southeastern, and if necessary, to "take possession of the road and rolling stock and hold the same subject to the order and control of the court."[94]
Isolated and alone, the only railroad workers in the city who had not had
their wages restored, the men of the Southeastern were in for a hard time.

Marshall Wheat acted quickly to limit the effect of the strike. Operating
on the basis of Judge Trigg's order, Wheat decided not to summon a posse
but instead "went in person and passed the trains through and beyond the
assemblages of strikers, endeavoring by gentle means and good council to
persuade the men to desist."[95] Boarding the mail train and riding it into the
yards at Edgefield on the outskirts of Nashville, Wheat convinced the men
to let the train pass unmolested. He told them if they uncoupled the mail
car he would just recouple it, and if they then uncoupled it again, he would
arrest them. He then began taking their names down, and the men decided
to let the train pass.[96] When the men argued with him, and with local agent
R. G. Butler, they insisted the strike was "the only redress they had," and
that "they would like to see the matter settled as early as possible." They also
reiterated their claim that "Gen. Wilson had it in his power to restore their
wages, if, by the exercise of such power, he could reduce them." The *Daily
American* reported further that "many of the employes express a good deal of
bitterness toward Gen. Wilson, who, they say, is rather abrupt and arbitrary
in his manner of treating them."[97] Despite these claims, Butler continued to
try to convince the men they would be better off if they would just go back
to work, suggesting that if Judge Trigg in fact ordered Wheat to take over
the line, they would all lose their jobs.[98] But the strikers knew that railroad
workers and others in Memphis, Louisville, and Nashville had already successfully used the turmoil of the Great Strike to advance their causes, and
they hoped to be able to do the same.

On Saturday morning, crowds gathered at the Southeastern depot, anxious
to see if the trains would run or not. As Nashvillians wondered what would
happen, the strikers themselves seemed unsure of what to do. The *Daily
American* reported that "the Southeastern employes were having frequent
consultations in squads, and then as a whole. While some were opposed to
allowing the coaches to go out, they finally yielded to the will of the majority,
though all seemed in doubt as to the best course to be pursued."[99] The men
of the Southeastern knew what they wanted, but they were not as sure about
how to get it.

Although the men rejected Wilson's claim that he had no authority to raise
their wages, the strikers decided to petition Judge Trigg directly. Meeting on
Sunday morning, the twenty-ninth, the strikers set forth their grievances,
which they delivered to the judge on Monday. Several specific issues were

addressed in addition to the reduction in pay, including the dismissal of an engineer and a conductor as well as the classification scheme the company had enacted. In their petition, the railroad workers specifically mentioned that not only was their pay inadequate, but that it was lower than any other road running into Nashville, and that all the other companies had "satisfactorily settled the difficulties between themselves and employes."[100]

Any hopes the strikers had that the judge would intervene on their behalf were crushed when the judge responded to their petition by sending instructions to Marshall Wheat "to summon a sufficient posse to protect the management in the running of the trains; and, if he could not get a posse in the Middle district of Tennessee sufficiently large to carry out this purpose, he should not hesitate to call for United States soldiers."[101] Based on the judge's new order issued July 30, Wheat "summoned a posse of men and took possession" of the railroad on July 31. Approximately three hundred people turned out to the depot hoping to be called, but, in all, only twenty-eight men served with Wheat, earning $3 per day and $3 per night of active duty; a number of men earned as much as $15 over the course of the four days Wheat controlled the railroad.[102] This compares to the reduced rate of $3.75 and $3.50 per day paid to engineers, or the rate of firemen, who were paid half that of engineers, or the less than $1.00 per day paid to laborers.[103] Wheat noted to the judge in his report that "many of the guards . . . [were] married men and need the pay for their services," making arrangements to secure their pay within the week.[104]

Although the strikers did not resort to violence, at least not such that was reported by Marshal Wheat or recorded in the newspaper, they did continue to press their demands and did what they could to keep the trains from running.[105] When six engineers were brought in from Evansville, Indiana, on Tuesday night, the strikers boarded the train they were on and convinced three of them to leave town. When Marshall Wheat discovered that three of his six engineers had "been 'snaked' away," he forbade the strikers from talking to the other three upon penalty of arrest.[106] The strikers, though, promised to use neither threats of violence nor intimidation, but only wanted to talk to the men. They promised Wheat that if any engineer could be found that would take a train out of Nashville, they would let him do so unmolested. They did, apparently, place two iron rails on top of the rails some distance out of town, which a southbound passenger train ran into, but no damage was done. By Tuesday, the strikers had also reduced their demands, promising they would return to work if the company abolished the classification scheme for newly hired engineers, and if it would restore the wages of the lowest paid laborers on the force to $1.00 and $1.25 per day, as it was before the reduction in June. Neither receiver Wilson nor Judge Trigg replied to their new offer.[107]

By Wednesday morning the strike on the Southeastern road was effectively broken when a freight train, complete with guards "armed with breech-loading rifles furnished . . . by his Excellency Governor Porter," pulled out of Nashville at 5:40 A.M.[108] On Thursday, the *Daily American* indicated that the strikers were willing to go back to work and expected that "the management will retain all but about six, who have been more prominent in the strike."[109] Reporting the next day, however, the paper noted that only "three or four engineers and firemen, out of the strikers, resumed their places. Some of the strikers said they did not propose to return to their labors on that line, while others would not have been permitted by the management to do so."[110] At 10:00 Thursday morning, August 2, exactly one week after it began, the only actual strike by railroad workers in Tennessee during the Great Strike of 1877 came to a dismal end. Marshall Wheat, after taking possession of the railroad and guarding it for four days, turned the railroad and its property back over to Wilson, the receiver, "in the same condition as when taken into my [Wheat's] control, so far as I have been able to learn."[111]

The larger effects of the strike, however, and the inspiration to working people in the Mid-South that it represented, did not come to an end. As it turned out, Louisville was not the only city in the region to experience strikes by workers outside the railroad industry during the Great Strike. Memphis, too, had problems with other workers seeking to take advantage of the general turmoil associated with the strike. On Wednesday, August 1, the brickmakers of the city went out on strike, asking for an additional twenty-five cents a day in wages, and were refused. The street force working for the gas company also demanded an increase in wages, and they were all fired.[112] The day before, just up the Mississippi River in Cairo, Illinois, a city technically in a northern state but southern in temperament and custom, African American laborers on the wharves of the Mississippi and Ohio rivers struck for an increase in wages from twenty to thirty cents an hour—a demand that was quickly granted.[113] Earlier in the strike, on Friday, July 27, African American longshoremen in New Orleans successfully went on strike, demanding a raise from thirty cents an hour to forty, the wage being paid to white laborers on other wharves.[114] The New Orleans strikers, perhaps because of the memory of that city's failed dock worker strikes of 1872 and 1875, attracted particular attention in Louisville, where the *Courier-Journal* noted that "a tendency to trouble with workingmen in New Orleans has been met by placing the city military on a war footing, with orders to use no blank cartridges in the event of a mob demonstration."[115] As far away as Galveston, Texas, black workers, ranging from railroad workers to day laborers to laundry women, struck over wage rates and working conditions.[116] During the course of the Great Strike, workers all over the region tried to take advantage of the opportunity for advancing their own interests, some more successfully than others.

Although it appeared that the strike, at least insofar as it threatened the Mid-South, was over, on Saturday, August 4, African American workers in Memphis employed on the wharves and elsewhere in the city reportedly planned to engage in a general strike. According to the *Appeal*, "several hundred colored laborers, instigated by evil-minded white and black men, have been holding meetings and agitating this movement for several days past."[117] At a meeting Friday night, August 3, a number of Memphis's African American workers resolved to strike for higher wages. The newspaper reported that the strikers planned "to visit the elevator of the Memphis and St. Louis packet company, at the foot of Beale street, and on the arrival of the down-river boat they would board her and compel the crew to quit work and strike for higher wages, and prevent anybody from going to work on board until the company's agents agreed to advance their wages." Earlier in the day, African Americans employed in various jobs throughout the city had, upon being paid, "informed their employers that they were not going to work again until their wages were raised." The majority of these workers were reportedly fired, but the action, the *Appeal* argued, clearly indicated "that an organized scheme had been concocted." And it was also clear that it was not the kind of action that would be tolerated by the white citizens of Memphis.[118]

In contrast to their earlier stance evincing sympathy for the plight of the railroad strikers in the North, the *Daily Appeal* was adamantly opposed to action of any kind on the part of the city's African American workers. The paper published an editorial notice "to the negro laborers who last night threatened the city with riot, we desire to say that the civil authorities of Memphis are prepared to and will maintain the peace at any and every hazard."[119] And they were right. In addition to the city police, the Chickasaw Guards, the Bluff City Grays, and Captain Reudelbuber's artillery company were all called out under arms to prevent any type of organized strike by the city's African American workers. A request to the governor for additional arms was granted on the fourth, but "due to the small number of arms in the State Arsenal," a mere two hundred rifles were shipped to bolster local forces.[120] Explaining that "should the black man come in collision with the white man, the former goes to the wall," the *Daily Appeal* boasted somewhat gleefully that "should the rioters attempt an outbreak, it will be no child's play on the part of the military, and but few blank cartridges will be used."[121]

The threatened riot never materialized. The *Appeal* noted that "acting upon the sober second thought, the colored men who on Saturday threatened the city with riot and bloodshed have resolved to seek peaceable means of redress." The *Appeal* continued, writing that "this is as it should be. If the packet companies and steamboats will not pay as much as they think they deserve for a day's labor, they have only to go out a few miles into the country to find plenty of work at good wages, with comfortable quarters and abundance of seasonable food." The South clearly had a place for African American workers, and that place was not in a labor action. "To the country, then, we would advise the discontented negro laborers to go. . . . The planters will reward their labor bountifully, and insure them against a possible visit from the traditional wolf who is always yelping at the poor man's door."[122] The South, the *Appeal* argued, knew the appropriate way to deal with its black citizens, and it did not appreciate the interference of northerners in its affairs. If the Great Strike proved anything, it proved to southerners that northerners should tend to their own problems, as they obviously had many. Uniformly making this point, the southern press editorialized on the general absence of violence in the South during the Great Strike, glossing over the labor actions that did arise.[123]

Both during and after the strike, many publishers minimized or ignored the participation of southern workers in the national uprising. In Allan Pinkerton's 1878 account of the strike, he characterized the riot as "bristling with piquant incidents to be laughed over in future years, that every Louisvillian can be very much obliged to them for an agreeable diversion from every-day business routine."[124] Two other accounts published in 1878, J. A. Dacus's *Annals of the Great Strikes* and Edward Winslow Martin's *The History of the Great Riots,* also downplayed the effect of the strike in the South, either barely mentioning or ignoring completely the disturbances in Louisville and Nashville.[125] Dacus mostly used the events in Louisville to highlight what he imaginatively termed the "complete restoration of good feeling between the North and South," noting that "hundreds of ex-soldiers of the blue and grey stood shoulder to shoulder in the ranks."[126] The uniform message seemed to proclaim that there was little real trouble in the South, as compared to the North, and what little occurred was easily resolved. Dacus praised both workers and management in Memphis for being able to "amicably" adjust their differences. The workers, according to Dacus (and the Memphis newspaper), "respectfully couched" their demands and expressed that they "appreciated the difficulties under which the management labored." The response by management was positive, leading Dacus to proclaim that it "justly entitles them to the lasting gradutude of the people of the entire country . . . [having] perhaps even saved the country from a revolution."[127] Although events in the North seemed to bring out the worst in people, these writers followed the lead of the southern press in highlighting the relatively positive nature of the events surrounding the strike in the South.

Although the southern press tried to minimize discussion about the participation of southern workers in the strike, the latent potential for labor violence revealed by the events of July clearly worried people. Like the iron fist covered by a white glove of humor, Pinkerton noted in his account of the Louisville events that, although the riots gave "a vast amount of amusement to the citizens of the city," the rapid military response should "remain as a perpetual warning to the turbulent and lawless elements of Louisville."[128] Basil Duke, basking in the success of his citizen army's restoration of peace to the beleaguered city, wrote the governor to say that hundreds of citizens wanted to establish military organizations armed by the state, but independent of the state guard and under the authority of the mayor. The governor refused, telling Duke instead that "the citizens of Louisville should immediately organize a sufficient number of State Guard companies to form a Battalion or Regiment and I will arm them and use all my power to make the organization effective and an honor as well as a safeguard to Louisville." Governor McCreary tried to explain that although Duke's fears of further turmoil might not be unreasonable, Duke was not the only one making such a request. "In every section of the state," McCreary wrote, "I have refused applications to furnish arms to independent military companies" because the law restricted the disbursement of public arms to state militia only.[129] Fear of further violence was widespread, if quietly expressed.

In Tennessee, private business owners, fearful of the potential for labor violence, petitioned the governor for troops and arms to protect their establishments. Responding to a letter from Germantown dated August 8, Governor Porter explained that in the absence of a declaration of emergency by the state legislature, it was the duty of county sheriffs to maintain order, not the state militia, and further, that "I have no arms that I can furnish you for your Company. All those on hand are already disposed of or engaged."[130] In a personal discussion at the capitol, however, Governor Porter apparently promised to provide the Knoxville Iron Company "with an order with which we could obtain some muskets for the use of guards to protect our buildings, tracks and improvements at our mines."[131] W. R. Tuttle, president of the Knoxville Iron Company, planned to introduce convict labor to work the mines. An agent of the East Tennessee, Virginia & Georgia Railroad Company, also based in Knoxville, wrote the governor, explaining that "Companies are being organized and being drilled . . . with the avowed purpose of resisting the introduction of Convict labor in the mines. That not only the miners but citizens are taking an active part in the matter. They threaten not only to drive off the Convicts—but to burn all the bridges on my Road." On behalf of the railroad, the letter writer continued, saying that "my object in writing at this time [July 27] is to acquire, in view of this state of affairs—and of the general disturbed condition of things throughout the country—all of which—you are well aware—what further demonstration you would want to justify you in affording as a strong guard to make these parties to place convicts in these mines—and to protect our Railroad property."[132] In a follow-up letter to the governor's promise of arms, on August 6 Tuttle told Porter that "[t]en years experience with these same miners convinces me that temporizing and argument with them is a waste of time. . . . They are chiefly Welsh and to use the sayings of one of their own people. 'They are as treacherous as the d—l.' They will say one thing and do another." Tuttle concluded by saying "that they are in *earnest* in their threats there is *no* room for doubt. Hence I say to you in all caution, that the sooner the question is settled the less time they and their supporters will have to perfect their schemes of resistance and to work up sympathy and public opinion."[133] The events of July proved that, even in the Mid-South, workers could and would engage in strikes and violence when they believed conditions gave them no alternative.

Although there continued to be pockets of concern over persistent labor violence in August 1877, what the purveyors of public opinion in the Mid-South wanted most was to return to doing business in the traditional way. On August 2, in the midst of some lingering local strikes but after the southern railroads were clearly running again and the worst of the danger from the strikes had passed, the *Appeal* ran an advertisement under the heading, "Workingmen's Demonstration." Leading off with the statement that "about eight o'clock yesterday evening a large crowd of workingmen assembled on Main street," the column continued with descriptions of the workers' "constantly-swelling numbers" and of their walking "steadily and quietly" toward a clear objective. "At a point between Adams and Jefferson," the paper continued, "The workingmen halted, and quickly took possession of the Great Western clothing-house. The genial proprietor of that far-famed establishment, well known to the workingmen as their best friend, gave them a cordial welcome, and then the 'strike' began. It is needless to say that the workingmen struck solid bargains in clothing and furnishing goods, and so ended the workingmen's strike in Memphis, to be reopened every Saturday night at the Great Western clothing-house, No. 227 Main street."[134] In Memphis, in the span of two weeks, the Great Strike of 1877 had passed from a symbol of what was wrong with northern urban society, to a threat of mischief and mayhem in the streets, to a marketing ploy to attract business for a dry goods store.

In some ways, perhaps, the Great Strike did not shake the foundations of society in the Mid-South as thoroughly as it did in other regions of the country. But it would be a mistake to suggest that it passed with no effect at all. Although Memphis's, Nashville's, and to some extent Louisville's experience with the Great Strike of 1877 did not mirror the experience of cities in the industrial Northeast and Midwest, it seems clear that the working people of the Mid-South were not the contented, happy workers the newspapers sought to portray. Even though the single railroad strike actually to occur in Tennessee failed to achieve its aims, and the South by and large remained unfriendly toward unions and strikes, many workers—not just those in the railroad industry—in Memphis, Nashville, Louisville, and elsewhere in the region pushed for, and in many cases received, real concessions from their employers, resulting in both higher wages and improved working conditions. The national crisis precipitated by the Great Strike created an opportunity for change, and the working people of the Mid-South, black and white alike, did what they could to make the most of it.

Notes

1. Although regional definitions vary, the Mid-South almost always includes Tennessee and Kentucky. Sometimes Alabama and Mississippi are also included, as are Louisiana, Arkansas, Missouri, Oklahoma, and Texas, depending on the organization doing the defining.

2. C. Vann Woodward, *Reunion and Reaction: The Compromise of 1877 and the End of Reconstruction* (Boston: Little, Brown and Co., 1951, 1966) presents the standard history of this series of events, an interpretation adopted by many writers on the South. For a more nuanced view of the end of Reconstruction as a result of conflicting ideologies revolving around notions of free labor versus class struggle, see Heather Cox Richardson, *The Death of Reconstruction: Race, Labor, and Politics in the Post–Civil War North, 1865–1901* (Cambridge, Mass.: Harvard University Press, 2001). See also Nancy Cohen, *The Reconstruction of American Liberalism, 1865–1914* (Chapel Hill: University of North Carolina Press, 2002), esp. 61–85, for a discussion of how the labor question affected the South.

3. Newspapers were an important component of the public dialogue during the second half of the nineteenth century, providing their readers with both news and an interpretation of events. Although the general press tended to write about similar topics in all parts of the country, mainstream newspapers tended to interpret events from a sectional or party perspective, thereby shaping the public's perception as well as providing information. The South, particularly the lot of the freedmen and their treatment by southern whites, was a frequent topic of the national press, and one that did not show the region or its white inhabitants in a particularly good light. Given the nature of the events of July

1877, southern papers, including the papers of the Mid-South, were only too happy to reciprocate; Richardson, *Death of Reconstruction,* xii.

4. For a good discussion of the historiography of the Great Strike, see David O. Stowell, *Streets, Railroads, and the Great Strike of 1877* (Chicago: University of Chicago Press, 1999), 1–11. See also Philip S. Foner, *The Great Labor Uprising of 1877* (New York: Monad Press, 1977); Robert V. Bruce, *1877: Year of Violence* (Chicago: Elephant Paperbacks, 1989 [1959]); Jeremy Brecher, *Strike!* (San Francisco: Straight Arrow Books, 1972); David T. Burbank, *Reign of the Rabble: The St. Louis General Strike of 1877* (New York: Augustus M. Kelley, 1966); David R. Roediger, "'Not Only the Ruling Classes to Overcome, but Also the So-Called Mob': Class, Skill and Community in the St. Louis General Strike of 1877," *Journal of Social History* (winter 1985): 213–39; Nick Salvatore, "Railroad Workers and the Great Strike of 1877: The View from a Small Midwest City," *Labor History* 21, no. 4 (fall 1980): 522–45; J. A. Dacus, *Annals of the Great Strikes in the United States* (Chicago: L. T. Palmer and Co., 1877; repr.: New York: Arno Press, 1969); Allan Pinkerton, *Strikers, Communists, Tramps, and Detectives* (New York: G. W. Carleton and Co., 1878; repr.: New York: Arno Press, 1969).

5. Eric Arnesen, *Waterfront Workers of New Orleans: Race, Class and Politics, 1863–1923* (New York: Oxford University Press, 1991); Peter Rachleff, *Black Labor in the South: Richmond, Virginia, 1865–1890* (Philadelphia: University of Pennsylvania Press, 1984); Donald G. Nieman, ed., *African Americans and Non-Agricultural Labor in the South, 1865–1900* (New York: Garland Publishing, 1994). Worker organization to achieve better pay was not restricted to urban workers, but can also be seen in the countryside. See esp. Julie Saville, *The Work of Reconstruction: From Slave to Wage Laborer in South Carolina, 1860–1870* (Cambridge: Cambridge University Press, 1994); John C. Rodrigue, *Reconstruction in the Cane Fields: From Slavery to Free Labor in Louisiana's Sugar Parishes, 1862–1880* (Baton Rouge: Louisiana State University Press, 2001).

6. Steven J. Hoffman, *Race, Class, and Power in the Building of Richmond, 1870–1920* (Jefferson, N.C.: McFarland and Co., 2004).

7. George C. Wright, *Life behind a Veil: Blacks in Louisville, Kentucky, 1865–1930* (Baton Rouge: Louisiana State University Press, 1985), 7; and Arnesen, *Waterfront Workers of New Orleans,* 52.

8. *Memphis Daily Appeal,* July 19, 1877, 1.

9. *Memphis Daily Appeal,* July 20, 1877, 1.

10. Jonathan Kennon Thompson Smith, "Genealogical Tidbits from the *Memphis Daily Appeal* during the Centennial Year of 1876," http://www.tngenweb.org/madison/smith/mda76-03.htm (accessed December 6, 2003).

11. *Memphis Daily Appeal,* July 21, 1877, 1.

12. See Joshua Brown's chapter in this volume for a fuller discussion of the ways in which newspapers, through the use of visual imagery, altered perceptions of workers in the public's imagination.

13. *Memphis Daily Appeal,* July 20, 1877, 1.

14. *Memphis Daily Appeal,* July 24, 1877, 1.

15. *Memphis Daily Appeal,* July 24, 1877, 2.

16. Foner, *The Great Labor Uprising of 1877;* Bruce, *1877: Year of Violence.*

17. *Memphis Daily Appeal,* July 24, 1877, 2.

18. Ibid.

19. *Nashville Daily American,* July 20, 1877, 2.

20. *Nashville Daily American,* July 24, 1877, 2.

21. Woodward, *Reaction and Reunion;* Edward L. Ayers, *The Promise of the New South; Life after Reconstruction* (New York: Oxford University Press, 1992), 332–33 and 340–41; C. Vann Woodward, *Origins of the New South* (Baton Rouge: Louisiana State University Press; rev. ed., June 1971).

22. Although not widespread public knowledge, many of these issues had been worked out by the various factions of the national political parties in the so-called Compromise of 1877. Woodward, *Reunion and Reaction.*

23. *Nashville Daily American,* July 25, 1877, 2; Woodward, *Reunion and Reaction,* 245–46.

24. *Louisville Courier-Journal,* July 23, 1877, 2.

25. *Louisville Courier-Journal,* July 26, 1877, 1.

26. *Memphis Daily Appeal,* July 24, 1877, 1.

27. Ibid.

28. *Memphis Daily Appeal,* July 26, 1877, 3.

29. *Memphis Daily Appeal,* July 24, 1877, 1.

30. Ibid.

31. *Memphis Daily Appeal,* July 25, 1877, 1.

32. Ibid.

33. Richardson, *Death of Reconstruction,* xii.

34. *Memphis Daily Appeal,* July 24, 1877, 1.

35. Ibid.

36. *Memphis Daily Appeal,* July 24, 25, 1877, 1.

37. *Memphis Daily Appeal,* July 25, 1877, 1.

38. *Memphis Daily Appeal,* July 26, 1877, 3.

39. Letter, Robert Duncan to Governor James D. Porter, July 27, 1877, Governor James D. Porter Papers, 1875–1879, GP 24, Reel 2, Box 3, Folder 8, Tennessee State Library and Archives, Nashville, Tennessee.

40. *Memphis Daily Appeal,* July 26, 1877, 1, editorial.

41. Woodward, *Reunion and Reaction; Memphis Daily Appeal,* July 26, 1877, 1, editorial.

42. *Memphis Daily Appeal,* July 26, 1877, 3.

43. *Memphis Daily Appeal,* July 27, 1877, 4.

44. Dacus, *Annals of the Great Strikes,* 468; *Memphis Daily Appeal,* July 27, 1877, 2, editorial.

45. *Memphis Daily Appeal,* July 28, 1877, 2.

46. *Memphis Daily Appeal,* July 31, 1877, 2, editorial.

47. *Nashville Daily American,* July 22, 1877, 4.

48. *Nashville Daily American,* July 24, 1877, 1.

49. *Nashville Daily American,* July 24, 1877, 4.

50. *Nashville Daily American,* July 25, 1877, 1.

51. *Nashville Daily American,* July 25, 1877, 4.

52. Ibid.

53. See esp. Stowell, *Streets, Railroads, and the Great Strike of 1877,* for a discussion of the role of urban crowds in the larger disturbances associated with the strike.

54. *Nashville Daily American,* July 25, 1877, 4.

55. Ibid.

56. Ibid.

57. *Memphis Daily Appeal,* July 25, 1877, 1.

58. Bill L. Weaver, "Louisville's Labor Disturbance, July, 1877," *Filson Club Historical Quarterly* 48, no. 2 (April 1974): 177–86; Pinkerton, *Strikers, Communists, Tramps, and Detectives,* 384–87.

59. *Louisville Courier-Journal,* July 25, 1877, 4.

60. Ibid.

61. Ibid.

62. *Nashville Daily American,* July 25, 1877, 1.

63. *Nashville Daily American,* July 25, 1877, 4; *Louisville Courier-Journal,* July 25, 1877, 4.

64. *Nashville Daily American,* July 26, 1877, 1; *Memphis Daily Appeal,* July 26, 1877, 1.

65. *Louisville Courier-Journal,* July 25, 1877, 4; Pinkerton, *Strikers, Communists, Tramps, and Detectives,* 385.

66. *Nashville Daily American,* July 25, 1877, 1.

67. *Louisville Courier-Journal,* July 25, 1877, 1.

68. *Louisville Courier-Journal,* July 25, 1877, 4.

69. Ibid.

70. "Proclamation," Broadside, July 25, 1877, Jacob, Charles Donald, 1838–1918 Papers, MSS C J, Filson Historical Society, Louisville, Kentucky.

71. *Louisville Courier-Journal,* July 25, 1877, 1.

72. *Nashville Daily American,* July 26, 1877, 1; *Memphis Daily Appeal,* July 26, 1877, 1.

73. "Report to Mayor Jacob from Basil W. Duke, Commander-in-Chief of the City Forces," July 31, 1877, Louisville City Records, Metro Archives, Louisville, Kentucky; August 2, 1877, *Minutes of the Common Council,* 14 Dec. 1877–12 Dec. 1878 (2nd Part), Reel #35, Louisville City Records microfilm, the University of Louisville Archives and Records Center, Louisville, Kentucky; August 2, 1877, *Minutes of the Board of Aldermen,* 1876, December 14–1878, December 12: reel 17, Legislative Records of Louisville, Kentucky, Bound Volumes, 1781–1929, microfilm, The University of Louisville Archives and Records Center, Louisville, Kentucky; Letter to John Baxter, March 24, 1870, Basil Wilson Duke Papers, 1838–1916, MSS 8, Filson Historical Society, Louisville, Kentucky.

74. "Report to Mayor Jacob from Basil W. Duke, Commander-in-Chief of the City Forces," July 31, 1877. According to the governor, more than half the arms available in the state were shipped to Louisville from the state arsenal in Frankfort. Letter from Gov. James B. McCreary to Gen. Basil Duke, 9 August 1877, McCreary, James Bennett, 1838–1918 Papers, MSS C, M, Filson Historical Society, Louisville, Kentucky.

75. *Louisville Courier-Journal,* July 25, 1877, 1; "Report to Mayor Jacob from Basil W. Duke, Commander-in-Chief of the City Forces," July 31, 1877.

76. "Proclamation by the Mayor," Broadside, July 25, 1877, Jacob, Charles Donald, 1838–1918 Papers, MSS C J, Filson Historical Society, Louisville, Kentucky; *Louisville Courier-Journal,* July 25, 1877, 1.

77. "Report to Mayor Jacob from Basil W. Duke, Commander-in-Chief of the City Forces," July 31, 1877.

78. *Louisville Courier-Journal,* July 26, 1877, 1.

79. Letter, Joshua F. Speed to Norvin Green, 27 July 1877, Green, Norvin, 1818–1893 Papers, MSS A, G 797, 21, Filson Historical Society, Louisville, Kentucky. Norvin Green was vice president of Western Union, a corporation he assumed the presidency of in 1878.

80. Maury Klein, *History of the Louisville & Nashville Railroad* (New York: Macmillan Company, 1972), 147.

81. *Nashville Daily American,* July 26, 1877, 1; *Memphis Daily Appeal,* July 26, 1877, 1.

82. *Annual Report of the Louisville & Nashville Railroad Company, 1877–78* (Louisville, Ky.: Bradley and Gilbert, 1878), 9.

83. "Report to Mayor Jacob from Basil W. Duke, Commander-in-Chief of the City Forces," July 31, 1877; and *Annual Report of the Louisville & Nashville Railroad Company, 1877–78,* 9.

84. Stowell, *Streets, Railroads, and the Great Strike of 1877;* Burbank, *Reign of the Rabble;* Roediger, "'Not Only the Ruling Classes to Overcome, but Also the So-Called Mob.'"

85. *Louisville Courier-Journal,* July 27, 1877, 4, July 28, 1877, 4, July 29, 1877, 4, July 31, 1877, 4.

86. *Nashville Daily American,* July 26, 1877, 1.

87. *Nashville Daily American,* July 26, 1877, 4.

88. Ibid.

89. Ibid.

90. Ibid.

91. *Nashville Daily American,* July 27, 1877, 4.

92. *Nashville Daily American,* July 27, 1877, 1.

93. Burbank, *Reign of the Rabble;* Roediger, "'Not Only the Ruling Classes to Overcome, but Also the So-Called Mob.'"

94. *Nashville Daily American,* July 28, 1877, 4.

95. "Report of Edward Wheat, U.S. Marshall, to Hon. Connally Trigg, Judge," Record Group 21, Records of the U.S. Circuit Courts, Middle District of Tennessee, Nashville Division, Equity Case 2184, in the holdings of the National Archives, Southeast Region, Atlanta, Georgia.

96. *Nashville Daily American,* July 28, 1877, 4.

97. Ibid.

98. Ibid.

99. *Nashville Daily American,* July 29, 1877, 4.

100. *Nashville Daily American,* July 31, 1877, 4.

101. Ibid.

102. *Nashville Daily American,* August 2, 1877, 4; "Report of Edward Wheat, U.S. Marshall, to Hon. Connally Trigg, Judge."

103. *Nashville Daily American,* July 28, 1877, 4; July 29, 1877, 4; August 1, 1877, 4.

104. "Report of Edward Wheat, U.S. Marshall, to Hon. Connally Trigg, Judge."

105. Ibid.

106. *Nashville Daily American,* August 1, 1877, 4.

107. Ibid.

108. "Report of Edward Wheat, U.S. Marshall, to Hon. Connally Trigg, Judge"; *Nashville Daily American,* August 2, 1877, 4.

109. *Nashville Daily American,* August 2, 1877, 4.

110. *Nashville Daily American,* August 3, 1877, 4.

111. "Report of Edward Wheat, U.S. Marshall, to Hon. Connally Trigg, Judge."

112. *Nashville Daily American,* August 2, 1877, 1.

113. *Memphis Daily Appeal,* August 1, 1877, 1; *Nashville Daily American,* August 1, 1877, 1.

114. *Nashville Daily American,* July 28, 1877, 2.

115. Arnesen, *Waterfront Workers of New Orleans,* 44–60; *Louisville Courier-Journal,* July 30, 1877, 1.

116. Philip S. Foner and Ronald L. Lewis, *The Black Worker during the Era of the National Labor Union* (Philadelphia: Temple University Press, 1978), 162–67; Jeremy Brecher, *Strike!* (San Francisco: Straight Arrow Books, 1972), 17.

117. *Memphis Daily Appeal,* August 5, 1877, 2.

118. Ibid.

119. *Memphis Daily Appeal,* August 5, 1877, 1.

120. Letter to G. W. Cooper, Memphis Tennessee, August 4, 1877, Governor James D. Porter Papers, 1875–1879, GP 24, Reel 5, Box 9, Folder 1, Tennessee State Library and Archives, Nashville, Tennessee.

121. *Memphis Daily Appeal,* August 5, 1877, 2. For information on the violent actions of Memphis whites involved in conflict in the streets with African Americans, see also James Gilbert Ryan, "The Memphis Riots of 1866: Terror in a Black Community during Reconstruction," *Journal of Negro History* (July 1977): 243–57; Altina Waller, "Community, Class and Race in the Memphis Riot of 1866," *Journal of Social History* 18, no. 2 (1984): 233–46; *Memphis Riots and Massacres,* reprint of *The Reports of the Committees of the House of Representatives, Made During the First Session Thirty-Ninth Congress, 1865–66* (New York: Arno Press, 1969).

122. *Memphis Daily Appeal,* August 7, 1877, 2, editorial.

123. Both the *Appeal* and the *Daily American* reprinted editorials from leading southern papers. See also Dacus, *Annals of the Great Strikes,* 428.

124. Pinkerton, *Strikers, Communists, Tramps, and Detectives,* 385–87.

125. Dacus, *Annals of the Great Strikes;* James Dabney McCabe, *The History of the Great Riots; The Strikes and Riots on the Various Railroads of the United States and in the Mining Regions, Together with a Full History of the Mollie Maguires* by Edward Winslow Martin [pseud.] (Philadelphia: National Pub. Co., 1877; New York: A. M. Kelley, 1971); Weaver, "Louisville's Labor Disturbance, July, 1877," 185.

126. Dacus, *Annals of the Great Strikes,* 430.

127. *Memphis Daily Appeal,* July 26, 1877, 3; Dacus, *Annals of the Great Strikes,* 466–69.

128. Pinkerton, *Strikers, Communists, Tramps, and Detectives,* 387.

129. Letter from Governor James B. McCreary to Gen. Basil Duke, 9 August 1877, McCreary, James Bennett, 1838–1918 Papers, MSS C, M, Filson Historical Society, Louisville, Kentucky.

130. Letter to A. G. Harrison, undated response to letter dated 8 August 1877, Governor James D. Porter Papers, 1875–1879, GP 24, Reel 5, Box 9, Folder 1, Tennessee State Library and Archives, Nashville, Tennessee.

131. Letter from W. R. Tuttle, President Knoxville Iron Company, to Governor James D. Porter, August 6, 1877, Governor James D. Porter Papers, 1875–1879, GP 24, Reel 3, Box 5, Folder 3, Tennessee State Library and Archives, Nashville, Tennessee.

132. Letter from East Tennessee, Virginia & Georgia Railroad Company, to Governor James D. Porter, July 27, 1877, Governor James D. Porter Papers, 1875–1879, GP 24, Reel 2, Box 4, Folder 1, Tennessee State Library and Archives, Nashville, Tennessee.

133. Letter from W. R. Tuttle, President Knoxville Iron Company, to Governor James D. Porter, August 6, 1877, marked "private," Governor James D. Porter Papers, 1875–1879, GP 24, Reel 3, Box 5, Folder 3, Tennessee State Library and Archives, Nashville, Tennessee.

134. *Memphis Daily Appeal,* August 2, 1877, 4.

5. The July Days in San Francisco, 1877: Prelude to Kearneyism

MICHAEL KAZIN

In the metropolis of the Far West, the great uprising of 1877 had one significant element in common with events that took place east of the Mississippi. Participants acted out of a strong feeling of antipathy toward the owners of big corporations, but the majority who took to the streets had little idea how to improve or replace a political economy mired in its fifth year of depression.

However, in San Francisco, white rioters lashed out more vehemently against a racial minority than against local employers and merchants. They attacked both Chinese immigrants and businesses that either hired them or transported them to American shores—but rioters injured and killed only the workers from Asia. The violence that occurred on the West Coast in July 1877 had major political consequences: the meteoric rise and rapid fall of a new third party, and then the reformation of strong and durable trade unions, which used the anti-Asian issue to portray themselves as the champions of all Californians with European backgrounds. If these were the wages of whiteness, they were, it must be acknowledged, rather good ones—at least for anti-Chinese labor leaders and the skilled unionists they organized and led.[1]

Railroad workers in California did not follow the lead of their eastern brethren who had touched off the great uprising. On July 22, as the strike wave was cresting elsewhere in the country, the directors of the mighty Central Pacific Railroad in San Francisco rescinded a 10 percent pay reduction they had ordered only a few days before for employees whose wages were more than $2 a day.[2] Most San Francisco dailies praised the railroad's move as a wise precaution, but it is not clear that a slash in trainmen's pay would have had the same consequence in California as it did in Pittsburgh and Baltimore. Even during the depression, wages on the West Coast were significantly higher—by 20 to 40 percent—than rates for similar occupations in the East, although the prolonged slump had forced a general decline in pay throughout the country.[3] Businessmen in San Francisco recognized that the miners on the rich Comstock Lode in the Sierra Mountains sympathized with the eastern strikers but correctly reasoned that they would not "resort to any violent measures" without a direct provocation from mine owners.[4]

Although no California workers seem to have walked off their jobs in solidarity with the national strike, many residents of the state's largest city did condemn the railroad corporations for the troubles. The two-hundred-member Typographers Union in San Francisco, though not condoning the "willful destruction of property" in the eastern strike, chided railroad owners for not recognizing "that a fair day's wage should be paid for a fair day's work."[5] The local press was almost unanimous in declaring, as the *San Francisco Chronicle* put it, "the bedrock cause of the trouble [is] the general, bad, wasteful, tyrannical, insolent, plundering and corrupt management of the great railway corporations."[6] Beginning with the assertion that the rioters should be crushed and order restored in the cities of the East, every daily newspaper except the conservative *Alta* raised the disturbing question of what had gone wrong in American society to cause such a tumultuous upheaval.[7] In contrast, the *Alta* defended the railroad magnates as a group and, while praising the Central Pacific's rescinding of its pay cut, reminded workers of their debt to the corporation. "The Company has paid out immense sums to laborers and employees," the paper editorialized, "and many a man and family has been made more comfortable thereby. It is hoped that this recent action will be properly appreciated."[8]

The mob violence that did come to San Francisco in July 1877 did not primarily target the property of San Francisco industrialists. It was directed at a different enemy: the almost twenty thousand Chinese immigrants who made up 10 percent of the population and close to one-fourth of the hired labor force in the city.[9] For several days, San Francisco was the scene of battles between whites and Chinese and between white rioters and the formidable police forces arrayed against them.

Although the violence of the "July Days" failed to destroy much of San Francisco's valuable real estate, it did propel the anti-Chinese movement on the West Coast to a new stage of political organization. Two months after the quelling of the mobs in San Francisco, Denis Kearney was chosen president of the newly formed Workingmen's Party of California.[10] Under Kearney's leadership, the WPC elected mayors and other officials in Sacramento, Oakland, and San Francisco and wrote a new state constitution (ratified by the voters in May 1879) that stringently limited the rights of Chinese and attempted to bar their further immigration into California. It also inaugurated an era of state regulation of public utilities and railroad corporations.[11] In 1882, Congress passed a law to exclude Chinese laborers from the country for ten years, for the first time restricting the immigration of people belonging to a specific national group. Whether or not the majority of labor activists desired such a law, national leaders of both major parties only began promoting it after the violent protests on the West Coast.[12]

In this chapter, I offer an interpretive narrative of the July Days in San Francisco and place the riot within the larger context of anti-Chinese politics in late-nineteenth-century America. Although the 1877 turmoil was the only event of its kind in the 150 years since the Gold Rush transformed a decrepit waterside military garrison into a burgeoning metropolis, the riots were but the most prominent (and one of the least deadly) examples of attacks on Chinese immigrants in cities, mining towns, and agricultural settlements throughout the Far West. These occurred from 1850 through the Gilded Age and froze Anglo-Chinese relationships in the region into an ugly mold that cracked only during World War II.[13]

Unfortunately, there is only scanty evidence touching on one of the more intriguing questions about the July Days in San Francisco: who were the rioters? Local observers at the time were unanimous in their opinion that "lawless hoodlums," the majority of them boys in their teens, were responsible for most of the violence. In the East, boys from white working-class families were certainly active in the riots touched off by the railroad strike, though the press there pinned the blame more widely on a "dangerous class" of chronically unemployed men influenced by radical groups like the Workingmen's Party of the United States (WPUS), an affiliate of the First Socialist International.[14] Alexander Saxton, in his pioneering study of labor and the anti-Chinese movement, was skeptical of the "hoodlum theory" as applied to San Francisco. Owing to "the massive character of the rioting and the degree of distress and unemployment"[15] in the city at the time, he believed that many adult working men must have been out on the streets, using stones and torches to drive their low-paid Chinese competitors out of the area.

According to the daily press, only fifty men were arrested for activities connected to the riots.[16] So few transgressors were apprehended because the forces of order were usually too occupied with driving crowds away from their intended targets to stop and make arrests.[17] Therefore, a majority of the men brought into court were caught while alone or in a small group. Only nine were still living in the city in 1880 when employees of the city directory and the U.S. census came by to record them. Because this sample is far too small to draw conclusions about thousands of riot participants, I have simply included information about various individuals in the body of the essay. A clear majority of those arrested did, however, have addresses in the South of Market Street neighborhood, the center of the unskilled white working class in late-nineteenth-century San Francisco.[18]

We will probably never know whether the majority of rioters were teen-agers bent on mayhem or merely unemployed workers out to avenge their frustrated dreams. But the intent of the July Days is clear. In response to unrest documented by telegraph from the faraway East, thousands of San Franciscans took part in a violent attempt to punish those they identified as their enemies. To understand why the Chinese in California became the target of such abuse, one has to examine the particular crisis facing the white working population of San Francisco at the end of the depression of the 1870s.

> From me shanty down on Sixth Street,
> It's meself have jist kim down;
> I've lived there this eighteen year
> It's in what they call Cork Town.
> I'm on the way to the City Hall
> To get a little aid;
> It's meself that has to ax it now
> Since the Chinese ruint the thrade
> —San Francisco song of the 1870s[19]

Before the depression, San Francisco manufacturers had enjoyed a period of rapid growth and high profits. The boom was primarily fueled by capital from the Comstock Lode and the existence of a thriving local market, one that eastern firms could not tap until the completion of the transcontinental railroad in 1869. By 1880, the city had become the ninth largest manufacturing center in the nation, with a factory workforce of 37,475 out of a total population of 233,959.[20]

But the coming of the national railroad utterly transformed the nature of San Francisco's labor market. In addition to the newly unemployed white and Chinese laborers who flocked to the metropolis after the driving of the golden spike at Promontory Point, Utah, more than fifty thousand easterners immigrated to the city immediately before and during 1869, in expectation of good times to come. When the depression broke on the Atlantic Seaboard in 1873 and a grasshopper plague wreaked havoc on the plains of Kansas and

Nebraska, within two years an estimated 154,300 men and women made the trip to California.[21]

Skilled workers who, aided by strong trade unions, had achieved high wages and secure employment in the 1860s were particularly affected by the new surplus of labor. In 1874, the contractor in charge of the mammoth Palace Hotel on Market Street signaled the change by hiring novice carpenters and plasterers instead of experienced union members. As the value of manufacturing output more than doubled in the period from 1870 to 1880, the development of a sizeable class of unemployed and underemployed men transformed what had been a boomtown into a city where the very rich and the desperately poor passed each other on the streets of a congested downtown.[22]

The general crisis of working-class San Francisco was accentuated in the mid-1870s by a regional economic downturn, the magnitude of which was new to the freshly settled Pacific Slope. In the beginning of the decade, speculation in Comstock silver mine stocks had become a feverish sport for anyone in the city who possessed a little free cash. An upper-class resident who was a young boy in the seventies remembered that "[t]here was hardly an individual who was not gambling," and that the hurried greeting in the midst of the brokerage houses on Pine Street was, "How's stocks?"[23] In August 1875, the euphoria was dampened when mining securities declined by $60 million in a single week.

The inevitable crash came early in 1877. The management of the rich Consolidated Virginia Mines announced that the firm's usual monthly dividend of one million dollars would not be forthcoming. The resulting panic registered a $140 million fall in mining stocks.[24] In late 1878, the value of Comstock shares was one-tenth what it had been three years before.[25]

Severe damage to an important source of California's capital was only one of the regional causes for the depression of the mid-1870s. A severe drought in the winter of 1876–77 cut the state's rainfall by two-thirds, causing massive crop failures and the decimation of cattle herds in the San Joaquin Valley. The volume of trade leaving San Francisco's wharves also dropped precipitously. Local manufacturers, already pinched by vigorous competition from Chicago merchants shipping their cheap goods west, laid off hundreds of workers in an attempt to cut expenses. The local brokerage firm of R. G. Dun & Company reported in late July that "failures have been unusually frequent."[26]

By 1877, the plight of the unemployed had become a constant theme in the San Francisco press. That year, as many as ten thousand people sought help through the private San Francisco Benevolent Association; four thousand applicants sought relief from April to June alone.[27] At least one-fifth of the available labor force was unemployed in the first half of 1877, and there was a widespread fear that farm workers would flock to the city as the full effects of the drought set in.[28]

The white working men of San Francisco were without a legitimate political remedy for their condition. The Democrats—the party to which the majority bore allegiance—was in power in both the city and the state, but its leaders ignored pleas to create public works jobs or to pass other emergency measures. Labor unions in the city reported only a skeletal membership of 3,835, itself probably an inflated total.[29] Henry George—then a zealous young journalist and Democrat—received a loud and long burst of applause when he charged in a July 4 oration, "Slavery is not dead. . . . The essence of slavery consists in taking from a man all the fruits of his labor, except a bare living; and of how many thousands, miscalled free men, is this the lot?"[30]

In 1877, there was one neighborhood where new and old enlistees in the army of impoverished laborers could find a cheap bed and a semblance of community life. South of Market Street was a tightly packed area of cheap hotels and lodging houses competing for space with the factories and warehouses of the industrial center. Stretching from the "Tar Flat" next to the docks at the foot of Mission and Folsom streets to relatively comfortable wooden houses west of 10th Street, South of Market was continually changing as new waves of migrants joined the jobless throngs.[31]

In the 1870s, South of Market was a predominantly male neighborhood with an even higher proportion of men to women than the 4 to 3 ratio for San Francisco as a whole.[32] This often made for a difficult family life because men hired for short periods and limited tasks often moved elsewhere to find work when a job was finished. In the early seventies, as native-born Protestants moved from the prosperous enclave of Rincon Hill adjacent to Tar Flat to the loftier peaks of Nob Hill, South of Market took on a decidedly Irish character.[33] The building of the churches of St. Rose and St. Patrick affirmed that fact. The thirty thousand Irish immigrants living in San Francisco at the time represented a greater total than in any other city on the West Coast.[34]

Large numbers of German, British, and other European immigrants also lived South of Market. Because four-fifths of San Francisco's common laborers in 1880 were foreign born (and 65 percent of *all* job holders), South of Market quickly became a mixed ethnic ghetto where a man could look for employment and relax at a saloon or corner grocery store owned by one of his countrymen.[35]

With the coming of the depression, many middle-class observers began to see the crowded working-class district as a repository of social evil. In 1876, San Francisco's health inspectors reported that poor drainage and open cesspools in South of Market were breeding outbreaks of diphtheria and other serious diseases.[36] Gangs of teenage boys, like their counterparts in poor urban neighborhoods throughout the world, roamed the city in search of thrills and cash. A Mexican political refugee, visiting San Francisco in the 1870s, described these "gangs of hoodlums" as daring practitioners of "robbery, seduction, and every kind of wickedness." He wrote of seeing young toughs stripping a "greenhorn" of his valuables after inviting him to a bar and drugging him, all with the tacit connivance of the saloon keeper.[37] Organized gangs even crashed evening performances of Verdi at the Grand Opera House and, according to the opera's manager, "beat [sic] themselves among respectable people in various portions of the gallery."[38]

The San Francisco press tended to view the hoodlums as more than teenage pranksters. The *Evening Post,* which sympathized with the plight of South of Market residents, constantly warned about the criminal character of the "thousands of young and desperate men at large in this city." After the conviction of a seventeen-year-old boy for the murder of a police officer, the *Post* counseled whipping for all young toughs and commented that the "average hoodlum" is "selfishness personified, and should be dealt with as the dangerous animal he is." When the burning of the town of Eureka in northern California was blamed on young "incendiaries," the *Post* and other papers predicted that similar attempts would be made in San Francisco.[39] The July Days appeared to be a fulfillment of that prophecy.

Prime targets of the young hoodlums were new and old Chinese residents of the city. New immigrants from Asia told of being "covered with wounds and bruises and blood" by the time they arrived in the comparative safety of Chinatown. Of course, the Chinese had faced informal and legal harassment in California since the Gold Rush; the Miner's Tax of 1850 required non-Mexican foreigners in the gold diggings to pay $20 a month to the state.[40]

The indictment of the "Celestials" had many parts. White Californians accused the Chinese of poisoning the nation's bloodstream through the introduction of "Asiatic germs" and of degrading its morals through gambling and prostitution.[41] But the most common complaint was economic. Chinese immigration, it was charged, imperiled the existence of free labor in the United States and threatened to reduce white workers to permanent pauperism or outright slavery. As San Francisco lawyer Henry Clement asked in 1877, "if one class of enterprises subsists upon cheap labor, is it not madness to suppose that another class, side by side with them, will pay higher wages?"[42]

Perhaps the most significant aspect of California labor history in the nineteenth century was the almost unified wrath of white workers, not against the employers of cheap labor but against Asian laborers themselves.[43] There was little social contact between white and Chinese workers in California.

Keeping to separate communities and following widely differing cultural patterns, the two groups were connected, if at all, only in the types of labor they performed in factories and small workshops producing for the consumer market.[44]

By the mid-1870s, even these common experiences were often lacking. Two of the city's largest industries, facing stiff competition from eastern manufacturers, switched over almost entirely to a Chinese workforce. As a result, the cigarmakers'—who first instituted the union label as an anti-Chinese tactic in an unsuccessful boycott—and the shoemaker's unions became, in effect, "anti-coolie" clubs. In such trades as construction and metal working, where production was geared to a local market, few Chinese were hired, and wage levels remained high. However, the depression of the seventies severely reduced the prosperity and workforce of those industries.[45]

By 1876, anti-Chinese agitation had reached a flash point in San Francisco. White workers may have been unable to find work, but they still could vote, and any politician who wanted to advance in his profession had to promise to fight for legislation to curb the "Mongolian menace." On April 5, the Democratic mayor of San Francisco, Andrew Jackson Bryant, and the Democratic governor of the state, William Irwin, presided over a mass anti-Chinese rally in the city. Irwin declared, "whoever would degrade the white laboring man to a lower level than he now holds is an enemy of his race."[46] With thousands of unemployed in the city and numbers of them filing out of the meeting hall, a riot seemed possible. Though one hundred extra police were sworn in for the rally, and private guards were stationed at the Pioneer and Mission Woolen Mills where many Chinese were employed, no violence occurred. After that point, however, assaults on individual Chinese immigrants increased to such an extent that the usually reticent Six Companies of Chinatown demanded greater police protection for their community.[47]

In July 1877, when almost 1,400 Chinese arrived in San Francisco in the middle of another summer of discontent, white men took to the streets in mobs, echoing the sentiments of a popular ditty:

> Twelve hundred honest laboring men,
> Thrown out of work today,
> By the landing of these Chinamen
> In San Francisco Bay . . .
> But strife will be in every town
> Throughout the Pacific Shore,
> And the cry of old and young shall be,
> "O, Damn, Twelve Hundred More."[48]

San Francisco was seemingly well equipped to handle a major riot in the summer of 1877. Though only 150 police patrolled the city, they were backed up by a state militia of 1,200 men divided into three regiments of infantry and one battalion each of cavalry and light artillery.[49] Thirty miles northeast in Benicia lay a major arsenal and the headquarters of the U.S. Army Department of the Pacific, with several thousand troops under the command of Gen. Irwin McDowell. At Mare Island, north of the city in San Rafael Bay, warships docked frequently to resupply and give their sailors shore leave.

Beneath this well-armed surface, however, lay some potential problems. Both the police force and militia were dominated by Irish immigrants, many of whom probably had family ties or friends in the South of Market area. One-third of the police force in 1877 was born in Ireland, and a clear majority of officers possessed Irish surnames.[50] In addition, seven of the twenty-two militia companies were entirely composed of Irish Americans. With the exception of the German-dominated companies, Irishmen were also active in the rest.[51] With a mayor elected largely on the strength of his anti-Chinese and pro-labor opinions and with the Board of Supervisors (the equivalent of a city council) dominated by Irish Democrats who identified politically with the grievances of their poorer countrymen, it is not surprising that San Francisco businessmen from English Protestant backgrounds feared for the safety of the city in the event of an anti-Chinese uprising.[52]

The spark that set off the July Days in San Francisco was struck in Pittsburgh on July 21. When news came by telegraph of the killing of forty men and women in the Pittsburgh streets at the hands of a Philadelphia militia detachment, a "whirlwind of excitement" hit the California city.[53] On Sunday the twenty-second, the Executive Committee of the local chapter of the Workingmen's Party of the United States called for a mass rally to be held the following night on the sandlots in front of the partially completed city hall between McAllister and Larkin streets off Market. The published notice of the meeting contained no reference to anti-Chinese sentiments, declaring the intention only "to express . . . sympathy and take other action in regard to [our] fellow workmen at Pittsburgh and Baltimore."[54]

By the morning of the twenty-third, it was clear that the rally would be large and potentially violent. The day before, police had arrested a peddler for walking through the downtown streets carrying a large sign advertising the gathering, which read, "To Sympathize with the Strikers in the East." After confiscating the "objectionable" notice, the man was released.[55] Rumors that "hoodlums" were planning to kill all the residents of Chinatown, to blow up a Chinese theater during a performance, and to assassinate several unnamed "railroad magnates" provoked Mayor Bryant to order the entire police force to be ready for action and convinced the state militia commander, Gen. John McComb, to summon his men to their armories.[56] Members of the avowedly anti-capitalist W.P.U.S. had been active in the rail strike in Chicago (headquarters of the socialist group) and in other cities, and San Francisco officials saw the specter of the Paris Commune in the pronouncements of party leaders.[57]

By half-past seven on the evening of the twenty-third, from eight to ten thousand people gathered in the sandlots.[58] As the audience buzzed expectantly, the meeting was called to order with typical Gilded Age formality. "A thin brass band" played "The Star-Spangled Banner," and a WPUS official named James D'Arcy—a part-time plasterer and full-time party activist—called the gathering to order and began the speeches. D'Arcy immediately warned his listeners that the meeting was not called to oppose Chinese immigration or for the "purpose of encouraging riot and incendiarism."[59] Then he went on to discuss the great strike and riots in the East. Violence was to be deplored, D'Arcy said, but some disruption was unavoidable owing to three million unemployed in the nation and "the political parties . . . the slaves of the money ring, the tools of monopolists."[60]

After D'Arcy spoke for about twenty minutes, seven other members or supporters of the WPUS took to the podium. A Dr. Swain quoted from ancient Greek in lambasting the government for not providing relief to the jobless. A Mrs. Laura Kendrick ended the speeches about 9 P.M. by urging the workingmen present to share their earnings with their wives, remarking that the depression was hurting women and children as badly as male wage earners. The daily press tended to assume that only men were activists in the overlapping ranks of the labor and anti-Chinese movements. But, on occasion, a female voice like Kendrick's revealed that both genders were represented in the working-class insurgency, and that women had their own reasons to promote the cause.[61]

As Kendrick's husband (his first name unreported) began to propose resolutions condemning the railroad corporations and criticizing the use of the military to quell strikes, three shots rang out from a second-story window behind the crowd on McAllister Street. After a few seconds of confusion, police located the apartment from which the gunfire had come. They quickly arrested a drunken suspect named John Griffin, just before the angry audience could avenge the wounding of three of its members.

However, some members of the already uneasy crowd took the shots as an excuse to raise the most popular local grievance. "Clean out the coolies!" one man shouted, and there were cries for a committee to be appointed to demand that the Central Pacific Railroad fire all its Chinese employees and hire whites in their places. D'Arcy took the podium again to repeat that the rally was not an anti-Chinese gathering, but members of the crowd persisted in their protests.

Minutes later, as the crowd passed Mr. Kendrick's resolutions, in a rather desultory mood, a colorful band approached the stage. It played loudly and was led by two men carrying huge transparencies that read "Workingmen, Protect Your Families" and "Self-Preservation is the First Law of Nature."[62] Instantly recognized as the musical contingent of the city's Anti-Coolie Clubs, who had been holding a convention that same evening, the horns and cymbals ended any remaining order in the mass meeting.

An anonymous man then jumped to the platform and suggested a raid on Chinatown in "a month or two . . . when the officers of the law and the Chinese are off their guard."[63] As he was speaking, a police officer saw a white teenager knock down a passing Chinese man and ran over to arrest the assailant. The prisoner yelled for help from his friends, and more than one hundred young whites from the crowd answered the call. In the first of many confrontations between rioters and uniformed keepers of order, they rescued him from the policeman's grasp. During the struggle, many of the departing spectators rushed to the scene. To the cry of "For Chinatown, boys; let's go for Chinatown!" as many as one thousand men and boys ran north up Leavenworth Street, "yelling like madmen."[64]

For the next four hours, the mob ran through the streets to the west of Chinatown, stoning and breaking into twelve Chinese "washhouses" (laundries) and attacking other targets they could identify as linked to the Asian population. These included a Presbyterian Mission on Washington Street at the edge of the Chinese quarter. Chief of police Henry Ellis, assuming the rioters would head for Chinatown, stationed the majority of his men there, leaving the growing mob to run almost at will through the rest of the central city. Here and there, an isolated officer attempted to scare the crowd away from a washhouse, but the rioters were moving too swiftly to be contained by a single policeman. Most often, officers could only force the attackers to split into smaller groups and alter their routes, making them even harder to suppress.

The next day, several reporters commented that the rioters seemed more bent on destroying property than hurting individual Chinese. One grisly exception to this, however, occurred in the sacking of a washhouse on the corner of Greenwich and Divisadero, in the northwest corner of town. The one-story laundry was charged by a gang of fifteen men and boys carrying cans of coal oil. They ran through a barrage of bullets from the eight employees inside, beat up the defenders, seized $150 from the cash box, poured their flammable liquid around the shop, and then ran down to Divisadero as the wooden structure began to burn. The next day, searchers found the charred body of a Chinese worker who had failed to escape the fire.

On Tuesday morning, the twenty-fourth, the pro-business *Alta* blamed "the lawless classes" who "are here, as they are in all great cities," for causing $20,000 worth of damage to private property.[65] After perfunctory praises for the night's police work, all three morning papers (the *Chronicle, Call,* and *Alta*) bemoaned "the deplorable insufficiency" of the force that had enabled the rioters to roam so freely. Meanwhile, prominent citizen were preparing their own response.

At two P.M. that day, more than two hundred of "the solid men of San Francisco" met at the Chamber of Commerce to revive the vigilante tradition of the Gold Rush era. They were responding to a call circulated around the city's largest businesses by General McComb of the state militia. The gathering—which included such notables as clothing merchant Levi Strauss, silver tycoon James C. Flood, sugar refinery president Claus Spreckels, and Mayor Bryant—selected William Tell Coleman to chair a new Citizen's Committee of Safety. Coleman was a wealthy import/export merchant whose operation did more than $100 million of business annually. More important, he had been a leader of the Vigilance Committees of 1851 and 1856, which were credited with stemming crime in the Gold Rush city, albeit through extralegal means. Now in his late fifties, Coleman was respected both for his political flexibility—he was a pro-war Democrat during the Civil War, then worked with the Freedmen's Bureau in the early years of Reconstruction, and became a moderate Republican in the 1870s—and his military experience.[66]

In his first statement as chairman, Coleman analyzed the violence and predicted the speedy suppression of the rioters. He wisely praised the great majority of the town's citizens as "staid, sober, honest, and industrious people" and blamed the previous night's violence on "a rough-scuff element of wild, reckless young men who are ripe for any mischief." Coleman expansively declared that twenty thousand "armed supporters of the law" could be organized in half an hour to make San Francisco "an unhealthy place for a mob."[67] After Mayor Bryant reported that the leaders of the WPUS would hold no more meetings until tensions had cooled, and would try to stop any violence by their supporters (an implicit retort to the "hoodlum" theory), Coleman outlined the organization of the Committee of Safety. Volunteers would be grouped by ward in companies of one hundred and would elect their own officers, subject to the confirmation of the chairman. The cavernous Horticultural Hall would be the general headquarters for the committee, but all companies would patrol their own wards unless needed to suppress a major concentration of rioters. The meeting of businessmen ended with twelve of the richest individuals in the city pledging an initial sum of $48,000 to pay members of the Committee of Safety.

Recruits were not slow to join. By nightfall, the committee reported that more than one thousand had signed up—including a self-employed drayman named Denis Kearney! Coleman then got busy securing weapons and potential reinforcements for his volunteer army. Avoiding the use of the militia, which was proving in eastern cities to be either too friendly with the rioters or too bloodthirsty, Coleman also decided to use firearms only as reserve weapons. He ordered the requisition of six thousand two-foot-long hickory pick handles and provided each man with both a club and a revolver.

Guns and ammunition seemed to be in short supply in the city. As Coleman wrote later, "[T]he larger part . . . had been bought up during the previous week by unknown persons."[68] So the chairman shot off telegrams to the governor in Sacramento and to General McDowell at the arsenal in Benicia, requesting the shipment of several thousand weapons and ammunition of all kinds. By the next day, the Committee of Safety had received 2,300 rifles, ample rounds, and the news that three warships from Mare Island would lay anchor in San Francisco Bay with fully armed contingents of marines aboard.

The city establishment also prepared psychologically for further rioting. In an ingenious argument, the *Alta* warned workingmen that they should help keep order because most of the money they had saved in local banks was lent on real estate, and fires would cause many of those loans to default.[69] The *Daily Stock Report* attempted to reassure the business community that "Every precaution is taken to avoid the enrollment of an unreliable person, so that the Committee [of] Safety . . . will form the most influential organization San Francisco has ever known."[70] Every paper appealed to the laboring population to separate itself from "the hoodlum fringe" while at the same time reporting that "a large majority of the workingmen" had no interest in violence.[71] Only the *Post* ventured even the mildest criticism of the forces of order. The paper endorsed the forming of the committee but reminded "the men of property and standing" that if they did not "restore to this city and the Pacific slope something like a healthy industrial and social tone," the rioting would recur.[72]

The evening of July 24 was quieter than the night before, though a few small groups of young men raided washhouses in the South of Market and beat up any Chinese unlucky enough to be in the area after dark.

But Coleman was preparing for bigger outbreaks. On the twenty-fifth, he let it be known that he was considering the arrest of up to 1,500 *potential* lawbreakers and confining them on naval ships waiting in the harbor. He also proposed ferrying hundreds more to tiny Goat Island, where small boats would circle and apprehend any would-be escapee as soon as he hit the water. Coleman later wrote that he abandoned the idea of prior detention because of "complications" and the "immediate legal action" that would have been brought on behalf of the prisoners. But the rumors of such measures, according to Coleman, did have the intended effect. Many a "rough and lawless man" left San Francisco for small towns on the surrounding peninsula to avoid arrest.[73]

Nevertheless, on the night of the twenty-fifth, official San Francisco was primed for trouble on a major scale. During the day, faithful Catholics had distributed copies of a statement by Archbishop Joseph Alemany that called on "all good citizens, the Catholics in particular, to stand by authority." The archbishop acknowledged that many of his flock had "suffered greatly" from the immigration of Chinese. But he counseled that "the remedy lies not in the mad torch of anarchy."[74] At 8 P.M., more than 1,500 members of the Committee of Safety jammed into Horticultural Hall, where their commander ordered them to "use your clubs on the heads of your opponents" and to protect fire hoses from mobs of arsonists.[75]

As William Coleman spoke, an unauthorized meeting that had none of the amenities of the mass gathering of two days before was taking place under a full moon at the city hall sandlot. An inebriated real estate agent, N. P. Brock, exhorted a crowd of eight hundred men to blow the ships of the Pacific Mail Steamship Company out of the water before they could discharge another cargo of Chinese laborers in San Francisco. The audience received Brock's dramatic suggestion with derision and drove him off the stand with stones. Two other speakers who advised the crowd to use legal channels to restrict Chinese immigration were trying to finish their own statements through the brickbats when the attention of the crowd was distracted by shimmering tongues of flame coming from the wharf area near Rincon Hill.

The fire had started a few minutes after 8 P.M. on the Beale Street wharf, where several lumber warehouses were located. It was probably an attempt to destroy the Pacific Mail dock, which lay right next to large stacks of milled wood. The steamship company enjoyed a virtual monopoly on the lucrative sea routes between East Asia and San Francisco, owned forty-six ocean vessels, and boasted the only wharf in the city equipped with a warehouse and gates instead of the open-planked structures of less profitable concerns.[76]

Such prominence bought protection. As thousands of dollars' worth of cedar and fir planks burned to ashes, private guards and city firemen surrounding the Pacific Mail dock made sure that the flames did not reach the company's property. Inside the warehouse, PMS Company employees stood ready with loaded cannons and repeating rifles in case a rioter somehow managed to break through the human barricade at the entrance.[77]

By 9:30, thousands of anti-Chinese rioters from around the city had converged at the foot of Brannan Street to watch the flames and harass the firemen trying to put them out. Earlier in the evening, several large gangs had marched through downtown and the South of Market, smashing windows of deserted Chinese washhouses and battling regular officers and Committee of Safety men at numerous locations. One mob was reportedly commanded by "a young man dressed in a black beaver suit, cleanly shaven and respectable appearing" who pointed out targets to more than one hundred boys and older men but committed no act of destruction himself.[78]

When news of the fire reached Horticultural Hall, Coleman quickly dispatched seven hundred men to aid the regular police. A few minutes after they arrived, the men charged the crowd, which was drawing closer to the Pacific Mail wharf. As the fire raged behind them, a phalanx of safety committee men with pick handles held high drove the jeering mob back up Rincon Hill. In the middle of the retreat, a woman stepped from one of the alleys off First Street and, "in full light," shot five times at the rioters. The crowd stopped and angrily rushed back down the hill.

Coleman's strictures against firearms were forgotten as committee men and police emptied their pistols wildly into the mass of yelling stone throwers. The shooting was so erratic that a confused eyewitness later wrote, "Whether any of the retreating crowd were wounded could not be told."[79] But within a few minutes, the forces of order had dispersed the rioters. The next day, newspapers reported that five men had been killed, all but one by gunfire. Only one of the dead was identified as a rioter.[80]

The day following the big fire was full of official activity. The Committee of Safety was flooded with applications to join; by nightfall, more than four thousand men had received their badges as special police and their distinctive white pick handle clubs. Coleman also organized a "Veterans Brigade" of eight hundred ex-Union and -Confederate soldiers and gave it a separate headquarters next to the Committee of Safety. More than ten thousand additional firearms were delivered from the Benicia Arsenal. On that night, with more men and weaponry ready than available in any eastern city, only two small fires were set, and both were quickly extinguished.

On the twenty-eighth, a force of several hundred police and Safety men with fixed bayonets escorted, from the dock to Chinatown, 138 Chinese who had just arrived on a Pacific Mail steamship. The "extra-ordinary pageant" attracted large crowds as it made its way through downtown streets, but it provoked no violence. On Sunday the twenty-ninth, Coleman relieved thousands of bored vigilantes from duty. Contingents of five men and an officer remained on call in each ward for another week. The "insurrection" was over, and only isolated acts of arson continued through the rest of the summer.

The end of the violence touched off a fierce debate about the merits of what had been done to quell the mob. As long as the city seemed in peril, political unity had prevailed. But in the final days of July, criticism of official actions began. Republican papers grumbled that lawbreakers were treated far too leniently. The *Chronicle* charged that Chief Ellis and William Coleman had allowed "several anti-coolie agitators" to join the Committee of Safety.[81] The *Alta* complained that only fifty rioters had been arrested, and questioned whether the presiding judge, Davis Louderback, whose anti-Chinese sentiments were notorious, would act to convict the guilty.[82]

On the other side, Democratic organs and others that spoke for the Anti-Coolie Clubs and trade unions belittled the seriousness of the riots and accused both Coleman and General McComb of seeking to increase their own power at the expense of the city's finances and patience. The *Post* took the city's incumbent Democratic administration to task for "surrendering by far too much . . . of their responsibility and their rights . . . to the hands of a body of men who . . . are in the eyes of the law irresponsible and without authority."[83] Questioning whether the Committee of Safety had even been necessary, the *Post* accused anonymous "civic captains" of shooting at unarmed crowds without attempting other methods of controlling them, a clear reference to the battle of Rincon Hill. The weekly *Illustrated Wasp,* in an article that staff member Ambrose Bierce may have written, commented wearily, "[N]ever was San Francisco so Committeed as during the past week." From inside the overcrowded and decrepit city jail, the anonymous reporter commented that it was "hardly right that persons charged with petty offences should suffer capital punishment."[84] Furthermore, a number of the "troops" were growing restless. A group of forty-eight Civil War veterans demanded to know when they would get paid.[85]

While white men were fighting to destroy or protect their property, the majority of the twenty thousand Chinese residents of San Francisco waited inside the narrow stores and apartments of Chinatown for the violence to end. The day of the Beale Street fire, a reporter from the *Chronicle* went to the Chinese district to interview some of the more prosperous members of the community. The whole neighborhood was boarded up, he wrote, and all money had been transferred to hiding places. Leaders of the Six Companies advised their contract workers to fight if attacked in Chinatown. An angry Chinese merchant told the reporter that the rioters were cowards. "They could attack a wash-shop in strength . . . and murder inoffensive Chinamen when they were twenty to one," the *Chronicle* man wrote, "but if they come to the Chinese quarter the Chinamen will not run."[86] Following the first night of violence, the Six Companies had purchased hundreds of rifles and hatchets for their men, and few rioters ventured into Chinatown during the entire week.

The only sign that the Chinese population of San Francisco was buckling under the strain was a sharp increase in the number of passengers returning to Asia on Pacific Mail steamships. In the last four months of 1877, more than twice as many Chinese returned home than had sailed back in the previous third of a year. And in September, as Denis Kearney began his oratorical offensive in the city hall sandlots, only ninety-four Chinese arrived in San Francisco, less than one-tenth the number of immigrants who had come from that country in July. Many more would depart over the next few years.[87]

The turbulence in the state's largest city frightened elected authorities and leading businessmen elsewhere in urban California. Across the bay in Oakland, thousands of unemployed workers gathered at nightly rallies on July 23 and 24, but no violence occurred. Nevertheless, that city's mayor and council set up their own Committee of Safety and recruited more than four thousand men to patrol the streets of what was the western terminus of the transcontinental railroad. The *Daily Stock Report* noted proudly that one company of Oakland's committee "numbers about 100 men and represents $10,000,000."[88] Before the end of the week, similar groups had been formed in San Diego, San Jose, and Sacramento—all with the generous support of local businesses. In none of the cities were there more than scattered attacks against Chinese immigrants.

The events in San Francisco had clearly provoked the fears and kindled the imaginations of many Californians. A letter writer from the small town of Vallejo, north of Oakland, reported on July 25 that "we can see on the street corners, narrow but compact groups of fours and fives attentively listening to the reading of the latest news from the Riot . . . which came with its murders and incendiarism, to make *even us* smell blood."[89]

* * *

What was the meaning of the July Days? Torn by conflict between two self-defined classes of whites and a Chinese population that appeared to be unified in its self-defense, San Franciscans tended to be vociferous in their opinions and strongly partisan in their politics. Their newspapers both engendered and reflected the passions of the time, as they did in other cities where the press had no rival as a forum for political debate, gossip, and innuendo. The seven English-language dailies were fiercely competitive in their zeal to give both a full report of the July Days and to explain what had happened and who was at fault. A contemporary business writer evaluated the press's impact in terms that might sound quaint to anyone raised in an era of instantly televised content: "Newspapers are, in truth, contemporary history," wrote Fred Hackett, "not always accurate, but none the less history . . . a terse newspaper paragraph is often quoted from Eastport to San Francisco and stirs up the hearts of millions."[90]

The majority of San Francisco dailies in the late 1870s took their ideology from the Jeffersonian-Jacksonian tradition of the Democratic Party. Democrats had often controlled California politics since statehood and had governed the city since 1873. But their press still spoke in the discourse of outsiders, blaming entrenched monopolies and plutocrats for grinding down the common man. This stance was particularly popular among white male wage earners. However, by the fall of 1877, many white workingmen were disgusted with the failure of the Democrats in power in city hall and the state house to lessen the pain they were feeling from Nob Hill businessmen and their Chinese employees. Stirrings that resulted in the formation of the Workingmen's Party of California later in the year were in the air by early August, and the Democratic press was responding to that as much as it was expounding a deeply felt perspective on recent events.

Democratic papers apologized for the riots, both in the East and the West, as the inevitable result of unjust treatment. On July 23, George Hearst's *Examiner,* the official organ of the party, commented, "when men are driven to desperation at the sight always before them of famishing women and children, they become as ravening as wolves." After unrest had gripped San Francisco and then subsided, the paper continued to blame big employers for provoking the violence. Behind the depression, the *Examiner* charged, was "the sinister influence of moneyed, landed and bonded plutocrats, in guilty partnership with venal and faithless representatives of the people," who, by their own policies, "have sown the dragon's teeth of civil commotion and possible revolution."[91]

The Democratic press consistently condemned the acts of the lawless while defending their beliefs. The July Days, they stated, should teach the employing class that Chinese labor would never be welcome in California. The weekly *Argonaut,* bewailing the armed escorting of Chinese laborers from their ship on July 28, was appalled that "the military . . . were held in readiness to shoot down our citizens, in event of interference with the immigrants." A Republican government, the magazine prophesied, could only survive as long as the native working class it ruled was content. "The government that does not provide work," intoned the *Argonaut,* "will be overthrown."[92]

While viewing the mass violence as a political lesson, the same publications paradoxically dismissed the size and seriousness of the riots. The *Argonaut* called them the "malicious mischief" of "a few hundred vicious boys,"[93] while the *Post* sought to refute the notion that any workingmen had belonged to a mob. "The disorders in this city have no class bias," the paper protested, "and the foolish talk which is too constantly going on does gross wrong to the industrial thousands upon whom rests . . . the whole fabric of material and economic society." Furthermore, it was claimed, San Francisco workingmen had no reason to disrupt the dominant order. Several papers stated that as many as 90 percent of the city's wage earners owned their own homes, and the *Post* invoked the image of the California dream when it claimed "a call for a meeting of laboring men in this city brings together men who would be classed among capitalists in any other city in the Union."[94]

Though their columns during the violence had been filled with details of fires and deaths, afterward, the Democratic press took pains to fault the Committee of Safety and the wealthy men who had initiated and supported it. In early August, the *Post* published a long eyewitness account of "Three Nights in the Ranks of the Safety Committee," written by a member of a Tenth Ward company. The anonymous correspondent had earnestly joined the "Pick-Handle Brigade," only to discover that his duties consisted of marching from place to place, hunting scarce rioters, and trying to stay awake on a diet of coffee and hardtack. He depicted his officers as pompous and incompetent. He and his fellow volunteers spent long hours discussing how their leaders would misuse the $70,000 that was donated for committee expenses. "I vote that Coleman has it for a senatorial fight," contributed one man, while the disgruntled group drank cold coffee with the grounds still in it served by Chinese servants, whom they detested. In a more serious tone, the *Post* inveighed against the bloodthirsty attitudes of prominent officers: "Mobocratic feelings displayed by men in broadcloth," the paper concluded, "are just as reprehensible as when they are displayed by men and boys in fustian and rags."[95]

Democratic officeholders and the workingmen's organizations they claimed to represent rushed to agree with such sentiments. Mayor Bryant, Governor Irwin, the Mechanics' State Council (which tried to coordinate the anti-Chinese activities of the area's troubled unions), and the local Anti-Coolie Clubs all depicted the riots as the actions of "thieves, idlers, and tramps" and denied that any of their constituents or members had been involved.[96] The "hoodlums" may have responded to anti-Chinese rhetoric, it was granted, but they did not help the cause of immigration restriction by their violent acts.

In sharp contrast, the two avowedly Republican papers in San Francisco—the *Alta* and the *Daily Stock Report*—proudly hailed the methods by which the riot was suppressed. Aware that they spoke for a majority of businessmen but for only a minority of voters, the two dailies saw the Committee of Safety as the necessary arm of solid citizens threatened by a half-crazed rabble interested only in anarchy and destruction. The *Stock Report* recommended that Coleman's organization be made permanent and that the police force should be vastly increased in size. It was indeed doubled that fall.

The Republican press saw the return to vigilantism in San Francisco as a model for the rest of the nation. "If all our cities are beset with considerable numbers of Communists, ready at the first opportunity to imitate the horrors of Paris," the *Alta* wrote, referring to the Commune of 1871, "they must be met with firmness."[97] The *Stock Report* lectured the authorities of Pittsburgh and Chicago on their failure to keep in check the railroad riots in their cities. If Committees of Safety had been organized in the East, the business paper admonished, the divisive effects of the militia would have been avoided. Several years later, William Coleman affirmed this position and then went on to contrast the welcome legitimacy of his committee of 1877 with the dubious legal standing of the vigilantes in 1856: "The greatest satisfaction given to Californians," Coleman wrote, "was that they had disproved the assertion often made that the Vigilance Committee was mobocratic and that Californians necessarily acted in an extra-judicial manner."[98]

Unlike the Democratic press, which denied that adult laborers had taken to the streets, conservative opinion makers directly attacked the manual working class directly. Hubert Howe Bancroft, historian and chronicler of the lives of California millionaires, blamed the unrest of the seventies on the unemployed, who "were, almost to a man, of foreign birth, and rarely of much intelligence."[99] Wealthy novelist Gertrude Atherton echoed Bancroft's opinion and added the charge that labor leaders were revolutionaries in search of a popular issue. "They were quite willing to appropriate all the capital in the state," she charged, "but as that drastic measure presented difficulties they concentrated on the unfortunate Mongolian."[100] In her account of the July Days, Atherton evinced no doubt that the riots were "to be a portentous uprising of the proletariat." Only the timely actions of "the superior class of citizens," she wrote, had stymied the evil designs of "the demagogues and their mistaken followers."[101]

The Republican press in 1877 was fighting to "civilize" a society that, since its birth, had been disorderly and rent with class and racial divisions. The merchants and manufacturers of San Francisco—the core of the party's support—agreed that Chinese restriction was inevitable; even the *Stock Report* felt the need to state its opposition to "the further introduction of Chinese."[102] But the nativist upsurge could not be allowed to disrupt moral discipline and civic peace. Thus, the minister of the opulent First Unitarian Church preached on the first Sunday after the riots that "the underground class . . . that do little else than burn and rob and howl and vote" was "the natural enemy of civilized man."[103] Thus, Committee of Safety leaders blamed skilled craftsmen for the participation of jobless boys in the riots, arguing that adult workers refused them training in order to keep wages high. According to the *Alta*, an unemployed youth automatically became a candidate for a life of hoodlumism, but, "Give the young employment, and they are like the bay that communicates with the healthy and purifying sea."[104]

There was a rational current to the anxieties of the newspapers, regardless of which major party they supported. White workers were quite serious about opposing politicians who did not move forcefully to curb Chinese competition and to stop new Asian immigrants from arriving. In the immediate aftermath of the violence, a thicket of small political groups briefly sprouted up in white working-class neighborhoods. There was a Workingmen's Party of San Francisco, a Workingmen's Municipal Convention, a Workingmen's Trade and Labor Union, and a National Labor Party (which, in spite of its grandiose name, was purely local in origin). Two months later, plebeian voters found a better vehicle to express their class antagonisms and to advocate a blatantly racist solution to their problems. The Workingmen's Party of California—led by the bombastic oratory of Denis Kearney—offered men from the South of Market neighborhood what one historian succinctly calls "a social movement which entered politics to achieve its objectives."[105] Though spokesmen for both major parties feared that the success of the WPC would initiate new and larger riots, the ascendancy of Kearney's organization, by legitimating the politics of white laborers, probably helped dissolve the frustrations that had led to the July Days.[106]

In 1879, pro-business residents of San Francisco viewed the mayoral victory of WPC nominee Isaac Kalloch as "the capture of the City by the enemy."[107] Ironically, the election was actually the Kearneyites' last hurrah. By 1880, after a series of spectacular trials, they faded away, bequeathing the legacy of a labor bloc that would elect candidates and promote pro-union legislation in San Francisco well into the twentieth century.[108]

In the history of mass violence in the nineteenth-century United States, the July Days of 1877 in San Francisco occupy a unique place. In contrast to the strike-inspired riot in Pittsburgh in 1877 and the draft riot in New York City in 1863, the toll of life and property in San Francisco was minimal. However, the western mob was remarkable for its single-mindedness of purpose and the impact its actions had on the ultimate success of its objectives.[109] Anti-Chinese riots had flared up before in California and the Far West and would again after 1877, particularly in rural areas. But because the July Days occurred in the unrivaled metropolis of the region, their significance was magnified. By inspiring the creation of a strong opposition to the major parties, the riots fused California politicians into an almost united body in the energetic movement for Chinese restriction.

Only a handful of labor activists spoke out for a different solution, arguing that the white working-class boys and men of San Francisco should turn their anger away from the relatively powerless Chinese and train it exclusively on major white employers. During the July Days, Patrick Healy, an organizer for the WPUS, counseled his class brethren to do just that in a letter to the *Post*. Healy blamed the "anti-coolie demagogues of this city" for inciting the poor to attack Chinese, and blamed the opportunistic rhetoric of Mayor Bryant, Governor Irwin, and "various other men in place and power" for inspiring violence against San Francisco's Asian minority.

Healy was hoping to change the subject. It was industrial capitalism itself that was the problem, he charged. With "labor-saving machinery," the Irish American bootmaker remarked, "the proprietors of large factories . . . can go on grinding out shoes and calico regardless of who had given years of their life to the acquirement of the technical knowledge necessary to follow such occupations in an individual capacity."[110] Healy was too realistic to propose an alliance between Chinese and white labor, but he did try to turn the attention of white working-class readers to changes in the political economy that he believed were largely responsible for their condition.

The opinions of Patrick Healy were never embodied in a significant political movement in late-nineteenth-century San Francisco. They provided no clear solution to the frustration and hunger for immediate relief that exploded in the streets of the city that July. White workingmen, many of whom had come to California from cities to the east and from Europe in search of a second chance, were unwilling to regard their misfortune as more than a temporary aberration.[111] In an environment long saturated with racialist ideology, the paucity of jobs and the miseries of daily life could easily be blamed on an alien people who worked for meager wages in shops and factories where whites had formerly been employed.

The widespread belief that Chinese "coolies" were the virtual slaves of their mercantile countrymen, rendering them passive and mentally inferior, motivated the righteous anger of men who took pride in their self-definition as "free laborers." By emphasizing Chinese restriction, white workers could retain the vision of an equality for members of their race alone, a notion that had ripened during the Jacksonian era and emerged strengthened after the divisive traumas of the Civil War. By blaming a group lower in status than themselves, the rioters of July convinced themselves that they were acting in the interests of an aggrieved majority. In so doing, they continued a tradition as old as the Democratic Party itself. They also presaged the right-wing populism of later groups of working- and middle-class white Americans. When, in 1968, George Wallace suggested that furious factory workers "with about a tenth-grade education" would make better governors than "genteel" politicians who coddled welfare mothers and sabotaged neighborhood schools, he was singing Denis Kearney's tune.[112]

Notes

1. This point is discussed in more detail in my article, "The Great Exception Revisited: Organized Labor and Politics in San Francisco and Los Angeles, 1870–1940," *Pacific Historical Review* 55 (August 1986): 382–84, and my book, *Barons of Labor: The San Francisco Building Trades and Union Power in the Progressive Era* (Urbana: University of Illinois Press, 1987), 162–71. On the concept of "whiteness" in labor history (inspired by David Roediger's well-known 1991 book, *The Wages of Whiteness*), see Eric Arnesen, "Whiteness and the Historians' Imagination," *International Labor and Working-Class History* 60 (fall 2001): 3–32, and responses by Eric Foner, Barbara Fields, James Barrett, and other distinguished scholars.

2. *San Francisco Alta California* (hereafter cited as *Alta*), July 23, 1877.

3. John Garraty, in his *The New Commonwealth, 1877–1890* (New York: Harper and Row, 1968), 130, claims wages on the West Coast were 40 percent higher than in the East; while Neal L. Shumsky, "Tar Flat and Nob Hill: A Social History of Industrial San Francisco During the 1870s" (Ph.D. diss., University of California, Berkeley, 1972), quotes Department of Labor figures for various trades in San Francisco and New York for 1870 and 1880 that show an average differential of 20 percent. See also Shumsky, *The Evolution of Political Protest and the Workingmen's Party of California* (Columbus: Ohio State University Press, 1991).

4. *San Francisco Daily Stock Report* (hereafter cited as *Stock Report*), July 27, 1877.

5. *San Francisco Evening Post* (hereafter cited as *Post*), July 24, 1877.

6. *San Francisco Chronicle* (hereafter cited as *Chronicle*), July 23, 1877.

7. See *Post,* July 23, 1877; *Illustrated Wasp* (hereafter cited as *Wasp*) 1, no. 52 (July 28, 1877): 2.

8. *Alta,* July 23, 1877.

9. Figures from U.S. Census, cited in Shumsky, "Tar Flat and Nob Hill," 49.

10. Ira B. Cross, *A History of the Labor Movement in California* (Berkeley: University of California Press, 1935), 96.

11. There is a large literature on the Workingmen's Party of California and Kearney's part in it. Illuminating accounts include Alexander Saxton, *The Indispensable Enemy: Labor and the Anti-Chinese Movement in California* (Berkeley: University of California Press, 1971), 113–56; Cross, *Labor Movement,* 88–129; Shumsky, *Evolution of Political Protest;* Philip J. Ethington, *The Public City: The Political Construction of Urban Life in San Francisco, 1850–1900* (Berkeley: University of California Press, 1994), 242–86.

12. Andrew Gyory argues that politicians in Washington seized on the issue of Chinese

exclusion as a way to mollify workers in California and elsewhere in the wake of the 1877 strike wave. Few white labor activists, he claims, demanded such a law. But the measure quickly became a staple of union legislative programs, both for the Knights of Labor and the new American Federation of Labor. See Gyory, *Closing the Gate: Race, Politics, and the Chinese Exclusion Act* (Chapel Hill: University of North Carolina Press, 1998).

13. For briefer accounts of the July Days, see Cross, *Labor Movement,* 89–93, and Shumsky, *Evolution of Political Protest,* 13–14, 131–39. On anti-Chinese violence, see Saxton, *Indispensable Enemy,* passim, and the forthcoming study by Jean Pfaelzer, *Driven Out: Roundups and Resistance of Chinese People in Rural California, 1850–1906.* My research was limited to accounts in the English-language press.

14. For a typical eastern description of the rioters, see *New York Times,* July 26, 1877; for the WPUS, see Howard H. Quint, *The Forging of American Socialism* (Indianapolis: Bobbs Merrill, 1953), 13–15. Robert Wiebe, *The Search for Order, 1877–1920* (New York: Hill and Wang, 1967), 10, agrees that most rioters were not "self-conscious wage-earners." On the brief but intense "Red scare" of late 1877 and 1878, see Gyory, *Closing the Gate,* 105.

15. Saxton, *Indispensable Enemy,* 115.

16. The individual arrest records, which would presumably be more authoritative than journalistic accounts, were destroyed in the massive fire that gutted San Francisco's City Hall just after the earthquake of 1906.

17. The official aggregate police arrest records for 1877 do exist in *San Francisco Municipal Reports for Fiscal Year 1877–78* (San Francisco: Board of Supervisors, 1878). They show that the total number of arrests for July 1877 was only slightly higher than the number for the following month of August—in which there were no riots. Only fourteen people were charged with "riot, rout, and unlawful assembly" in July 1877. It is possible that the police records only count persons arrested by the 150 members of the regular city force and not arrests by the more than three thousand "special officers" of the Committee of Safety. However, the newspapers record only fifty arrests by any authority.

18. The remaining eight men lived in several different neighborhoods north of Market Street. I could verify occupations for only eighteen of the men, ranging from a milkman to three common laborers. There was no correlation between occupation and residence (as many low-status job-holders lived north of Market as south of it).

19. From *In Their Place: White America Defines Her Minorities, 1850–1950,* eds. Lewis H. Carlson and George A. Colburn (New York: Wiley, 1972), 169–70; attributed to an Irish immigrant (no date given).

20. Shumsky, "Tar Flat and Nob Hill," 22.

21. Cross, *Labor Movement,* 60–61, 69. Cross states that one-fourth of the immigrants were trained only as unskilled factory hands.

22. Shumsky, "Tar Flat and Nob Hill," 23–24, 120. Gunther Barth, *Instant Cities: Urbanization and the Rise of San Francisco and Denver* (New York: Oxford University Press, 1975), passim.

23. Anson S. Blake, "A San Francisco Boyhood, 1874–1884," *California Historical Quarterly* 37, no. 3 (September 1958): 218–19.

24. Cross, *Labor Movement,* 69–71.

25. Shumsky, "Tar Flat and Nob Hill," 118.

26. *Stock Report,* July 26, 1877.

27. Cross, *Labor Movement*, 71; Frances Cahn and Valeska Barry, *Welfare Activities of Federal, State, and Local Governments in California, 1850–1934* (Berkeley: University of California Press, 1936), 199.

28. Saxton, *Indispensable Enemy*, 106.

29. See the union-by-union account in the pro-labor *Post*, July 21, 1877.

30. *San Francisco Morning Call* (hereafter cited as *Call*), July 5, 1877.

31. Alvin Averbach, "San Francisco's South of Market District, 1858–1958: The Emergence of a Skid Row," *California Historical Quarterly* 52, no. 3 (fall 1973): 197–99.

32. Shumsky, "Tar Flat and Nob Hill," 141.

33. Albert Shumate, "A Visit to Rincon Hill and South Park" (San Francisco: privately printed, 1963), 15–17. The invention of the cable car made possible the development of Nob Hill as a wealthy residential neighborhood.

34. Shumsky, "Tar Flat and Nob Hill," 137.

35. Ibid., 143.

36. Ibid., 139.

37. Guillermo Prieto, *San Francisco in the Seventies: The City as Viewed by a Mexican Political Exile* (in Spanish), trans. and ed. Edwin S. Morby (San Francisco: J. H. Nash, 1938), 75–76.

38. Letter of A. C. Ranger to Chief Henry H. Ellis, October 13, 1876, Bancroft Library, Berkeley, California.

39. *Post*, July 21, 23, and 25, 1877.

40. Quote from Iris Chang, *The Chinese in America: A Narrative History* (New York: Viking, 2003), 126.

41. Stuart C. Miller, *The Unwelcome Immigrant: The American Image of the Chinese, 1785–1882* (Berkeley: University of California Press, 1969), 163–65.

42. Special Committee on Chinese Immigration of the California State Senate, *Chinese Immigration: Its Social, Moral, and Political Effect* (Sacramento, Calif.: F. P. Thompson, 1878), 271.

43. Saxton, *Indispensable Enemy*, details the history of the early California labor movement in relation to the Chinese. Pioneer labor historian John Commons reflected the inaccuracy as well as the racism of many white workers when he commented in 1918: "The anti-Chinese agitation in California was . . . doubtless the most important single factor in the history of American labor, for without it, the entire country might have been overrun by Mongolian labor, and the labour movement might have become a conflict of races instead of one of classes." Quoted in Isabella Black, "American Labour and Chinese Immigration," *Past and Present* 25 (July 1963): 73.

44. Cross, *Labor Movement*, 136.

45. Saxton, *Indispensable Enemy*, 75–76.

46. Quoted in Elmer C. Sandmeyer, *The Anti-Chinese Movement in California* (Urbana: University of Illinois Press, 1939), 59. On taking office on December 4, 1875, Bryant had pushed through the Board of Supervisors a host of anti-Chinese measures later found unconstitutional (as with most such laws passed since 1850). Bryant's restrictions included a 2 A.M. curfew on San Francisco sidewalks. See Oscar Lewis, *San Francisco: Mission to Metropolis* (Berkeley: University of California Press, 1966), 139.

47. Victor G. and Brett de Bary Nee, *Longtime Californ': A Documentary Study of an American Chinatown* (Boston: Houghton Mifflin, 1974), 47.

48. Quoted in Carlson and Colburn, *In Their Place,* 170–71.

49. *S.F. Municipal Reports,* 1877–78, 59–60; Henry G. Langley, *The San Francisco Directory for the Year Commencing March, 1877* (San Francisco: privately published, 1877), 1082–83.

50. *S.F. Municipal Reports,* 1877–78, 73–82.

51. 1877 *City Directory,* 1082–83; Hugh Quigley, *The Irish Race in California and on the Pacific Coast* (San Francisco: A. Roman and Co., 1878), 265.

52. Quigley, *Irish Race,* 264–65.

53. Frank Roney, *An Autobiography,* ed. Ira B. Cross (Berkeley: University of California Press, 1931), 268. Roney was a prominent socialist and trade-unionist in late-nineteenth-century San Francisco.

54. *Call,* July 23, 1877.

55. *Call,* July 24, 1877; *Post,* July 23, 1877.

56. *Chronicle,* July 24, 1877; Cross, *Labor Movement,* 89.

57. *Alta,* July 26, 1877; Quint, *Forging,* 14.

58. The following narrative is based on accounts published in San Francisco's daily newspapers and the secondary sources already cited, including Cross, *Labor Movement,* 89–93; Roney, *Autobiography,* 268–69; and Bruce, *1877: Year of Violence,* 267–68. In order to retain the flow of the narrative, citations will be provided only for additional sources or for a direct quotation.

59. *Alta,* July 24, 1877.

60. *Call,* July 24, 1877.

61. See Martha Mabie Gardner, "Working on White Womanhood: White Working Women in the San Francisco Anti-Chinese Movement, 1877–1890," *Journal of Social History* 33 (1999): 73–95.

62. Ibid.

63. *Chronicle,* July 24, 1877.

64. *Call,* July 24, 1877.

65. *Alta,* July 24, 1877.

66. Hubert Howe Bancroft, *History of the Life of William T. Coleman: A Character Study* (San Francisco: The History Company, 1891), 350–51; Ethington, *The Public City,* 106–8, 144–45.

67. *Call,* July 25, 1877.

68. William Coleman, "San Francisco Vigilance Committee," *Century Magazine* 43 (November 1891): 133–50, published in *The San Francisco Vigilance Committee of 1856: Three Views,* ed. Doyce B. Nunis Jr. (Los Angeles: Los Angeles Westerners, 1971), 40.

69. *Alta,* July 25, 1877.

70. *Stock Report,* July 25, 1877.

71. *Alta,* July 25, 1877.

72. *Post,* July 25, 1877.

73. Coleman/Nunis, *S.F. Vigilance Committee,* 40.

74. *Chronicle,* July 26, 1877.

75. *Post,* July 26, 1877.

76. 1878 *City Directory* for San Francisco, 23; Blake, "A San Francisco Boyhood," 219.

77. *The Spark* (weekly), July 29, 1877, 2.

78. *Call,* July 26, 1877.

79. Ibid.

80. The fullest report of casualties is in the *Post,* July 26, 1877. Of the twenty-five reported wounded from the Rincon Hill battle (there were probably many more), seventeen were injured by gunfire and the rest by rocks.

81. *Chronicle,* July 26, 1877.

82. *Alta,* July 28, 1877; for Louderback's vehement racism, see his testimony in California State Senate, *Chinese Immigration,* 158–59. In fact, the majority of the accused were convicted, though no rioter was sentenced to more than a year in jail.

83. *Post,* July 30, 1877.

84. *Wasp,* August 4, 1877, 12. The back page of the same issue contains a pastel drawing of the Beale Street fire of July 25, 1877.

85. Letter from C. Mason Kinne (officer in the state militia) to Chief Henry H. Ellis, July 30, 1877, Mss. #657, Ellis Papers, California Historical Society, San Francisco.

86. *Chronicle,* July 26, 1877.

87. *S.F. Municipal Reports, 1877–78,* 258; Chang, *Chinese in America,* 128.

88. *Stock Report,* July 28, 1877.

89. *The Spark,* July 28, 1877, 2.

90. Hackett, *Industries of San Francisco,* 50.

91. *San Francisco Examiner,* July 23, 28, 1877.

92. *Argonaut* (weekly) 1, no. 20 (August 4, 1877): 4.

93. Ibid.

94. *Post,* July 26, 28, 1877. Also see *Argonaut* 1, no. 19 (July 28, 1877): 4.

95. *Post,* August 4, July 27, 1877.

96. Heintz, *San Francisco's Mayors,* 102–3; Saxton, *Indispensable Enemy,* 115; *Call,* July 29, 1877; *Post,* July 26, 1877. As Saxton notes, Coleman agreed with these views as well. Though a "hard-liner," he was too smart a politician to condemn, even indirectly, a majority of the voting population.

97. *Alta,* July 26, 1877.

98. Nunis/Coleman, *S. F. Vigilance Committee,* 43.

99. Hubert Howe Bancroft, *History of California,* vol. 7 (San Francisco: History Company, 1890), 351.

100. Gertrude Atherton, *California: An Intimate History* (New York: Harper and Brothers, 1914), 289.

101. Ibid., 294.

102. *Stock Report,* July 31, 1877.

103. Sermon of Reverend Horatio Stebbins, quoted in *Call,* July 30, 1877. The 1877 City Directory called Stebbins's $115,000 church "one of the most beautiful structures our city contains, and is remarkable for the purity of its architectural design and its interior beauty"(1054). No Protestant church in the city cost as much to build. Richard Hofstader describes the Protestant clergy as being "bloodthirsty in its reaction" to the 1877 strikes and riots; Richard Hofstadter, *Age of Reform* (New York: Knopf, 1955), 150.

104. *Alta,* July 28, 1877.

105. Shumsky, "Tar Flat and Nob Hill," 252.

106. Ibid., 310. Shumsky finds that the WPC was a unifying force in San Francisco because it "released the energy which produced the July riots."

107. Blake, "A San Francisco Boyhood," 224.

108. See Saxton, *Indispensable Enemy*, 139–52, and my *Barons of Labor: The San Francisco Building Trades and Union Power in the Progressive Era* (Urbana: University of Illinois Press, 1987).

109. According to the *Chronicle*, July 29, 1877, forty-one washhouses in all were raided, accounting for $50,000 of damage to Chinese property. Materials and buildings destroyed on the night of July 25 on the Beale Street wharf amounted to about $100,000 in value. As far as we know, seven people were killed during the riots in San Francisco. In contrast, the violence in Pittsburgh caused $5,000,000 damage to railroad property alone, and more than fifty people were killed. In the 1863 New York draft riots, several hundred were killed, and property destruction was in the millions of dollars.

110. Letter to *Post*, July 25, 1877.

111. See the discussion on this point in Shumsky, "Tar Flat and Nob Hill," 17–18.

112. See the classic arguments on this point in regard to blacks in George M. Frederickson, *The Black Image in the White Mind: The Debate on Afro-American Character and Destiny, 1817–1914* (Hanover, N.H.: Wesleyan University Press, 1987), 130–64, and in Saxton, *Indispensable Enemy*, 19–45. For a discussion of Wallace and his ilk, see my *The Populist Persuasion: An American History*, rev. ed. (Ithaca, N.Y.: Cornell University Press, 1998), 220–42.

6. California's Changing Society and Mexican American Conceptions of the Great Strike

DAVID MILLER

El Jefe de Policía concentró anoche su fuerza en nuestra ciudad, para estar listo en cualquier emergencia que pudiera ocurrir con motivo de los acontecimientos que tienen en alarma al resto del país.
—*La Crónica,* July 28, 1877

[Last night the police chief concentrated his city forces to be ready for whatever emergency could occur induced by the events that have alarmed the rest of the country.]

On the night of Friday July 20, 1877, fire razed the Southern Pacific Railroad Hotel located adjacent to the Los Angeles depot. This clandestine attack on railroad property occurred under the cover of darkness, absent the public spectacle that accompanies mob action. In fact, no Los Angeles newspaper reported if authorities ever apprehended the arsonists. But the event, along with news of the violent strikes in the East, raised concern sufficiently to result in a specially organized "police guard" at the city depot by the following weekend intended to prevent potential outbreaks of violence. The chief of police, "ready for whatever emergency," ordered the engines out of the roundhouse with boilers lit. The volunteer force then patrolled railroad property every night until the eastern strikes had ended.[1]

Meanwhile, events just west of the city in Santa Monica further reveal the limited commitment Angelenos had to disrupting railroad operations. On July 23, a determined and unusually large crowd descended on the Santa Monica Railroad, jamming city trains and demanding admittance. These patrons came not in protest but in their shared desire to escape the summer heat by traveling to local beaches.[2] Hardly the mob of Baltimore or Buffalo, the largest gathering in Los Angeles looked to the railroad for summer recreation. The only attack in Santa Monica came on the twenty-fifth. The *Santa Barbara Daily Press* reported that on Wednesday an unidentified assailant sabotaged the Santa Monica Railroad by cutting a signpost and laying it across the tracks. Fortuitously discovered by passers-by, the potentially deadly roadblock was quickly removed and resulted in no harm to any trains or passengers. A July 27 telegraph to California railroad baron Collis Huntington declared "the best of feeling among railroad employees all along the line" and that the potential for violence was low.[3]

The eastern strike and uprisings in San Francisco did make for a tense several days in Los Angeles and San Diego. But just like the limited violence targeting railroads, labor rallies similarly created a lot of smoke and little fire. For one, the major Californian railroads acted quickly to assuage their workers, rescinding an earlier decision to cut wages and effectively extinguished any potential labor trouble. Rather than protest their own wages, several working groups met in Los Angeles during the last two weeks of July to address the situation in the East. These meetings remained small and received limited mention in the city press. But in the wake of San Francisco's mob violence and the increasing momentum of the region's Granger and Workingmen's movements, tension surrounding the labor meetings grew. By the first week of August, the *Los Angeles Star* reported that a particular meeting had induced the formation of yet another police force of about one hundred men to serve, if needed, to prevent a riot. The *Star* attributed the precaution to rumors that "the roughs" from San Francisco had traveled south and might instigate violence in Los Angeles and Santa Barbara Counties. The Los Angeles press rebuked sensational reports in San Diego's papers that fear and mob rule had gripped the city. The "roughs" never appeared, the meeting ended uneventfully, and all the apprehension "amounted to nothing."[4]

With the notable exception of anti-Chinese violence in San Francisco, Californians reacted to news of the strike in discourse rather than in action. As a result, southern California might at first appear far less significant relative to the radical demonstrations in the East. It is no surprise that historians of the Great Strike have paid little attention to California. However, the strike assumes a new meaning when we reconsider the long-absent voices in southern California because the Great Strike is more than labor history. In California, those who wrote about it were not just industrial workers, they were "white" and "nonwhite"; laborers and Rancheros; Americans and Mexicans.

I argue that despite a lack of strike-related action, southern Californians remained far from passive, engaging in a sustained debate about relevant issues of labor, capitalist development, and race. The press turned the strike into a forum of important civic debate suggesting how the strike, the end of Reconstruction, and new labor questions were framed in a multiethnic West. The dialogue it created tells historians something about the meaning of the strike to southern Californians in a time of rapid social and economic change.

Framing the strike in the workplace, among the roundhouses and engineers, limits the conclusions one can draw about the diverse meanings of the strike. Scholars are increasingly expanding their search. David Stowell's work, by placing the action in city streets, allows historians to consider the meaning of the strike in a new way. It was not only important as a blow by workers against the strains of capitalism in the workplace, it was also a blow by common citizens against the strains of capitalism in the social space of the streets and community. Though the historiography of the strike has recently expanded to include social and urban history, consideration of race and the West remains conspicuously absent from this body of literature.

This essay explores the Great Strike of 1877 from the experience of southern Californians, especially people of Mexican descent.[5] It takes the action out of the workplace and instead locates it in the rhetoric and dialogue among southern Californians. Events outlined in this essay will contribute to a broader understanding of the Great Strike of 1877 by offering discussion of these heretofore-neglected aspects by placing the Great Strike within the context of southern California's anti-Chinese movement, regional and transcontinental railroad debates, and Mexicans' struggles against the onslaught of white hegemony.

Events in southern California also complicate the notion of the strike as a watershed moment in labor and industrial history.[6] Californians had faced the intrusion of capitalist development for decades. By 1877, Mexican Americans were near the culmination of a three-decade-long struggle to resist white hegemony. Mexican Americans had become, in David Weber's term, "foreigners in their native land."[7] To them, the strike served as another defensive moment in this struggle, and thus cannot be considered a breaking point with the past.

Recent scholarship on the railroad, the Compromise of 1877, and the end of Reconstruction in the South highlights the tensions of capitalist development and racial equality in a democratic society.[8] Events in southern California suggest likewise: that a new synthesis of the strike's legacy would interpret the strike within the context of Reconstruction and the transcontinental railroad debate in southern California as a particularly salient moment in the ongoing struggle in United States history between capital, labor, and race. By 1877 southern Californians were engaged in a sustained campaign to bring a second transcontinental line while debating the consequences of the early stages of massive railroad development and capitalist expansion. Meanwhile,

Chinese laborers were becoming the "indispensable enemy" to white workers, and Californios lost much of their land, culture, and authority.[9]

Mexicans, Anglos, and the California Railroads

We begin our survey of the Great Strike not in 1877 but when the United States obtained California in 1848. The Spanish (1769–1821) and Mexican (1822–48) governments oversaw California's development into an agrarian society based primarily on subsistence farming and, later in the south, large cattle ranches. Spanish institutions mixed with indigenous peoples formed the foundation of California's society and culture. When possession of California transferred to the United States, a fifty-year transition from "Mexican" to "American" California began.[10]

The gradual loss of Mexican authority to Anglos resulted from a complex interaction of several factors, not the least of which involved dramatic demographic shifts. The discovery of gold in 1848 created an almost overnight change in the state's population. The Mexican majority in northern California, consisting of about eight thousand in 1849, quickly became the minority when more than one hundred thousand "forty-niners" flocked to the gold fields. Though many Mexicans attempted to immigrate to northern California (between five and ten thousand by the 1850s), violence and discriminatory laws drove the majority from the diggings. In fact, Mexicans succumbed to the same legislation that victimized the Chinese. As a result, native and foreign Mexicans returned home to Mexico, but others traveled south to Santa Barbara and Los Angeles, where they would remain the majority population until the 1860s.[11]

The Mexican way of life in politics, culture, and the economy slowly gave way to Anglo institutions, the result being the gradual distancing of native Californios from the centers of political and economic authority. A process in which Anglos increasingly identified Mexicans as nonwhite, characterized by their supposed inherent laziness and role as shiftless outsiders, accompanied the gradual loss of Californios' political and property rights.[12] Meanwhile, Mexicans of all classes, native and immigrant, increasingly performed menial labor.[13] Thus, California's Mexican population simultaneously lost their rights as American citizens, their economic status, and their "white" identity.

Of course, Mexicans did not allow these threats and changes to go unchallenged. Historians have identified at least three models of Mexican survival strategies: "separation," "accommodation," and "the third space." Mexican Californians who *separated* resisted white authority by rejecting Anglo institutions completely. But peaceful separation also meant exclusion from authority in Anglo civic life. For example, in order to divide the electorate in Los Angeles, Anglos gerrymandered voting districts where many Mexicans had grouped together in barrios. This effectively removed Californios and Mexicans from party politics by 1880, whether as candidates or voters.[14]

Those Mexicans who adopted English, formed business arrangements with Anglos, and utilized Anglo courts and social systems, *accommodated* to Anglo culture and social norms rather than fought against them. Unlike in Los Angeles, many Californio leaders in San Diego accommodated to the Anglo takeover as a means of protecting their own interests. When, for example, Anglo legal culture dominated court proceedings, many Californio property owners abandoned the Iberian system to dispute their losses in American courts. Others, San Diegan Juan Bandini being perhaps the most successful, entered into lucrative business partnerships with prominent Anglos.[15]

But the majority of Mexican Californians occupied a *third space,* accommodating to some Anglo institutions and at the same time maintaining many separate culturally Mexican ones. The third space tactic was often difficult because Mexicans had to negotiate the middle ground with important choices every day. How would they fight for political participation? How would they identify themselves? The range of responses was broad, but Mexicans increasingly identified themselves as Mexican Americans, spoke both English and Spanish, and sought to incorporate issues specific to their needs into political debate. Recent scholarship suggests that rather than have "whiteness" thrust upon them, "many Southwest Hispanic elites were white or passed for white using Mexican, not Anglo criteria." In this way, Mexicans were agents shaping the terms of a white identity "to resist the annihilation of their own class."[16]

Coverage of the strike in the Hispanic press suggests another example of this third space tactic to define the terms of their whiteness. Though Anglo institutions, labor and economic structures, as well as race and class ideologies provided the context within which Mexicans would have to operate, Mexicans themselves shaped and defined them to their advantage. Assertions of whiteness were an important defensive weapon for California's Mexican population in 1877 because by the early 1880s, Mexicanos and Mexican Americans had become "people of color" to most Anglos.[17]

The tension between legal ideals and ideological realities led many Mexican Americans to appropriate the rhetoric defining the Anglo white working class.[18] This survival tactic of asserting Anglo- and European-oriented conceptions of whiteness has a long history in southern California, extending as far back as the Spanish period. Californios emphasized their European blood to distinguish themselves from indigenous populations. A number of Mexicans tried again in the 1850s to reassert that whiteness, but this time in terms of free-labor ideology. This legacy mixed in 1877 with new paradigms of American whiteness and resulted in what I argue was for some a conscious effort to critique capitalism while aligning with an American white citizenry.

During the presidential campaign of 1856, many Mexicans in Los Angeles attempted to link themselves with the larger body of Anglo white workers by accepting the racialized components of free-labor ideology. The logic of free-labor ideology for Republicans in 1856 necessarily meant the preservation of wage labor and free land for white men.[19] Anglos in California utilized the rhetoric of white exceptionalism to justify claims to the traditional lands of ranchero elites. In return, Californios attempted to identify themselves as white while distinguishing themselves as something *other* than black. The political debate in *El Clamor Publico*, the leading Hispanic and Republican organ in Los Angeles during the 1850s, shows how Californios appropriated racialized political rhetoric employed against them for their own use.

Early in the campaign, *El Clamor* editorials included the white supremacy embedded in free-labor ideology by connecting *"la raza blanca"* to "free labor." The editors elaborated on the intent of the Republican campaign and weighed in on the heated abolition debate, arguing that the party "opposes the extension of black slavery, within our national territories, as it [slavery] conflicts with the work interests of free whites, with the development of national resources, [and] as it raises resistance to the absorption of the National territories for the white race [people]. . . ." Frequent editorials mentioned "the security of the white race" and "the preservation of the national territories for colonization of the free white race." One letter to the editor, received from a recent immigrant to Los Angeles, articulated the point clearly. The author declared, "I am not any rabid abolitionist. I believe firmly in the non-extension of slavery, if the settlement so desires it." In this way, the newspaper offered an appeal—in Spanish—to the Mexican community that placed them within the ideological body of white citizens uniting the Republican Party.[20]

I speculate that many Californios aligned themselves with the Republican Party in 1856 because its ideology provided a space to negotiate whiteness. Disproportionately high election returns in southern California suggest that the Republicans received strong Mexican support.[21] But Mexican Americans did not vote for the Republican candidate John Fremont, abolitionism, or the Republican's nationalization agenda. Californios voted for the opportunity to unite with whites that the highly racialized free-labor ideology offered. By identifying with Republican Party ideology and denying a "colored" identity (which Democrats projected onto Mexicans), Mexican Californians could place themselves in the shared racial community of the majority of white northerners and their "white" California neighbors.

Thus Mexicans, since the 1850s, set a precedent of negotiated accommodation and conceptions of whiteness framed in terms of Anglo political economy. A similar, though slightly different, process unfolded in 1877 as new labor questions emerged, debate about a transcontinental railroad raged, and hostility against the Chinese increased. By 1877 California had suffered a significant depression aggravated by the presence of the railroad linking the West to eastern markets. Farmers, railroad barons, politicians, and a growing labor movement stood at odds over how best to solve the problem of California's economy.[22]

Debate regarding abusive monopolies, land fraud, regional economic development, and a southern transcontinental railroad stood at the forefront of California's political agenda on the eve of the Great Strike of 1877. In the spring one year prior to the Great Strike, Charles Pickett outlined many of the central political issues facing the residents of California. Pickett, in a series of letters and speeches addressed to the people of California, articulated what many believed was the corruption and economic subjugation the Central Pacific Railroad unleashed on California. The Central Pacific had used its power, he explained, to influence and corrupt the political operations of the state. The people must arise, he urged, utilizing Congress and appropriate legal channels to end the abuse. In addition, Pickett pointed out that because Mexican grants covered much of the Central Pacific's land, the corporation resorted to extortion to obtain the land shares. He also argued for a second transcontinental railroad, south along the thirty-second parallel, in order to end the Central Pacific's economic subordination of southern California. A second line would effectively end the Central Pacific's monopoly and thereby reduce prices and rates, increasing commerce in southern California.[23]

Looking to familiarize themselves with their new opportunities, immigrants to California just one month prior to the strike may have obtained and read "The Lands of the Southern Pacific Railroad Company of California." The Southern Pacific Railroad's pamphlet, directed to perspective landowners and immigrants, advertised the nearly twenty thousand square miles of corporate land for sale. The pamphlet reassured immigrants that low wages, the Chinese threat, and the accusations made of corporate land monopolies were not significant problems in California. While on the eve of the strike southern Californians still worried about the problems Pickett identified, they increasingly added the "Chinese threat" to that list.

According to the Southern Pacific, California offered settlers the best possible prospect for economic independence. Land, business, agriculture, and climate were all better than in any other part of the West. The railroad also discounted claims that its land monopoly denied farmers the chance to own land. Citing national tenant rates, the pamphlet claimed that California had the lowest laborer to farm ratio in the nation, at two to one. This appeal to the yeoman ideal reminded settlers that "it is better to be poor for a few years on your own land than to be moderately poor as a tenant for others."

The guarantee of success was made all the more certain by Mexico and the greater Southwest's rapid integration into the regional economy. Subtly referring to the Southern Pacific's own plans, the pamphlet noted that it is "considered a certainty" that a railroad would be built from Texas. Indeed, the Southern Pacific's president, Collis Huntington, had been battling Tom Scott for command of the southern route since he assumed control of the Texas & Pacific Railroad in 1871. Huntington attempted to cement his claim by arguing that the "inhabitants of Mexico will do much to enrich Southern California." "There must be a railroad from Mazatlan to Yuma," connecting Mexico to Los Angeles, Sacramento, and Puget Sound, thereby creating "one of the most important channels of travel and trade on the continent." To the Southern Pacific, the claim of Mexican integration into the southwestern economy by way of the railroad was a means of reassuring prospective land-owners of the future viability of the region and their own livelihoods.

The Southern Pacific also claimed that the Chinese did not pose a threat to the white worker. "Wages are higher in California than in any other part of the world," the pamphlet declared, besting the rates in the Atlantic states by nearly two times and Europe by as much as three. Future workers need not worry about a degraded state of white labor. The Chinese were paid "higher wages than are paid to persons in the same occupation in the Atlantic states" and they "own little land, labor little on their own account, and have not engaged in any of the higher mechanical pursuits." In short, the pamphlet underplayed one of the most volatile issues in California, arguing that the reality of large numbers of Chinese laborers did not threaten the future success of white Americans. Reaction to the strike suggests that the majority of Californians did not share the Southern Pacific's confidence.

Of course, the pamphlet is much more problematic than its authors wished to acknowledge. Much of the land for sale came to the Central Pacific by way of seized Mexican lands, despite claims to the contrary. And many of the purchasers were not independent families, but large-scale corporate agriculture that eventually challenged and displaced independent producers. In addition, many white Californians continued to blame the Chinese for the perceived threat of low wages and the real condition of high unemployment.[24]

The Strike and the Great Debate of 1877

> Until this Chinese problem is solved on principle[s] that will
> secure our working-classes from the evils of degrading and ruinous
> competition with the hordes of pariahs now inundating our coast
> there will always be danger of sudden and serious disorder.
>
> —Los Angeles *Evening Express,* August 11, 1877

> Con las huelgas de obreros en el Este ha coincidido el movimiento
> anti-chino en California y los disturbios en San Francisco; pero
> uno y otro movimiento son independientes entre si; no tienen
> punto de contacto mas de que una cosa, y es que lo mismo la
> immigración de chinos aqui como la opresión de las corporaciones
> alla redunda en perjucio del proletario.
>
> —*La Crónica,* August 1, 1877

> [The workers' strikes in the East have coincided with the anti-
> Chinese movement in California and the disturbances in San
> Francisco. But both movements are independent; they do not
> have more than one meeting point, it is the same that Chinese
> immigration here and corporate oppression there results in the
> harm of the proletariat.]

> It is enough to say that the outbreak is one of the best evidences
> that could be given us against the idea of railroad monopolies, and
> that those we have should be controlled.
>
> —*San Diego Press,* July 26, 1877

Coverage of the strike in the southern California press became a forum to negotiate the contested issues of race, citizenship, railroad monopolies, and capitalist development. Analysis of that debate reveals a range of responses and interpretations between both Anglo and Mexican populations. Both offered a labor-oriented critique of the strike, but in decidedly racialized terms. Leading Hispanic papers linked the strike to California's debate about Chinese labor, articulating a white identity and thus allying themselves with the nascent Workingmen's movement. The strike also became a means to critique capitalism in general and challenge the power of California's railroad monopoly in particular. Mexican papers articulated a vision of class antagonism, while Anglos believed in the ultimate cooperation of capital and labor. Both groups, however, agreed on the need for government intervention in the economy and direct regulation of California's railroad. Southern Californians also used the strike to make new arguments in favor of a second, southern, transcontinental railroad. Ultimately, the strike served as an impetus for widespread discontent as economic development became intricately tied to notions of whiteness and exclusion.[25]

California's vitriolic anti-Chinese movement framed the labor critique of the strike. Not surprisingly, Anglo papers quickly related the labor unrest in the East to the racist elements of the perceived "labor problem" in California. The *Express* invoked the violence of the strike to further the anti-Chinese cause. The paper characterized the riots in the East as "epidemic" in that they "spread from place to place as if they had been connected with each other by a train of inflammable sympathy." Such was not the case in California. According to the *Express,* the San Francisco riots had ended with much less destruction than might have been were it not for the "good people" of the city. But, "had a serious riot got headway in that city [San Francisco]," the *Express* reasoned, "there is no telling how disastrous an influence it might have had elsewhere." Noting that labor in California "has not reached the same degree of hardship that it has in the thickly populated Atlantic states," the paper warned that there still remained "in our midst an ever-present cause of discontent and source of injury to labor . . . which may yet cause us very serious trouble on this coast." The editors concluded, "Until this Chinese problem is solved on principle[s] that will secure our working-classes from the evils of degrading and ruinous competition with the hordes of pariahs now inundating our coast there will always be danger of sudden and serious disorder."[26] To the Anglo press, Californians had narrowly escaped disaster in the summer of 1877. Most important, the causes of the strike suggested that they might not be so lucky if their own "labor problem" was not soon resolved.

Relatively few Chinese lived in San Diego in 1877, but San Diegans, much like their Los Angeles neighbors, nonetheless linked themselves to the statewide discussion of "the labor question." The *Press,* throughout the week of the most prominent coverage of the strike, reported on anti-Chinese actions throughout the state. Most important, San Diego Democrats could support the Los Angeles Democrats' anti-Chinese and anti-monopoly platform while cheering reports from Oakland that a crowd had demanded the Central Pacific fire all Chinese workers.[27] In this way, the *Press* linked San Diegans to the larger imagined body of white Californians agitating against the Chinese. The extent of anti-Chinese rhetoric in a city with a relatively small Chinese population also suggests how the strike fanned the flames of racialized labor antagonism throughout the state.

The *Los Angeles Evening Express* explained that the strike offered a solution to "the labor problem" in California. The *Express* reasoned that the strike's "evil has a deeper root" than simply a few upset wage earners. Technological advancement and the concomitant increase in productivity had not enjoyed a correlated rise in consumption because wages had decreased. Wages had decreased because a glut in the labor market meant labor was willing to accept pay cuts. The *Express* reasoned that the market needed to cut production by instituting an eight-hour workday. The paper then took the significant step of applying the same logic to California, reasoning that unemployed white men could not get jobs the Chinese had taken, creating a situation where only three in every four men were currently employed. "We are glad to see that the movement to give preference to white labor in industries that have heretofore been wholly monopolized by the Chinese, is gaining ground." The editors continued, "There is enough work for all our white people, but there is not enough if a great portion is given to Mongolians." The paper called on the railroads to dismiss and repatriate all Chinese labor because "their example would soon be followed by all other corporations."[28] Ridding the state of excess Chinese laborers would ensure full white employment, keeping wages high and the likelihood of violent riots low.

Anglos in southern California took the opportunity to rhetorically connect events in the East with "the labor problem," concluding that the Chinese represented a threat to white workers similar to ethnic workers in the East. Anglos refrained from targeting Mexican laborers and thus presented an interpretation of the strike with which Mexicans could agree. The Hispanic press blamed labor and wage injustice on the Chinese workforce and in so doing united Mexican workers with their Anglo counterparts.

La Crónica connected directly the eastern strikes with the question of Chinese labor in California, concluding that both represented a threat to the working class. *La Crónica* asserted a decidedly racialized argument with regards to the anti-Chinese movement in California and the Workingmen's movement in San Francisco. The paper claimed that events in the East and the labor movement in California, although occurring at the same time, had "no more than one meeting point" in common: both the immigration of the Chinese in California and the oppression of corporations in the East resulted in the harm of the proletariat. Mexicans had been victimized because the presence of the Chinese in California had been a hindrance "to our progress in the most important branches of our wealth." The solution to the Chinese problem followed from the same logic *La Crónica* applied to the strike. Editors suggested that legislatures needed to oppose Asian immigration, although they had been "delinquent" to remedy the situation. Whether in the Hispanic *Crónica* or Anglo *Express,* Los Angeles's Hispanic population both articulated and received a view of the strike consistent with the anti-Chinese rhetoric sweeping the state in the summer of 1877.[29]

Anti-Chinese rhetoric in the Hispanic press did not end with the strike, nor was it limited to southern California. The Hispanic press continued to support the racialized arguments of both the Workingmen's movement and Democratic Party. San Francisco's *La Voz del Nuevo Mundo* encouraged its readers to support the "anti-coolie" Democratic candidate to the party's nominating convention, Mr. Taylor. San Franciscans read, "For our part, we hope that all our friends give their vote in his favor as an act of justice and a tribute to his merit." The paper also advised its readers that "Hispanic-Americans of the city" had worked "with unflagging toil for the triumph of his candidacy."[30] But the strike was discussed in broader terms than simply an elegant warning of California's racialized "labor problem."

Both Anglo and Hispanic papers generally recognized the strike as a crisis in capitalism and sympathized with the striking workers, coloring the strike as a "giant struggle between capital and labor."[31] But the Hispanic press rejected the idea that because capital and labor shared mutual interests the consequence of the strike would be equally burdensome. This position was becoming increasingly common after a more immediate challenge to free-labor ideology appeared following the Civil War. Two competing visions of political economy were emerging, one based on free labor and the notion that shared interests of capital and labor would increase production, and the other that argued capital and labor were in fact inherently at odds. Rhetoric of the strike suggests that though many Anglos clung to the older belief, Mexicans were asserting an ideology of class conflict.[32]

La Crónica, referring to the strike as "the battle between capital and labor" and sympathizing with an "enslaved proletariat," suggested to its readers the tension inherent in capitalist transformation. In addition, *La Crónica* recognized that the strikers would suffer again when it came time to pay for the damage they wrought. Reflecting on the strike in an August editorial, the editors concluded that it had not accomplished any lasting change because the strikers, not government or corporations, would pay for property damage. Corporations had emerged relatively unharmed. The strike had revealed, *La Crónica* lamented, capital's "double domination over the proletariat."[33]

In a lengthy *La Crónica* editorial, Angelenos read an important interpretation of events that reveals much about Mexican sensibilities in 1877. Conscious of the "serious and grave" topic, the editors argued that the strikes, now over, required extended study and presented "an eloquent warning to the proletariat." Criticizing the process of the consolidation of capital, the editors noted that monopolies represented the real threat, "struggling with the united spirit of the proletariat." The changing nature of the American economy had left capital unharmed while it "shaved cruelly salaries much below the necessity for living." If left unchecked, these changes would inevitably lead to more violence.

Unfortunately, corporations had become the "masters" of elections. Thus,

La Crónica reasoned, workers had no other recourse but "extreme remedies: strikes and revolution." The real tragedy of the strike was not only that democracy had failed, but that the nature of capitalism would continue to burden workers so long as the cost of the strike came not from the government or employers but from the workers themselves. Despite this seemingly grave outlook, *La Crónica* offered a solution that suggested a strong faith in the possible compatibility of capital and representative democracy.

La Crónica predicted future crisis if American democracy failed to restrain unbridled capitalist corruption. "We proclaim that in a free country and [one] governed by democratic institutions . . . look for a remedy to all of this in legislative bodies." The paper demanded that the legislatures (presumably both state and national) had the power to remedy the "disastrous social economic situation" by "establishing better harmony and more justice between capital and workers." But just as monopolies dominated elections, corporations had an "iron fist" of interest that controlled legislatures. Thus, the eventual remedy would come after elections and the nation's legislative bodies became free of corporate interests. Short of that, workers would have no recourse but violence, although it would not result in real change because capital did not pay for damage and had no incentive to prevent strikes. Workers then might have but one choice left, revolution.[34]

On the other hand, the Anglo interpretation of the strike in California suggested a natural ability of capital and labor to reconcile. The *Star*'s editors lamented the rioting and violence, placing their "sympathies with the unfortunate men who have been driven to such a degree of desperation by the iron hand of greed and gain." They concluded that the strike represented "a triumph of labor over capital." Unlike *La Crónica*, the *Star*'s editors reasoned that in the interests of resuming business, "the rich will have to foot the bill," and did not predict that the consequences of the strike would create any additional burden for workers. The *Star*, quoting the *San Francisco Herald*, agreed that "capital should learn some degree of moderation" because the "capitalist and laboring man [are] dependent on each other."[35]

The *Star* suggested the solution to preventing further outbreaks of labor violence involved realizing capitalism's mutual interests. Citing the example of an Austrian railroad corporation that had reportedly earned considerable profit and "cared for" employees, the paper asserted that capital and labor could cultivate their mutually agreeable interests. The European example, the *Star* concluded, "goes far to take away all the friction between master and men, and shows that there is room for the soul even in industrial affairs." Returning to the strike, the *Star* reminded its readers of the Central Pacific's "lessons learned" when it rescinded the planned wage cut.[36]

Yet at the same time that the *Star* embraced the ability of capital and labor to reconcile, it too advocated government intervention to regulate capitalism. An editorial in the *Star* claimed that most of Los Angeles's press agreed that "the more we examine this matter [the strike] the more we are impressed with the fact that the states of the general government should regulate fares and freight, and even the wages of such employees." Thus Anglos and Mexicans differed on their interpretation of the relationship of capital to labor while they agreed in principle that government should regulate capitalist development.

Such an interpretation made perfect sense to Angelenos who had for years advocated government regulation of the Central and Southern Pacific's rate monopoly. After government regulation, southern Californians put their hope in competition to break the monopoly. Californians advocated loudly and indeed had been successful making their discontent known. Mark Hopkins of the Central Pacific warned Collis Huntington in a September letter of the growing agitation regarding the Central Pacific's "gobbling up the Santa Monica railroad." Hopkins explained that the "Los Angeles people have been raising the devil in public meetings, and their newspapers are howling all the time."[37]

Why would the Hispanic press identify fundamental tensions in capitalism as the source of the strikes in the East and then blame the Chinese for similar labor problems in California? For one, *La Crónica* did not believe that Californians had experienced the same level of "deprivations" as had the East, commenting, "you [Californians] know weakly the tyranny of capital. We are in an infinitely superior condition to that afflicting the population where the disturbances occurred." To the editors of *La Crónica,* although Californians had not yet felt the full brunt of capitalist development, they believed capital and labor were inherently at odds.[38] Should the "harm of the proletariat" in the East spread to the West because of the Chinese "problem," California workers would also experience capital's "double domination over the proletariat." In this case, the Hispanic press does not seem to have identified the dominant capitalist force in California, the Southern Pacific Railroad, as the source of their problems. They had reason to join forces with whites in their effort to demonize the Chinese.

La Crónica was projecting itself, consciously or not, as part of the imagined community of United States citizens. *La Crónica* distinguished American democracy from European and, perhaps implicitly, Mexican, democracy. The editors had faith in an eventual resolution because the success "of the American people" showed that the majority "of the American people are wise." Therefore, "disturbing elements always met resistance in the citizenry," unlike in Europe, where one "can not comprehend a pacification of enraged masses without great use of powerful military forces." The United States citizenry were distinct in that American society remained "founded on law."

Adopting class language such as "proletariat" served rhetorically to place Mexicans in California's white working class, but in some ways as antagonistic workers. Incorporating the racialized anti-Chinese rhetoric served to place Mexicans alongside, ideologically at least, whites. But by speaking of a unique "American" democracy, *La Crónica* argued that Mexicans in California shared the unique identity of the American citizen. Interpreting the strike, *La Crónica* and its readers identified themselves as sharing a white working-class American identity in contrast to Chinese or European others.[39]

Many in southern California discussed the strike within a larger debate about California's regional development and the politics of opening the Texas & Pacific rail link to San Diego. In Los Angeles and San Diego the familiar complaints about capitalism's systemic inequality, prominently low wages, and high freight rates that harmed small producers and stifled regional economic development lent weight to the regional movement to end the Central Pacific's freight and rate monopoly.

Many in San Diego agreed with the sentiment in Los Angeles. Oblivious to the causes, the *San Diego Press* presented the strike as a losing proposition for workers, but more importantly, for free trade and good business. "Whatever reason the strikers may have had for their war upon commerce and trade, and upon the rights of all to avenge themselves of a real or fancied wrong, will result to their detriment, and largely to their loss."[40] San Diegans did not pay much attention to the labor issues behind the strike. Given the limited coverage of the strike as a labor action and San Diego's long-suffering call for an intercontinental rail link, it is little surprise that the *Press* soon couched the strike in terms familiar to its residents.

The strike suggested to San Diegans that the government should regulate the railroads on behalf of small producers. "We do not propose to moralize," began one editorial, "nor do we mean to denounce capital or labor" because both were relevant to the causes of the strike. "It is enough to say that the outbreak is one of the best evidences that could be given us against the idea of railroad monopolies, and that those we have should be controlled." The editorial made explicit that "control" included state regulation of freight rates and workers' wages so "they [railroad policies] shall not wear out the people."[41]

If regulation could not sufficiently reduce the tension between capital and labor, then opening competitive railroad lines would. Among southern Californians, San Diegans were probably the most hostile toward the Southern Pacific monopoly and most vociferous in their attempts to secure a second, southern, transcontinental railroad. Not surprisingly, San Diegans thought of the strike in terms of the dangers monopolies posed to small producers and workers while casting the violence in the East as a warning to southern Californians who might oppose a second rail link.

Ending the Central Pacific's monopoly with the addition of the Texas & Pacific was on the minds of San Diegans well before Reconstruction ended and the strike erupted in 1877. Before coverage of the strike even appeared in San Diego's press, editorials and city officials actively promoted a southern rail link. The *Union* ran a letter on July 20 that argued the extension of the Texas & Pacific Railroad to San Diego represented the best, if not only, means to undercut the Central Pacific, posing as "an obstacle to monopoly." For the next two days, San Diegans followed articles detailing the Texas & Pacific meetings in Louisiana and Los Angeles, while carefully scrutinizing the railroad bill in Congress. On the twenty-third, the *Press* editorialized on behalf of small farmers, claiming that San Diego needed a rail link for "the poor" with only "a lot or two" of land.[42]

Revolt in the East, reasoned the *Press,* demonstrated that competitive lines of trade remained the best way to destroy a monopoly, outside of the law. The paper continued, "The present trouble ought to bring that fact prominently before the people, and especially before Congress. It will perhaps aid in doing so" and "it may be that out of the great evil will come something good after all." If the strike created a "war on commerce" and resulted in "the detriment" of the workers in the East, at least it would advance southern California's call for corporate regulation and the arrival of the Texas & Pacific.[43]

The *Evening Express* in Los Angeles had also become an outspoken opponent of the railroad monopoly by 1877. J. J. Ayers had served as its editor since 1873 and purchased the *Express* in 1872 to prevent its "falling under the control of the railroad company, whose iron grip they [Angelenos] had even then begun to feel."[44] The paper ran regular updates on the negotiations of the Texas & Pacific Railroad, especially in San Diego. The *Express* also articulated its opposition to the Central Pacific's rate monopoly that separated Los Angeles from the Arizona market. These issues would resurface in less than a year at the California State Constitutional Convention.

The Strike at the State Constitutional Convention, 1878

An amendment: "To prevent the temporary lowering of rates below the cost of operation in order to kill off a rival."

—J. J. Ayers, California State Constitutional Convention, Fall 1878

"Provided no native of China, no idiot, insane person, or person convicted of any infamous crime . . . shall ever exercise the privileges of an elector of this State."

—California State Constitution, 1879

The very issues at stake in the public dialogue in July resurfaced at the 1878 California State Constitutional Convention, and their resolution suggests the contested nature of California's new political economy after the strike. Calls for a convention to revise the constitution of 1849 occurred as early as 1857 and 1859. Because the Workingmen's Party and the realization of a constitutional convention occurred immediately after the strike, we might speculate about how the Great Strike of 1877 played an important role in shaping those two events.

The conditions breeding grievances had been set in California before the summer erupted in violence—bank failures, farm debt, the perception of high numbers of Chinese, and the presence of a powerful railroad monopoly. And the movement to control monopolies was well underway by July 1877. It is no surprise that southern Californians would interpret the strike in these terms. It is also but a small jump from the rhetoric of the press at the time to the issues at the convention. (In fact the *Los Angeles Evening Press*'s editor, J. J. Ayers, served as a delegate from Los Angeles.) Armed with this appreciation of the strike for southern Californians, it seems that extensive coverage of the strike hastened convening the convention, placed old concerns in new terms, and shaped the new California constitution.

Certainly we see the same central issues at stake at the convention all discussed extensively in the press during the strike. The issues of anti-Chinese legislation, control of freight rates, the jurisdiction of the state over certain corporations, an eight-hour work day, a board of railroad commissioners, state-owned railroads, and the protection of wages were all proposed as amendments at the convention.[45] But more than a mere correlation, the press interpreted and gave meaning to the strike in these terms, thus setting the stage for large-scale discontent at the convention. And as working-class Sinophobia grew throughout the 1870s, the strike provided the impetus to couch anti-Chinese rhetoric in terms of the dangers of massive labor violence.

The Workingmen were ultimately unsuccessful in their efforts to limit the power of capital in the new state constitution. What amendments they did pass were heavily diluted, including J. J. Ayers's demand for legislation to protect against unfair elimination of competition. The Workingmen also failed to gain the most traditional labor demands, such as the establishment of a bureau of labor statistics or mandating an eight-hour workday.[46]

Although the convention may be best characterized by the "ineffectiveness of the Workingmen in Sacramento," the anti-Chinese goals met with great success. One clause forbade Chinese suffrage and Article XIX forbade their employment. The latter also suggested enforced ghettoization or police action against "aliens 'dangerous or detrimental to the peace or well-being of the State,' on the grounds that such aliens would be the cause of breaches of the peace directed against themselves."[47] Despite writing laws that seemed impossible to reconcile with the U.S. Constitution, the Workingmen reflected their fears of labor insurrection induced by the threat of Chinese labor. Here we see how rhetoric employed to explain the strike reappeared as California constitutional law.

The new constitution met with approval by the majority of southern Californians. Three of four papers in Los Angeles supported it, along with one in San Diego and one in San Bernardino. The *San Francisco Chronicle* listed the opposition to the constitution as "corporations, railroads, banks (previously exempt from taxation), dealers in mining stocks (previously exempt from taxes), land monopolists, pro-Chinese aristocrats, the newspapers who sell out to the above classes, and the preachers who serve the above." All southern California counties voted a majority in favor of the constitution, consistent with the split in northern California between the cities that opposed it and the rural districts that favored it.[48]

For Mexican Californians, the strike was both more, and less, significant than it was for working whites and farmers in California. Interpreting the strike in terms consistent with the anti-Chinese movement may have facilitated formation of the Workingmen Party among both Anglos and Hispanics. However, any rhetorical gains Hispanics made in 1877 do not appear to have parlayed into influence, as it had for whites. For Hispanics, effectively excluded from the convention, the strike represented one of a precious few opportunities to ally themselves with the white workers' movement in California and advocate for their place in the imagined white nation.

Indeed, Hispanics' absence from the convention would very much be to their detriment. One proposal, for example, called for the publication of laws in English only, and many pieces of anti-Chinese legislation would end up affecting Mexican immigrants as well. The clause disenfranchising natives of China also provided that no "idiot, insane person, or person convicted of any infamous crime . . . shall ever exercise the privileges of an elector of this State."[49] Such a definition was all too readily applied to Mexicans. Debate surrounding the strike represented another moment in the long and often unsuccessful struggle of Mexican inclusion in racialized American institutions. And the whole episode through to 1879 suggests another aspect of the complicated story of racial and class solidification in California.

Conclusion

Though in no way spreading massive labor violence to California, the Great Strike of 1877 did play an important role in how Californians conceived of corporate railroad regulation, competitive railroad expansion, anti-Chinese sentiment, and Mexican resistance strategies. The significance of the strike in southern California lies not so much in violent actions but in the ways in which Mexicans and Anglos gave meaning to the strike within the context of their own experience. It allows consideration of the strike in broader geographic, temporal, and thematic terms than before. If the significance of the strike in southern California had its roots decades before 1877 and extended beyond the 1880s, then the strike fits into a larger national story not neatly divided at 1877.

The significance of the strike for southern Californians lay in how they linked California's labor, race, and railroad monopoly issues to the strike. For one, Californians joined other Americans in reconceptualizing the relationship of capital and labor. Mexicans tended to argue a vision of antagonism much at odds with the older version of American free-labor ideology. But many Mexicans also understood the strike in terms similar to those of white workers, namely the perceived threat of Chinese labor and railroad monopolies. This explanation of events served as another moment since conquest when some Mexican Californians projected themselves part of the imagined community of white working citizens. While the evidence does not show conclusively whether this was a conscious strategy or not, it nonetheless suggests that one result of the strike was a new dimension to the history of the consolidation of racial identity in California. Before Hispanics adopted a new "Mexican American" identity, they utilized public and political debate regarding the "American" nationalist white identity.

A second point is that much of the southern California press seized upon events in the East to articulate the need for a southern transcontinental railroad in new terms. In previous debates, southern Californians argued that the Central Pacific's monopoly hindered the region's economic development and therefore needed to be ended by bringing the Texas & Pacific to southern California. The San Diego press, in particular, maintained this argument. During the strike, the press also began to argue how the strike demonstrated that the danger a monopoly posed to workers' rights and well-being could result in a civil disaster. Ending the Central Pacific monopoly would help avoid both a riot similar to the eastern strikes and regional economic subordination. In this way, the strike strengthened southern California's argument for a second transcontinental railroad through Texas to San Diego. Ultimately, the strikes in the East *against* the presence of the railroad became a powerful argument *for* the presence of a railroad in southern California.

Third, the issues at stake for southern Californians colored their views of the strike and promoted the formation of the Workingmen's Party and the constitutional convention in 1878. Important ideas and laws that characterized the Workingmen's movement and the later Progressive movement received plenty of public discussion among both Anglos and Mexicans. Questions concerning the appropriate role of government and corporations, the balance of capitalism and democracy, and the natural relationship of labor to capital dominated public debate. The Great Strike and the debate surrounding it shaped the outcome of California's constitutional convention and the lives of California's Mexican citizenry for decades.

Finally, a fourth significant point needs to be made concerning the strike in the West. Often excluded from the "main" narrative of United States history, the West has been long overlooked as a viable and dynamic factor in the nation's development. The West must be taken into consideration because without it, a very different synthesis of United States history emerges. In the case of the Great Strike, East-centered histories might quickly conclude that 1877 marked a watershed moment in the nation's transition to industrial capitalism. But this research suggests that the significance of the strike to Californians, especially Mexicans, was part of a broader development not neatly cut in 1877.[50] Mexicans' decades-long fight to survive in an increasingly white California, the development of California's railroad, and the rise of the Workingmen's movement are stories that do not include 1877 as a watershed. With this consideration, one can appreciate the salience of the strike but not so neatly conclude that it marked a period of *national* transition.

Notes

1. *La Crónica,* July 28, 1877.

2. *Los Angeles Daily Star,* July 24, 1877.

3. Telegraph to Collis Huntington, July 27, 1877, Collis P. Huntington Papers, Series I, Reel 13, Henry E. Huntington Library, San Marino, California.

4. *Los Angeles Daily Star,* August 5, 1877; J. A. Dacus, *Annals of the Great Strikes in the United States: A Reliable History and Graphic Description of the Causes and Thrilling Events of the Labor Strikes and Riots of 1877* (New York: Arno Press, 1969 [1877]).

5. A note on terminology: I will use the terms Manuel Gonzales employs in his work, *Mexicanos: A History of Mexicans in the United States* (Bloomington: Indiana University Press, 1999), because his usage is based on the first national survey to provide empirical evidence about how Latinos see and identify themselves. Accordingly, I use *Mexican* to refer to people of Mexican background in the United States. If there is a need to distinguish between native-born and immigrants, I use *Mexican American* for the former and *Mexicanos* (and/or *Mexicanas*) for the latter. I refer to elite native Californians of Mexican, Latin American, South American, and/or Spanish heritage as *Californios.* I use *Latinos* when referring to Americans of Latin American descent. Finally, I use *Hispanic* only as a linguistic term in reference to Spanish-language newspapers.

6. Karl Marx commented from Europe that the workers' uprising against the strains

of capital in the workplace "could serve as the beginning of the establishment of a serious labor party" in the United States. Similarly, the majority of historians studying 1877
have portrayed the uprising as a *labor* strike, marking the beginning of a new era of
labor antagonism in the United States. In their assessment of the legacy of the Great
Labor Strike, these historians have identified the strike as a "watershed" event in United
States history. Despite variations of perspective and emphasis, most of the literature falls
within a broad consensus of the strike as a labor uprising, the participants having a wage
relationship with the railroads. David O. Stowell, *Streets, Railroads, and the Great Strike
of 1877* (Chicago: University of Chicago Press, 1999), 1–11.

7. David Weber, *Foreigners in their Native Land: Historical Roots of the Mexican Americans* (Albuquerque: University of New Mexico Press, 1973).

8. See Scott Nelson, *Iron Confederacies: Southern Railways, Klan Violence, and Re-
construction* (Chapel Hill: University of North Carolina Press, 1999), and Heather Cox
Richardson, *Death of Reconstruction: Race, Labor, and the Politics of the Post–Civil War
North, 1865–1901* (Cambridge, Mass.: Harvard University Press, 2001).

9. The anti-Chinese and Workingmen's movement played an important role in how
Mexican Californians discussed the strike. See Alexander Saxton, *The Indispensable Enemy: Labor and the Anti-Chinese Movement in California* (Berkeley: University of California Press, 1971), for the essential analysis of the development of anti-Chinese movement
in California by 1877.

10. For analysis of this process, see Tomás Almaguer, *Racial Fault Lines: Historical
Origins of White Supremacy in Southern California* (Berkeley: University of California
Press, 1994); Albert Camarillo, *Chicanos in California: A History of Mexican Americans
in California* (San Francisco: Boyd and Fraser Publishing Co., 1984), and *Chicanos in a
Changing Society: From Mexican Pueblos to American Barrios in Santa Barbara and South-
ern California, 1848–1930* (Cambridge, Mass.: Harvard University Press, 1979); Richard
Griswold Del Castillo, *La Familia: Chicano Families in the Urban Southwest, 1848 to Present*
(South Bend, Ind.: University of Notre Dame Press, 1984); Leonard Pitt, *The Decline of the
Californios: A Social History of the Spanish-Speaking Californians, 1846–1890* (Berkeley:
University of California Press, 1966).

11. Camarillo, *Chicanos in California,* 14–15. See Camarillo for his analysis of how the
introduction of the Anglo legal system and discriminatory land laws meant that within a
decade, the majority of Mexicans in northern California had lost their lands, while their
southern brethren experienced a similar process once they succumbed to population
parity with Anglos in the 1860s. Trouble in translation, costly litigation, high interest
rates, and overt violence prevented most Mexicans from successfully challenging Anglos
in court.

12. This transformation occurred despite the guarantees in the Treaty of Guadalupe
Hidalgo. That treaty, which ended the Mexican-American War, officially recognized Cali-
fornia's Mexican population as white American citizens and guaranteed "the enjoyment
of all the rights of the United States according to the principles of the Constitution."
For more on the effects of the Treaty on Mexican Americans, see Richard Griswold Del
Castillo, *The Treaty of Guadalupe Hidalgo: A Legacy of Conflict* (Norman: University
of Oklahoma Press, 1990). Along with demographics, economic and labor changes in
California also affected racial attitudes. As Anglo Americans began to view Mexicans as

"permanent laborers" and never as American citizens, Mexicans became a more stigmatized racial other. Anglos simply could not imagine Mexicans as white citizens or white workers, only as "people of local color." See Elliot West, "Reconstructing Race," *Western Historical Quarterly* 34 (spring 2003): 22–23, for a useful summary of race identity in the nineteenth-century West.

13. Gonzales, *Mexicanos*, 87–88.

14. Camarillo, *Chicanos in California*, 21–25. Some might also have challenged Anglo authority outside the law. The bandit Joaquin Murieta became a folk hero to Mexican peoples as he sought revenge against "gringos," killing and robbing as a means of resisting Anglo authority. Mythical heroes such as Joaquin go a long way in illustrating how violent and contested the struggle between California's Anglo and Mexican citizens had become.

15. Camarillo, *Chicanos in California*.

16. F. Arturo Rosales, "'Fantasy Heritage' Reexamined: Race and Class in the Writings of the Bandini Family Authors and Other Californios, 1828–1965," in Erlinda Gonzales-Berry and Chuck Tatum, eds., *Recovering the U.S. Hispanic Literary Heritage, Vol. 2* (Houston: Arte Publico Press, 1996), 100.

17. For more on the "third space" especially as it manifested itself in the early twentieth century, see David Gutierrez, *Walls and Mirrors: Mexican Americans, Mexican Immigrants, and the Politics of Ethnicity* (Berkeley: University of California Press, 1995). Elliot West has summarized that to many Anglos, Mexicans "posed little cultural threat and played useful economic roles." Mexican Americans were thus "either rendered invisible, segregated in cities and countryside, or they were re-imagined as a bit of American exotica." He concludes that "these people of color became what was much tamer: people of local color"; West, "Reconstructing Race," 22–23.

18. For more on the relationship between the formation of working-class and white identity, see David Roediger, *The Wages of Whiteness: Race and the Making of the American Working Class* (New York: Verso, 1991), and *Toward the Abolition of Whiteness: Essays on Race, Politics, and Working Class History* (New York: Verso, 1994).

19. Eric Foner, *Free Soil, Free Labor, Free Men: The Ideology of the Republican Party Before the Civil War* (Oxford: Oxford University Press, 1970), remains the essential summary of free-soil ideology. The ideology rested on four basic assumptions: labor and capital shared the same basic interests; employers and employees were equal partners in the construction of contracts; waged work, protected by the right to vote and equality under the law, would guarantee equal opportunity; and wage work was a temporary condition en route to small-scale ownership (assuming capital consolidation would not occur.) Free-labor ideology also included an explicit racial understanding that free labor and the western territories were reserved for whites.

20. *El Clamor Publico*, August–November 1856.

21. Republican candidate John C. Fremont fared poorly in California relative to his national returns, receiving 18 percent of the California vote compared to 33 percent nationally. However, Fremont fared well in California counties with prominent Mexican populations, receiving *more* votes than either of the other two candidates in Santa Barbara, Santa Clara, and San Luis Obispo counties and placing second in Los Angeles County. Returns compiled by the author from the *San Francisco Herald*, September–October 1856.

22. William Deverell, *Railroad Crossing: Californians and the Railroad, 1850–1910* (Berkeley: University of California Press, 1994), 37–39.

23. Charles Pickett, "Pickett's Pamphlet in the Railway, Chinese, and Presidential Questions" (San Francisco: Henry E. Huntington Library, 1876). By 1877, Collis Huntington, Leland Stanford, Charles Crocker, Mark Hopkins, and David D. Colton owned 85 percent of California railroads. See Deverell, *Railroad Crossing*, for a detailed history of the antagonism between California's citizens and the railroads.

24. Jerome Madden, "The Lands of the Southern Pacific Railroad Company of California" (San Francisco: privately published, 1877). Madden, acting as the official land agent of the Southern Pacific, published this pamphlet in June 1877.

25. Founded in 1872, *La Crónica* served as the major Hispanic organ in Los Angeles. *La Crónica* identified itself as "the organ of the moral, political, and commercial interests of the Spanish people in particular and the 'raza Latina' in general"; June 6, 1877. Reaction to the strike in Hispanic papers shows the role the Hispanic press played in articulating resistance and opposition to Anglo hegemony. The two major Anglo newspapers, the *Daily Star* and *Evening Express*, targeted English readers and Anglo society. Yet it seems reasonable to conclude that many bilingual members of the Hispanic community might have received much of their news from the *Express* and would give meaning to the strike, in part, in terms this wing of the Anglo press articulated. The *Express* was particularly Hispanic-friendly, advocating, for example, "the urgent reasons why the Spanish language should be taught in public schools" and providing sustained coverage of legal cases involving disputed ranch land; July 28, 1877. It also championed the Democratic Party, workers, farmers, and was decidedly anti–railroad monopoly.

26. *Los Angeles Evening Express,* August 4 and 11, 1877.

27. *Press,* July 24, 26, and 28, 1877.

28. *Evening Express,* August 11, 1877.

29. *La Crónica,* July 28 and August 1, 1877.

30. *La Voz del Nuevo Mundo,* August 22, 1877.

31. *Daily Star,* July 22, 1877.

32. Heather Cox Richardson, *Death of Reconstruction,* xiii. See Richardson for a useful summary of this ideological divide and how it ended African American efforts to obtain equality after the Civil War. See also John Mason Hart, *Border Crossings: Mexican and Mexican-American Workers* (Wilmington, Del.: Scholarly Resources, 1998), where he outlines the emergence of a Mexican working-class consciousness that by the 1870s appeared in Mexican workers on both sides of the border. It is reasonable to conclude that much of what the Hispanic press in southern California was articulating regarding the harm of the strike on the proletariat had its roots in Mexican, not American, labor ideology.

33. *La Crónica,* August 1, 1877.

34. The preceding analysis appeared in the August 1 edition of *La Crónica.*

35. *Daily Star,* July 25, 1877.

36. *Daily Star,* July 19 and 25, 1877.

37. *Daily Star,* July 26, 1877; Mark Hopkins, ed., *Letters from Mark Hopkins, Leland Stanford, Charles Crocker, Charles F. Crocker, and David E. Colton to Collis P. Huntington* (New York: J. C. Rankin Co., 1891), 108.

38. *La Crónica,* August 1, 1877.

39. *La Crónica,* August 1, 1877.

40. *Press,* July 25, 1877.

41. *Press,* July 26, 1877.

42. *San Diego Union,* July 20, 1877; *San Diego Press,* July 20–23, 1877.

43. *Press,* July 26, 1877. San Diego's newspapers also reported extensively on the Granger movement. See the *Press,* July 24–26. It is difficult to make connections between the strike and that action mainly because San Diego's press did not. Though papers did not link directly the issues of the strike to the numerous Granger lectures and meetings, the farmers' movement did relate to the rate and monopoly argument insofar as it was the small producers who voiced the most consistent attacks on railroad shipping rates. By the constitutional convention in 1878, San Diego would ally with the "rural" farm representatives against the "urban" corporate interests. See Carl Brent Swisher, *Motivation and Political Technique in the California Constitutional Convention 1878–1879* (Claremont, Calif.: Pomona College, 1930).

44. H. D. Barrows, "Two Notable Pioneers, JJ Ayers and George Hansen (with Portraits)," *Annual Publication of the Historical Society of Southern California and Pioneer Register* 4 (1897): 61.

45. Swisher, *Motivation and Political Technique,* 80, 105–33. Swisher's work remains the only authoritative study of the State Constitutional Convention.

46. Saxton, *The Indispensable Enemy,* 128–29; Swisher, *Motivation and Political Technique,* 61.

47. Saxton, *The Indispensable Enemy,* 128–29.

48. Swisher, *Motivation and Political Technique,* 102, 110.

49. Proposed by Representative Edward Martin of Santa Cruz, E. B. Willis and P. K. Stockton, *Debates and Proceedings of the Constitutional Convention of the State of California,* vol. 1 (Sacramento, 1880), 100. Review of the convention materials and biography of delegates reveals no Spanish surnames. In fact, only two of the 152 delegates were native to the state. This was a significant change from the 1849 convention that included six native Californians and one Spaniard. Swisher, *Motivation and Political Technique* 27–36; Saxton, *The Indispensable Enemy,* 129.

50. Another potential area of research might be in Arizona. Manuel Gonzalez speaks briefly of the fight in Tucson to develop a rail line in the 1860s and 1870s that had the effect of reshaping Hispanic and Mexican society. See Gonzalez, *Mexicanos: A History of Mexicans in the United States* (Bloomington: Indiana University Press, 1990), 91–98.

Contributors

JOSHUA BROWN is executive director of the American Social History Project/Center for Media and Learning and a professor of history at the Graduate School, City University of New York. He is the author of *Beyond the Lines: Pictorial Reporting, Everyday Life, and the Crisis of Gilded Age America* and coauthor of *Forever Free: The Story of Emancipation and Reconstruction.* He also has collaborated on award-winning films, including *1877: The Grand Army of Starvation* and, most recently, noted digital projects including the two-part multimedia CD-ROM *Who Built America?* He writes frequently about the history of U.S. visual culture, and his cartoons and illustrations have appeared in popular and scholarly print and online publications.

STEVEN J. HOFFMAN is a professor of history and coordinator of the Historic Preservation Program at Southeast Missouri State University in Cape Girardeau. His research interests include studying the role of race and class in the city-building process. Recent publications include *Race, Class and Power in the Building of Richmond, 1870–1920* and "Progressive Public Health Administration in the Jim Crow South: A Case Study of Richmond, Virginia, 1907–1920," an article in the *Journal of Social History.*

MICHAEL KAZIN is a professor of history at Georgetown University. He is the author of *A Godly Hero: The Life of William Jennings Bryan; Barons of Labor: The San Francisco Building Trades and Union Power in the Progressive Era; The Populist Persuasion: An American History;* and coauthor of *America Divided: The Civil War of the 1960s.*

DAVID MILLER is a Ph.D. candidate in history at the University of California, San Diego. He specializes in nineteenth-century United States political and cultural history, with a special interest in the California borderlands. His dissertation, "Heroes of American Empire: John C. Fremont, Kit Carson, and the Culture of Imperialism, 1842–1898," investigates how popular representations of Fremont and Carson shaped the evolving, and intricately related, contours of American freedom and empire as Americans engaged in a national dialogue concerning the anxieties and contradictions aroused by western expansion.

RICHARD SCHNEIROV is a professor of history at Indiana State University. He is the author of *Labor and Urban Politics: Class Conflict and the Origins of Modern Liberalism in Chicago, 1864–97* and coeditor with Shelton Stromquist and Nick Salvatore of *The Pullman Strike and the Crisis of the 1890s: Essays on Labor and Politics.*

DAVID O. STOWELL is the author of *Streets, Railroads, and the Great Strike of 1877* as well as two articles on the Great Strike. His most recent article, "The Free Black Population of Columbia, South Carolina, in 1860: A Snapshot of Occupation and Personal Wealth," appeared in the *South Carolina Historical Magazine.* He is a project specialist for SEIU Local 200United.

SHELTON STROMQUIST is a professor of history at the University of Iowa. He has written on the history of railroad labor, working-class politics, and progressive reform. His first book was *A Generation of Boomers: The Pattern of Railroad Labor Conflict in Nineteenth-Century America,* and his most recent, *Reinventing "The People": The Progressive Movement, the Class Problem, and the Origins of Modern Liberalism.*

Index

Page numbers in *italics* refer to illustrations.

The Working Class in American History

The University of Illinois Press
is a founding member of the
Association of American University Presses.

Composed in 10.5/13 Adobe Minion Pro
by Jim Proefrock
at the University of Illinois Press
Manufactured by Cushing-Malloy, Inc.

University of Illinois Press
1325 South Oak Street
Champaign, IL 61820-6903
www.press.uillinois.edu